unspoken facts

unspoken facts

a history of
homosexualities in Africa

Gays and Lesbians of Zimbabwe
Private Bag A6131
Avondale
Harare
Zimbabwe

Layout and typesetting by Frances Marks
Cover design: Danes Design, Harare
Printed and bound in Mauritius by Précigraph

ISBN 978-0-7974-3483-7

contents

glossary   *vii*
list of acronyms   *x*
preface   *xi*

1 • introduction   1

Shungu (Willpower)   *18*
Asikhulumeni (Let's Talk)   *21*

2 • sexuality in ancient African societies   24

A cave painting, near Guruve, Zimbabwe   *42*
Unyankwabe: A wife for Zodwa's ancestors   *43*

3 • early European influences on African sexualities   49

A Difference of Opinion   *65*

4 • sex behind bars   72

Zimbabwe's first gay rights activist: *87*
    Sarmiento, 1788

5 • early Colonial Zimbabwe   92

Women loving women   *106*

6 • homophobia in settler society   *114*

April 1968. My Dearest John   *129*

7 • homophobia in the African nationalist movement   132

    Face-to-Face   156

8 • in the rurals ...   161

    Finding love on the gold mines   177

9 • gay rights to sexual rights   182

    A special sort of sisterhood   201
    A lesbian affair on Nigerian video (a film review)   206

conclusion: homophobia hurts everybody   210

further reading and watching   220
notes on contributors   245
index   248

glossary

bohali – (Sotho) brideprice.

boukontchana (also spelled **boukoutchana**) – (Sotho) thigh sex.

bukhonxana – (Shangaan, Tsonga) thigh sex.

catamite – an old-fashioned word usually meaning 'passive' male homosexual 'partner'; also sometimes used as 'male prostitute' or 'concubine'.

chibado – (**Umbundu**) a powerful diviner/medicine man said to gain his powers by ritual sodomy among the Ovimbundu of southern Angola.

chibanda – [see **chibado**].

chibudo – [see **chibado**].

chidhoma [pl. **zvidhoma**] – (Shona) [see **tokoloshi**].

chikwambo – (Shona) charm purchased by someone to make others suffer.

chitsina – (Shona) 'bad luck' in not being able to marry.

divisi rakaipa – (Shona) a charm that works through illicit sexual acts like incest or male-male sex.

dunuzaing – (Zulu) 'protruding, or presenting the buttocks'.

gangisa – (Tsonga, Shangaan) thigh sex.

gayle – white South African gay slang or secret language.

hlobonga – (Zulu) thigh sex.

hlonepha – (Sotho) respect.

hungochani – (Shona) homosexuality.

hunhu – (Shona) traditional African philosophy stressing community and mutual obligations.

huroyi – (Shona) witchcraft.

ibbi – (Wolof), also spelled **woubi** or **oubi**, meaning passive male homosexual partner throughout francophone West Africa.

induna – originally a Zulu word for a military leader, it later came to be used to mean 'boss-boy', or an African put in charge of a group of other African workers.

inkotshane [pl. **izinkotshane**] – (Shona) colonial-era spelling of ngochani.

kuchu – (origin unknown), widely used throughout east Africa for male homosexual.

kupindira – (Shona) 'raising seed' [see **kusika rudzi**].

kupinganyika – (Shona) 'to protect the land' by ritual incest in Manyika (eastern Shona) tradition.

kusenga – (Shona) manual stretching of the *labia majora*.

kusika rudzi – (Shona) keeping the family line going in cases where a husband cannot make his wife pregnant.

likopano – (Sotho) African women's mutual help associations.

lobola – (Ndebele, Zulu) brideprice [now used widely used in other southern African languages].

mamuna – [see **mbonga**].

mapoto – (Shona) an informal marriage of convenience.

matanyera {also spelled **matenyero**} – (Shona from Chewa) street or latrine cleaner, or a man who has thigh sex with another man.

matanyola – (Sotho) 'male prostitution'.

matanyula – (Zulu) 'male prostitution'.

maotoane – (Sotho) thigh sex.

mashave – [see shave].

mbonga – (Shona) a female 'guardian' whose celibacy protects the chief and his people.

mhondoro – (Shona) the most powerful of the Shona ancestral spirits.

moffie – originally an insulting Afrikaans term for homosexual but now widely used humorously even by LGBT.

motsoalle – (Sotho) intimate friend.

mukadzirume – (Shona) 'woman-man', a woman who lives as a male-gendered person.

mupfuhwira – (Shona) 'husband-taming herb' or love potion.

muroyi – (Shona) witch.

murumekadzi – (Shona) 'man-woman', a man who lives as a female-gendered person.

muthi – (Ndebele, Zulu) medicine, magic.

muti – (Shona) medicine, magic.

n'anga – (Shona) doctor or diviner.

ngaka – (Sotho) traditional healer.

ngozi – (Shona) avenging spirit.

ngochani – (Shona) {also variously spelled as **ngotshana, nkotshane, bukhontxana, boukontchana**} sodomy, or homosexual.

njuzu – (Shona) water sprite or mermaid; sometimes explains unusual behaviour.

roora – (Shona) brideprice.

sahwira – (Shona) intimate male friend.

sangoma – (Ndebele, Zulu) doctor or diviner.

sanusi – (Ndebele, Zulu) doctor or diviner.

setsoalle – (Sotho) intimate relationship, potentially with either sex.

shave [pl. **mashave**] (Shona) – 'stranger spirit' that often possesses neglected wives.

skesana – (slang, Tsotsitaal) passive or effeminate sexual partner [possibly comes from **inkotshane**].

thigh sex – when the active partner ejaculates between the thighs of the passive partner, hence no anal penetration.

tinconcana – (Shangaan) plural form of **ngochani**.

tokoloshi – (Zulu) a goblin-like evil spirit who often brings dreams of sexual misbehaviour or lust.

ubuntu – (Ndebele, Zulu) traditional African philosophy stressing community and mutual obligations.

ukumetsha – (Xhosa) thigh sex.

umfaan {also spelled **umfaana**} – (Tsotsitaal, from Zulu) slang term for boy, sometimes also used to mean boy-wife.

umteto ka Sokisi – (Zulu) 'Sokisi's rules' or the proper manners governing male–male mine marriage or prison relationships.

unyakwabe – (Zulu) a person who is possessed by an ancestral spirit in order to provide a wife for a **sangoma**. Sometimes explains a certain type of woman-woman marriage.

wyfie – (Afrikaans) passive male homosexual partner; also 'wife' or 'bitch'.

'yan daudu – (Hausa) male homosexual, transvestite or prostitute.

list of acronyms

ACDP – African Christian Democratic Party.

ANC – African National Congress.

ASO – AIDS Service Organisation.

GALA – Gay and Lesbian Archives of South Africa.

GALZ – Gays and Lesbians of Zimbabwe.

GASA – Gays and Lesbians of South Africa.

GLOW – Gay and Lesbian Organisation of the Witwatersrand.

HIV/AIDS – Human Immunodeficiency Virus and Acquired Immuno-deficiency Syndrome, now usually considered together rather than separately in order to stress the close relationship between infection with the virus and the development of symptoms.

HUMCC – Hope and Unity Metropolitan Community Church.

LGBT – Lesbian, gay, bisexual, transgender.

LeGaBiBo – Lesbians, gays, and bisexuals of Botswana.

LEGATRA – Lesbians, Gays, and Transsexuals of Zambia.

MSM – Men who have Sex with Men who do not necessarily identify as gay or bisexual.

NCGLE – National Coalition of Gay and Lesbian Equality.

OLGA – Organisation for Lesbian and Gay Action.

PF-ZAPU – Zimbabwe African People's Union.

TAC – Treatment Action Campaign.

UDF – United Democratic Front.

WSW – Women who have Sex with Women who do not necessarily identify as lesbian or bisexual.

ZANU-PF – Zimbabwe African National Union (Patriotic Front).

preface

This book is a collective effort.

The principal author is Marc Epprecht, whose original research was published as *Hungochani: The History of a Dissident Sexuality in Southern Africa* with the financial support of the Canadian Federation for the Humanities and Social Sciences. Additional research since then has been supported by the Faculty of Arts and Science, Queen's University, Canada. A generous grant from the Open Society Institute made the current publication possible.

The inspiration for a 'popular' version of the research comes in part from a proposal first floated by Bev Clark of Kubatana Trust but subsequently endorsed by the executive committee of GALZ. The need for a book that speaks to a wide, non-academic audience has been amply shown in recent years by African leaders who have fuelled homophobic prejudices.

Gerald Mazarire of the Department of History at the University of Zimbabwe had the task of wrestling *Hungochani* into a form that could be made accessible to a wider audience. This involved removing cumbersome footnotes and translating highly specialised language into more-easily understood terms. Epprecht then reworked the draft into a stylistically consistent form and added new evidence and arguments to broaden the appeal of the book. Further towards that end, Keith Goddard, the GALZ Director for Programming, provided both additional research insights from the point of view of an activist directly involved in some of the struggles discussed and the final copy-editing of the manuscript. Additional editorial suggestions came from Jeff Piker, a writer and community worker living in Canada.

Small sections of the text have been adapted from Epprecht's contributions to David Gerstner (ed.) *The International Encyclopedia of Queer Culture – Contemporary Gay, Lesbian, Bisexual and Transexual Cultures* (New York: Routledge, 2006) and the Homophobia fact sheet edited by Rosemary Forbes and published on the website of the Interagency Coalition on AIDS and Development, www.icad-cisd.com.

The shorter pieces between the historical chapters were gathered in three ways. First were contributions directly from GALZ:

- *Shungu*, by Poliyana Mangwira (also known as Tsitsi Tiripano).
- *Asikhulumeni* – Let's Talk (anonymous) was previously published in Shona and Ndebele, respectively, in the book *Sahwira* (Harare: GALZ, 2002). Dumisani Dube and Keith Goddard translated them into English.

Marc Epprecht directly solicited input from colleagues who have done research into same-sex sexuality in Africa. Contributions came from:

- Nkunzi Nkabinde and Ruth Morgan of GALA (*Unyankwabe*).
- Chris Dunton (*Face to Face*).
- Lindsay Clowes (*April 1968. My Dearest John ...*).
- Drew Shaw (*A Special Sort of Sisterhood*).
- T. Dunbar Moodie (*Finding Love on the Mines*).

Marc Epprecht himself contributed *A Difference of Opinion*.

Taiwo Oloruntoba-Oju wrote *A Lesbian Affair on Nigerian Video*, a review of a genuine film, *Emotional Crack*: Lancelot Imasuen (director), Emem Isong and Bob Emeke Eze (story) and Emem Isong (screenplay), Lagos: RJP Productions, 2003.

'A Cave Painting, near Guruve, Zimbabwe' is taken, with the permission of the author, from Peter Garlake's *The Hunter's Vision* (London: British Museum, 1995), p. 141.

Sarmiento's speech by the Marquis de Sade was translated and abridged by Marc Epprecht from the original French, found in G. Lely (ed.), 'Aline et Valcour' in *Œuvres complètes du Marquis de Sade: Édition définitive* (Paris: Édition Tête de Feuilles, 1973). It was previously published on the website, *Behind the Mask.*

Doug Jack, Oliver Phillips, Cary Alan Johnson, Barbara Kaim, Charles Gueboguo, Stephen O. Murray, and Anthony Manion all either helped to network the concept, offer insightful critical suggestions or provide other assistance and encouragement along the way.

Contributions in *Women Loving Women* come from previously published sources. These include:

- *Hungochani,* for which 'Anonymous' gave permission to publish an excerpt from an exchange of letters on file at the Gay and Lesbian Archives, Johannesburg.
- Bev Clark for her weblog entry <http://slate.msn.com/id/2086560/entry/2086672>.
- Calixthe Beyela, *Femme nue, femme noire* (Paris: Michel Albin, 2003), translated by Marc Epprecht.
- Kenda Mutongi, 'Dear Dolly's Advice: Representations of Youth, Courtship, and Sexualities in Africa, 1960–1980', *International Journal of African Historical Studies* (2000), 33(1), pp. 1–23.
- Human Rights Watch and International Gay and Lesbian Human Rights Commission, *More Than a Name: State-sponsored Homophobia and its Consequences in Southern Africa* (New York: HRW and IGLHRC, 2003).
- Mark Gevisser and Edwin Cameron (eds), *Defiant Desire: Gay and Lesbian Lives in South Africa* (Johannesburg: Ravan, 1994).
- Mpho 'M'atsepo Nthunya, *Singing Away the Hunger: Stories of a Life in Lesotho* (Pietermaritzburg: University of Natal Press, 1996).
- Caroline Zilboorg, *The Masks of Mary Renault* (Columbia: University of Missouri Press, 2001).
- Renée Liddicoat, 'Homosexuality', *South African Journal of Science,* May 1962.
- GALZ, *Sahwira* (Harare: GALZ, 2002).

- Marie Nagadya with Ruth Morgan, '"Some say I am hermaphrodite just because I put on trousers": Lesbians and tommy boys in Kampala, Uganda', in R. Morgan and S. Wieringa (eds), *Tommy Boys, Lesbian Men and Ancestral Wives: Female Same-sex Practices in Africa* (Johannesburg: Jacana, 2005).

Finally, this book would not have been possible without the commitment and professional support of Weaver Press in Harare.

1 • introduction

Homosexuality. Lesbians. Gay rights. Homophobia.

These terms have come up quite a bit in recent years in Africa to the shock, embarrassment and even anger of many people. This book is about that, and about the coming out (into public view) of individuals who in the past tended to keep a low profile. What does the history of homosexuality and the reactions against it tell us about African history in general? And how might this knowledge help us in struggles against HIV/AIDS, gender violence and other social inequalities in contemporary Africa?

Let us start by getting our definitions clear, as there are so many misconceptions, fears and prejudices around this topic. A big misconception is implicit in the very words 'homosexual' and 'homosexuality', for example. These words are typically taken to mean a single, basic type of person or behaviour when in fact they refer to a wide variety of people and sexual behaviours. The English language, like many others, has developed quite a rich and constantly expanding vocabulary to capture that variety. This obviously includes Women who have Sex with Women (WSW) who may or may not identify as lesbians, and Men who have Sex with Men (MSM) who may or may not identify as gay. But even within these terms there are many different expressions of sexuality – the active, penetrating partner ('husband', 'macho', 'top', 'butch-dyke'), the passive, penetrated partner ('wife', 'femme', 'bottom'), mutual partners, or women and men who just like to cuddle or to express intimate affection in non-genital ways. There are also people who are sexually attracted equally to men and women (bisexuals), and people who enjoy

1

'cross-dressing' – wearing the clothes or cosmetics associated with the opposite sex – but not necessarily engaging in homosexual relations (transvestites). People who think of themselves as living in the body of the opposite sex are termed transgendered persons (transwomen, transmen or simply trans) although in Zimbawe, a transgendered man will generally identify as a queen and a transgendered woman as a dyke. Although also termed trans, transsexuals, more strictly speaking, are people who feel they are 'born in the wrong body' and they often seek hormonal therapy and sex-reassignment surgery (sex-change opera-tions) to change their sex. There is as well a rare group of people who possess both male and female sex organs (intersexed, formerly called hermaphrodites). There are people who consider themselves heterosex-ual, or 'straight', yet will engage in sex with members of their own sex at different times of their lives or simply as they find convenient.

The possibilities are in fact so varied that many gay rights activists now avoid the words 'homosexual' and 'homosexuality' altogether. These, they say, feed into simplistic stereotypes that have been used to justify discrimination. They therefore now prefer to use the plural form (homosexualities, or same-sex sexualities, or sexual minorities). LGBT.(short for Lesbian, Gay, Bisexual, and Transgender) is another term that is growing in popularity and lgbt is sometimes placed in lower case to avoid the appearance of overconfidence in the categories. Queer is also debated as an identity, but queer politics is fairly clear. It refers to any kind of political activism that publicly challenges stere-otypes about homosexualities and that seeks to win public recognition of sexual rights as human rights.

Sexual rights does not mean freedom to copulate without restric-tion, as opponents sometimes loudly proclaim; rather, it means putting an end to both discrimination against LGBT persons because of their sexual orientation or identity, and the violation of any individual's sexual autonomy and human dignity; it therefore excludes pederasty (man–boy relationships), in most cases, and the heterosexual abuse of children (paedophilia).

Queer politics and the struggle for sexual rights are a very new development in most of Africa, dating generally from the 1990s. Africans, however, have known for a very long time about people who somehow do not fit the heterosexual ideal. In the main African languages of Zimbabwe, for example, the concept of 'homosexuality' goes by the terms *hungochani* (Shona) and *ubunkotshani* (Ndebele). These words can be traced back at least a hundred years. Versions of them are also found in other African languages in the region. In Zulu, for instance, *nkoshana* refers to sexual intercourse between male persons, or sodomy, while in Tsonga (Shangaan) *tinconcana* or *bukhonxana* mean 'boy wives' or 'mine marriages'; the widespread urban slang word *skesana* probably comes from the same root. Other African words for same-sex sexuality found in the region include *maotoane* (Sesotho), *matanyera* (from Nyanja), *mashoga, mabashaa* and *misago* (Swahili) and *esenge* or *eshengi* (Ovambo) and 'yan daudu (Hausa). From Wolof comes *woubi, oubi* and *ibbi* used across francophone West Africa, while *kuchu* (origins unknown) is understood to mean homosexual across much of east Africa.

The origins of these words are impossible to know for sure. We do know, however, that they mostly suggest a strong stigma or social disapproval. Despite this, some gay rights activists in recent years have adopted them to describe themselves with a touch of pride. They say the mere fact that such words exist in African languages is proof that people like themselves have always been known in traditional culture. It gives a strong support for their case that LGBT people in Africa are fully deserving of the same rights and respect that are theoretically enjoyed by all other citizens.

The majority population may need more convincing on this. Zimbabwean gays and lesbians who choose to publicly admit their *hungochani* are in fact often perceived as a threat to the morals of black African society, aping a western perversion or prostituting themselves for tourist dollars and European-style beer (as another term of contempt in Zimbabwean popular culture hints: 'clear drinkers'). President Robert Mugabe has encouraged this anti-homosexual or homophobic attitude. Among other names, he has called homosexuals 'worse than dogs and pigs', 'gangsters' and 'an abomination, a rottenness of culture'.

He even suggested that Britain's supposedly 'gay government' was attempting to impose homosexuality upon Africans as part of a wider programme of western imperialism. The king of Swaziland, the presidents of Namibia, Kenya, Zambia and Uganda as well as top church leaders around the continent have all echoed similar views, sometimes in quite violent language. The Archbishop of the Church of Nigeria (Anglican), to give one example, in 2003 termed homosexuality both a 'Satanic attack' on his church and a form of slavery. The Minister of Home Affairs in Namibia, in an even more chilling speech, urged new police recruits to 'arrest on sight gays and lesbians and eliminate them from the face of Namibia'.

Such threats have in many cases hardened people's negative attitudes towards homosexuality. They have contributed to a climate where individual gays and lesbians have experienced blackmail, job discrimination, police harassment, shunning by their families and even mob violence. Lesbians in this climate are especially at risk from family members who arrange forcibly to get them pregnant, or from gangs of young men who seek to 'cure' them by rape. The stigmatisation also leads to self-hatred or 'internalised homophobia' amongst gays and lesbians. This in turn exposes them to relatively high rates of emotional depression, alcoholism, or even suicide.

For many Africans, therefore, any association with *hungochani* can spark violent reaction and shameful or angry denials. A case in point was the Zimbabwean police officer Jefta Dube shooting and killing a fellow officer in 1996 after the deceased had called him *'ngochani mukadzi'*. Dube did not deny that he had been sexually assaulted by the former president of Zimbabwe, Canaan Banana. But his defence was that the experience of being homosexually assaulted had made him emotionally unstable. For his part, Banana angrily denied the charges against him and hinted at a foreign or white conspiracy for making them in the first place. He later fled the country in disgrace.

These painful events and accusations in Zimbabwe have taken place at a time of rapid development of human rights and democratic governance elsewhere in Africa. In fact, as early as 1991, Lesotho and

Ethiopia became the first two African nations to uphold the idea of gay rights as part of promoting democracy for all citizens. Then, soon after democratic elections in 1994, South Africa included in its constitution the principle of freedom from discrimination based on sexual orientation, one of the first countries in the world to do so. The first black president, Nelson Mandela, met with gay activists and publicly endorsed their causes, as did fellow Nobel Prize-winner Archbishop Desmond Tutu. Was this because South Africa is not 'really African' or was succumbing to western pressure, as some opponents suggested? On the contrary, South Africa has actually been well ahead of many western countries in overturning its discriminatory laws. The government has shown a mature and independent appreciation of the ways that homophobia relates closely to other discriminatory attitudes in society, including racism and hatred or contempt of women (sexism, misogyny). It holds to the view that all of these attitudes feed upon each other to frustrate the advancement of civil rights generally, to improve health for all and to achieve economic development with a fair distribution of wealth.

Interestingly, even the more homophobic regimes such as Zimbabwe and Namibia have hinted that they, too, understand those interconnections and that they support research about homosexuality and gay rights. The Declaration on Gender and Development signed by all eleven heads of state of the Southern Africa Development Community in September 1998 called for, amongst other things:

- Promoting the eradication of elements in traditional norms and religious beliefs, practices and stereotypes which legitimise and exacerbate the persistence and tolerance of violence against women and children
- Introducing and promoting gender sensitisation and training of all service providers engaged in the administration of justice
- Undertaking and sharing research, gathering of statistics and other information on the causes, prevalence and consequences of violence on women and children.

Since lesbians are women, and since gays usually begin to understand their homosexual feelings when they are still children, this declaration is clearly gay-friendly. And indeed, despite the homophobia of some

African leaders, gay movements have flourished in recent years in many countries. Gays and Lesbians of Zimbabwe (GALZ) now openly provides counselling, legal and other support services to its members. The Equality Project in South Africa, The Rainbow Project and Sister Namibia, LeGaBiBo of Botswana, and Ligueey (Senegal) and Alliance Rights Nigeria, amongst many others, all seek to challenge hurtful stereotypes of homosexuals and to end discriminatory laws and practices.

These contradictory developments and controversies have drawn the attention of scholars and human rights activists from around the world. They raise provocative questions about culture, democracy, race and the nature of imperialism in the modern day. Talk of sexuality also brings us to reflect on HIV/AIDS. Although this was once widely assumed to be a 'gay plague' or a 'white man's disease' it is now devastating the black majority population throughout Africa. Can anything further be done to help protect the next generation of young people in Africa from this scourge? Could the frank discussion of the diversity of human sexuality help to provide Africans with the kinds of knowledge that might begin to slow the terrible progress of the HIV/AIDS pandemic?

This book will try to answer some of these questions by taking a close look at the history of same-sex sexuality. It will focus primarily on three African countries – Zimbabwe, South Africa and Lesotho - but will also refer to cases studies from elsewhere around the continent. This is very unbalanced, we know. But we also know from many of the studies discussed in the final chapter, and from our close discussions with researchers and activists around the continent, that there are strong similarities between southern Africa and elsewhere in Africa. We are therefore not suggesting that our research is the answer to all questions; rather, we hope that our research will suggest questions or ways to look for evidence in the wide variety of specific situations around Africa that still need to be investigated. The aim is to gain a better understanding of who these homosexuals are, where they came from in historical terms, and what they really want through their present-day activism. As well, it will try to shed light on how such strong attitudes both for and against gay rights have come to be and how those attitudes towards same-sex relationships have affected so-called normal society. Finally, we would like to suggest ways in which societies in the region might move to heal the hurtful impacts of homophobia and other prejudices.

All of this is not to present gays and lesbians as blameless heroes in the struggle for democracy. On the contrary, we hope that gay rights activists and sympathisers can learn from this history as well so that they can better recognise political mistakes or errors in judgement that were made in the past. Such knowledge of the past may strengthen the effectiveness of their activism and their ability to offer counselling in the future.

Before reviewing this history, we want first to address a number of basic questions that are commonly raised in popular discussions around the issue. What causes homosexuality? Is it not 'unnatural'? Can it be spread to the heterosexual population? Is it a lifestyle choice? Are there cures for it? How commonplace or rare is it? Are some cultures relatively immune to same-sex sexuality compared to others? Given all the taboos and the secretive nature of same-sex affairs in most cultures, is it even possible to uncover their history? If so, why is it important for us to know about it?

The answer to the first of these questions – what causes homosexuality – is much argued. All that we can say with a fair degree of certainty is that ... well, we just do not know. While many theories try, none can definitively account for the great variety of same-sex sexual behaviours that appear around the world in different cultures, across time and in many animal species. The last fact alone – that homosexuality appears frequently in nature – clearly destroys the argument that homosexuality is 'unnatural'. In fact, nature is unquestionably one of the many factors to play a role in determining a person's sexuality. It is almost certain, for example, that some people have a genetic predisposition to homosexual orientation or preference – they are born that way. The attraction to people of their own sex is in these cases 'hard-wired' into their brains and cells. For others, family socialisation or a traumatic sexual experience (such as rape) at a young age may be the most important influence affecting long-term sexual preference. Physical closeness, gender imbalance in society, alcohol consumption, age, one's stage in the life cycle and innumerable other idiosyncratic factors can also affect short-term decisions about sexual partners and conduct (so-called situational homosexuality).

This suggests that the question of what causes homosexuality is ultimately misguided. One might equally ask, what causes heterosexuality, or even why humans are sexual at all? The answer is simply, they are.

Our approach then is to follow what scientists, doctors, leading Christian theologians and other social science scholars generally agree about the nature of homosexuality. This is a consensus that has emerged from decades of research and reflection primarily from the west but also increasingly from queer communities in underdeveloped and former colonial countries such as Mexico, India and Algeria. It regards human sexuality as a continuum from one theoretical extreme to another, with the majority of the population somewhere in the middle. The small percentage of the population found at either extreme in terms of their innate sense of sexual preference (that is, 'pure' homosexual or 'pure' heterosexual) is probably constant across the world and throughout history. The percentage of people who act in accordance with more ambiguous or bisexual feelings in their choice of sexual partners, however, varies enormously over time, across cultures and in relation to economic, political and other social considerations. Sexuality, in other words, is thus not merely a natural or instinctive phenomenon; rather, it is to a large extent learned or 'constructed'.

We can see this quite clearly when we look at the changing ways that homosexuality has been treated by society in the west. In ancient Greece, the homosexual relationship between a man and a youth was highly regarded, even idealised. This kind of homosexuality was thought to allow deeper spiritual and intellectual exchange than procreation-oriented sex with women (which was regarded as animalistic or soulless). That notion fell out of fashion in the Christian period of the later Roman

Empire. But male–male sexual relations came back into respect, even to the extent of being sanctified by church marriages, in the Middle Ages. The Protestant Reformation, and the infamous Catholic Inquisitions in the 16th and 17th centuries, once again brought renewed hostility against 'sodomites'. But this too gave way to a period when same-sex affairs were widely tolerated. The Code of Napoleon in 1803 actually forbade the persecution of people on the basis of their sexual preference.

The pendulum swung against homosexuals in the west once again in the late 19th century. At that time new theories arose about the supposed 'cause' of homosexuality, shifting the blame away from moral sin and constructing it as a medical problem. This implied that homosexuality somehow should and could be cured, typically through combinations of rigorous physical exercise, psychiatric therapy and shaming. Worse was to come in the aftermath of World War II. During the Cold War both sides portrayed homosexuals as a weak link in the struggle between capitalism and communism (that is, adding treason to the list of their supposed medical and moral failings). Probably the most intense fear and hatred of homosexuality in western history occurred during the 1950s and 1960s, when suspected gays and lesbians were entrapped by the police and hounded out of their jobs. Only since the 1970s has a culture of limited tolerance re-emerged in the west, although even this limited tolerance is under constant threat of backlash and renewed repression by the political right and Christian fundamentalists.

All of the above makes it clear that there is indeed a history of homosexuality and of ever-changing social attitudes towards it. But why should the majority population bother about such a presumably small minority, especially in a place like Africa where questions of poverty, land reform and ill-health are so urgent? The answer is twofold. In the first instance, the small minority in question is not so small as is commonly thought. Exclusively homosexual people may number only 1% to 5% of the population, but men who sometimes have sex with men, and women who sometimes have sex with women, number many more, possibly even a majority in certain settings. Second, in looking at European history we can see a clear pattern that should be of great concern to the majority population. Increasing intolerance or hatred of homosexuals fairly clearly coincides with periods of intolerance and hatred of foreigners (xenophobia). The Protestants of England and the Netherlands, for example, blamed homosexuality on the Catholics and the Spanish, with whom they were at war. The British later accused the Portuguese and Arabs, their rivals for control of trade in the Indian Ocean. In each case the accusation of homosexuality served to fuel greater contempt for and hatred of the foreign enemy.

This history also reveals an obvious connection between stigmatising homosexuals and the oppression of women who step out of traditional feminine roles. The most intense persecution of 'sodomites' in the 16th and early 17th centuries coincided with the burning of tens of thousands of female witches in western Europe. The homophobia of the Cold War period in North America coincided with enormous tensions around moving women out of the workforce, which they had entered during World War II, and back into suburban, domestic roles.

Both xenophobia and sexism against women present huge obstacles to the economic development and political rights of the majority. It thus follows that exposing the sources of prejudice against the homosexual minority might improve our ability to attack prejudice against other groups that experience discrimination and systemic disadvantage.

Finally, there is strong consensus amongst scholars that the history of homophobia can help us to understand, and then to move away from, some very old but very dangerous habits or conventions in our language. Perhaps above all is the tendency we seem to have of wanting to divide societies neatly into two categories. Such dichotomies are almost always simplistic and misleading. The dichotomy of homosexuality versus heterosexuality is clearly such a false dichotomy, but so is that between masculine and feminine. Even 'man' and 'woman' are not necessarily as self-evidently distinct as we commonly assume. In fact, appearances can be deceiving. A person with a male body may have a highly masculine or macho personality and still be homosexual. Equally, a male may have an effeminate personality but be lustily heterosexual. A woman may wear trousers for comfort or to make a political statement about her civil rights but not as a sign of lesbian orientation. A woman may acquire the status and titles of a man (and in many parts of Africa may even formally marry another woman) without for a moment desiring the masculine role in a sexual relationship.

All of this suggests that we need to be more careful in our use of words that imply or impose false dichotomies on complex social relations. We also need to be careful not to base our judgements of people on the incorrect assumption that there is a direct and predictable relationship between the physical body (sex), social behaviour (gender) and sexual feeling (sexuality). The relationships between sex, gender and sexuality are in fact constantly negotiated. The study of these negotiations is particularly hazardous since so much takes place non-verbally – a fleeting touch, a look, a smile – and leaves very few solid traces that can be followed back through time. Matters are complicated further by the fact that many of the words we use carry unintended and unhelpful cultural 'baggage'. The words gay, queer and lesbian, for example, all derive from the modern west – the word homosexual did not even exist until its invention in 1869. These words are closely associated in people's minds with a very specific type of behaviour or identity that is alien and in some cases even offensive to non-western gays and lesbians. Using those terms may suggest misleading parallels with the western experience and thus blind us to important differences or shades of meaning in local cultures.

For all these reasons, researchers now stress the need for great caution in approaching the language around sexuality. We will try to heed those cautions here and be careful with the words we choose, even if it sometimes results in clumsy-sounding phrases. So, for instance, rather than 'homosexuality' and 'bisexuality,' from now on we will use the expressions 'homosexualities' (plural) or 'same-sex sexuality'. These terms are more accurate in that they do not imply a permanent condition or a single, unchanging cultural identity that is either diametrically opposed to heterosexuality or perfectly stuck between the two extremes. Likewise, rather than 'gay' we will say 'males who have sex with males' (unless we know for certain that the men we are talking about really did in fact regard themselves as gay in the modern western sense). The same applies to 'lesbian', which we will avoid in favour of 'female–female sexuality' or 'lesbian-like'. Rather than 'queer' we will use 'gay rights activist or sympathiser' and so on. Of course, wherever there are indigenous terms we will use them rather than importing foreign ones and will use the local words and spelling of the time (such as *inkotshane* in 1907), even when the modern Shona spelling is *ngochani*.

One of the central arguments we hope to make is that the oppression of gays and lesbians today, like the oppression of women, is, to a large extent, structured into or rooted in our language, often so deeply that we can't even see it. Challenging the language can therefore help us to see the blindspots and prejudices that are otherwise taken for granted. New words, even if they sometimes sound clumsy, can make invisible oppressions in a culture visible for people to see and fight against.

Before addressing the history of same-sex sexuality in Africa, it helps to know what people have already said and written about the topic. There are some real surprises in this respect. For example, the first people to claim that same-sex sexual relations are 'unAfrican' were not African themselves, nor even in some cases had they ever been to Africa. They were European men. Sir Edward Gibbon was the first, writing in 1781 about the decline and fall of the Roman Empire. He knew nothing about Africa from direct experience or learning, but he wanted to 'believe and hope' (his words) that Africans were 'exempt from this moral pestilence' (i.e. sodomy).

In the following century, another Englishman was even more assertive. In an appendix to his translation of the *Arabian Nights*, Sir Richard Burton divided the world by whether homosexual behaviour was supposedly native to the region or not. Although he made little mention of Africa in the essay, nor had he travelled much outside of Dahomey, this English aristocrat placed the 'Negro' parts of the continent together with northern Europe in the non-homosexual zone.

Why would Burton have made such a huge claim without proper

research (and in fact contrary to numerous earlier first-hand accounts of male–male sexuality from West Africa and of Africans enslaved to the Americas)? He did not explain his reasons but we may make an educated guess from his other assumptions. Firstly, working on the assumption that homosexuality was a 'by-product of modernity', he excluded Africans because he regarded them as primitive. Secondly, this emphasis on African primitiveness justified the imperial conquest of Africa by supposedly virile northern Europeans. Burton's eccentric interpretation, in other words, breathed new life into the arguments for British and German imperialism. By seizing new territories in Africa, they would protect hapless Africans from the sodomistic Portuguese and Arabs.

In the case of Zimbabwe, the topic was hardly mentioned before a remarkable two-page 'study' published in 1979. Like Burton before him, the author used the topic to make sweeping moral claims to a European audience rather than to find out what was really happening in Zimbabwe. Indeed, anthropologist Michael Gelfand used the apparent infrequency of male homosexuality in Shona culture to make negative judgements about homosexuality and modern society in general. 'The traditional Shona seems to have none of the problems associated with homosexuality,' he pronounced. 'Obviously they must have a valuable method of bringing up children, especially with regard to normal sex relations, thus avoiding this anomaly so frequent in western society.' These conclusions were based on a small number of stories from non-homosexual persons, no research amongst traditional healers or diviners, and no reference to scholarship on sexuality from elsewhere in Africa or the world.

European claims about the rarity or non-existence of same-sex sexuality in African traditions prepared the ground for blaming homosexual behaviour amongst Africans in modern times upon external influences. In the colonial era, as noted, the British regarded Arabs and Portuguese as the key culprits. Some in South Africa blamed imported Chinese labourers. The French-trained psychologist Frantz Fanon later argued that colonialism itself was to blame (regardless of whether it was Portuguese or French or British). By its very nature, he maintained, colonial rule empowered white settlers to sexually humiliate (or emasculate) African men. This led some to insanity, some to violence, and some to homosexuality.

This theme of emasculation occurs in a number of novels from around Africa and was also developed by the historian Charles van Onselen in his study of male migrant workers in colonial Zimbabwe. Van Onselen argued that the mining companies turned a blind eye or even 'forced' African men into homosexuality. Why would they do such a thing? Because the mine-owners were worried that their workers, separated for long periods from their wives and children and labouring under stressful and dangerous conditions, might rebel unless distracted by cheap sex. Since the government did not want female prostitutes in the mine compounds or nearby towns, this left only each other or animals to afford men the necessary release. Van Onselen wrote about a similar phenomenon in the Johannesburg area, and about sexual relations amongst African men in the criminal gangs there. He tells of a Zulu gang leader in the mid-1890s, Nongoloza Mathebula, who was said to have ordered his men to have sex with each other or with boy servants. To this day, more than a century later, the gang now known as the 28s remains loyal to the 'Ninevite system'.

Van Onselen's studies reveal much about the horrendous conditions faced by African men at mine compounds and other such institutions in southern Africa. But they also leave many questions unanswered. How can a man be forced to have sex with another man? If a man's sexual urge is really that strong, how do we explain the existence of males who take a passive role in the sexual act? Can mass change in sexual behaviour come about because of a single individual (and be kept up for over a century after he ceased giving orders)? And what about the women left behind in the rural areas: Did they know or care about their men's behaviour at the mines? Were they themselves driven by loneliness into lesbian-like affairs? How did all this supposedly shameful, un-traditional behaviour affect people's understanding of their own culture?

Scholars of Zimbabwe have largely avoided these questions. By contrast, a number of studies, memoirs and films have appeared from elsewhere around the continent that show, and in some cases praise, indigenous African homosexualities. South Africa has produced the majority of these, beginning with T. Dunbar Moodie's 1988 examination of 'mine marriages' on the Witwatersrand and Patrick Harries' study of Mozambican migrant labourers. Both these studies showed that male–male marriages amongst African mine-workers were commonplace at the beginning of the 20th century, so much so that they were not regarded as shameful, even by the female wives left behind. On the contrary, almost everyone seems to have approved, as long as it was kept quiet. The men liked it because they did not need to go to female prostitutes, with all the risks of disease and the high expense that that involved; their wives liked it because they did not need to fear their husbands would get a second family with town women; the youth or male 'wives' accepted it because they earned money and gifts and acquired a protector in the violent surroundings of the mine compounds; and, of course, the mine companies liked it because it saved them from the expenses and higher wages that would need to be paid if women and children were allowed into the urban areas. Only the Christian missionaries protested, but without much effect.

In more recent years, there have been further studies of gay rights activists in the anti-apartheid struggle and in the fight against the spread of HIV/AIDS. Gays and lesbians themselves have also started to come out with their own autobiographical accounts of growing up or dealing with sexuality issues in southern Africa (*Sahwira* in Zimbabwe, for example). Some of these are discussed in the final chapter on further reading and watching. For now, though, we want simply to mention the work of Zackie Achmat. As a historian, Achmat warned researchers against repeating negative stereotypes about gays and lesbians and against assuming that African men could not love men out of sensual desire (rather than economic or cultural need). Along with gay rights activists and scholars of women and gender such as Patricia McFadden and Evelyn Zinanga in Zimbabwe, he called for culturally sensitive research that questions the myth of the exclusively heterosexual African. They make a strong case that such research might contribute to our understanding of how cultural change around intimate personal life occurs in relation to the global political economy. This knowledge can then be put to the service of the wider community. Indeed, Achmat's own career is a powerful role model in that respect. From self-described 'adult molester' to scholar and gay rights activist, Achmat went on to found the hugely successful Treatment Action Campaign. TAC was nominated for the Nobel Peace Prize for spearheading a broad, international social movement for equitable access to health care and to treatment of HIV/AIDS.

~ ⌣

This book takes up these many challenges by interpreting the evidence for popular audiences in Africa. It follows the basic structure and draws upon data first presented in an academic book entitled *Hungochani: the history of a dissident sexuality in southern Africa* (Montreal: McGill, 2004) which followed the history from the ancient Bushmen, through 'medieval' Shona and other Bantu-speaking kingdoms, to the early colonial societies and the establishment of industrial economies. It then examined how settler culture trickled into the emerging African 'middle class' and from there into the anti-colonial and anti-apartheid struggles. Finally, it examined the rise of the modern gay rights movement. We shall stick to the same basic path, with one new chapter to guide readers towards other works that discuss homosexualities in Africa.

We have also woven into the narrative a number of personalised or fictionalised vignettes ('little pictures') of the lives of people who engaged in same-sex relations in the past. The reason for this is simple: often, especially in an area of study like the history of sexuality, the evidence is scanty, if not entirely hidden between the lines. We may suspect emotions, but we cannot prove them when we rely on the dry descriptions left by colonial bureaucrats and police, or on the hazy memories of old people. We therefore allowed ourselves a little artistic licence to imagine what people may have felt in the past. For this purpose, we invited a range of activists and scholars to draw upon their experience, research and imaginations to fill in the gaps and silences that they have come across in the historical sources. These vignettes are not true in the literal sense, but we believe that they capture important truths in a poetic or dramatic sense. Our hope is that they humanise the people we are talking about and help to bring the history to life.

Shungu (*Willpower*)

Poliyana Mangwiro was one of the first Shona women to publicly defend the rights of lesbians and was an early, active member of GALZ. For this, she was harassed and forced to flee from her home in the small town of Marondera. Yet, despite her courage and outspokenness for gay rights, she caused some confusion and controversy in the LGBT movement on account of her bisexual lifestyle. Her choice of sexual partners also put her at high risk of contracting HIV. When she became sick, her second husband deserted her. Poliyana died in 2000 of AIDS, cared for to the end by her long-time lesbian partner, Zandile. Following her story is another told by a man who prefers to remain anonymous. Like Poliyana's, it tells of learning to find self-acceptance in a society torn by conflicting individual awareness, family pressures and outside influences.

My name is Shungu. I was raised in the rural areas and it was there that I began to realise that I was different from other girls of my age. I was not happy playing with the girls; I wanted to play with the boys. I used to herd cattle, hunt and play soccer with the boys. At that time I never once thought that my ways were different from others: there was not a lot that I ever gave thought to in that matter. My parents then started to see that my behaviour was different from the others. My mother used to scold me roundly, forcing me to do housework like the other girls. I used to dodge this as much as I could. I wanted to do work that was done by the boys. I got distracted watching the men at work.

After some time, when I became a teenager, I felt happy whenever I saw other girls naked. This often used to happen when I went down to the river to wash. I never wanted to be touched by a boy and if ever this happened, I used to fight with him and I often used to defeat anyone I fought with.

Eventually I grew up and got married just like every girl must do according to the customs of our culture. It was like a forced marriage because, in our culture, they would not consider me a full woman if I were not married. Again, they thought there was something wrong with me because they saw I had no desires for men. My parents did everything to find a boy that they thought would be suitable for me to marry, and so my parents and his parents started negotiations.

From the beginning, it was clear that the man I was married to would never satisfy me in bed. He started to complain that when we went together (had sex), it was like he was going with another man. After a few months, he started to delay coming home in the evenings. The marriage started to fail. At times he ended up sleeping elsewhere and not coming home. This continued until I left the man and returned to my parents even though there was no happiness in my home.

After a couple of weeks, I met another woman called Gertrude who came from the same village as me. I started to feel attracted to this girl. After only a short time of knowing each other, we started to spend the day together, helping each other and having fun.

We then went to live in Harare where I worked as a maid. We lived together at the house where I was working. It was at that time that we fell in love. That relationship was one of true feelings of love, without anything being forced as had happened when I got married. We then left to go and live in Dzivarasekwa where we were lodging. After that we went to live in Epworth. Gertrude became ill until she died. It is a year since she left me. Until today, I have not found anyone *else who loved me as Gertrude did. I am going on with my life but I know that I was created differently from others. I wish that one day I might find happiness like that which I found with Gertrude.*

Asikhulumeni – Let's Talk

I am 26 years old. I was born in Bulawayo. My parents are respectable people. I grew up being greatly cared for and loved by them. They sent me to the best schools and I owe it to them for what I am today.

From a tender age I could tell that I was different from other boys of my generation. I used to like playing with girls as I saw boys as being violent. The thing is, I was born beautiful and some boys used to say I was a girl. I grew up to like the things that girls did. Of course I am still able to perform some manly duties such as digging in the garden, fixing utensils, mending punctured car tyres and the like. This shows that I learnt things that might be of use to me as a man.

The fact that I was different from other boys always bothered me. When I was a teenager and had reached the age of puberty, other guys were going out with girls; but I had no real desire to do that. At this point my friends were boys and I wished I could love them as they loved their girls. This feeling bothered me for a long time and I wondered where it came from. I had no one to ask. I could not even approach my parents. At this time, my communication with my parents was not something that gave me any sense of freedom. Sometimes I sensed that they were seeing what was inside me, but at the same time I would get angry when they did nothing to let me know that they understood something was bothering me. I was always troubled and I was a loner.

Going to college was a blessing in disguise as this helped

me to discover who exactly I was. When I tried dating girls I felt there was something unclean about it: I never liked them; I had no feelings for them whatsoever, no matter what kind of a girl it was.

I went to a boys-only college. I had a hard time, as there were so many cute boys and very little time. I became attracted to most of these guys. One day I met a guy who had just the same feelings as me. We talked about our lives and, amongst other things, our sexuality. This moment was so emotional; we cried, hugged and kissed. From that moment I felt relieved; I felt I belonged. Learning now became easy for me and my performance at school improved dramatically.

As time went on, I met other gay people who were in the closet for fear of being criminalised by the laws which did not approve of homosexuality. Because of my education I managed to read a lot of books in my research into whether my feelings were normal or not. I got to know that most white people had accepted this condition though there were still some who had not. As I continued to read, I learnt that those who lived in the past lived a life punctuated with war and the kidnapping of other tribes. So, in those days, gay people were never tolerated as they were said to be a threat to the nation; and so were looked down upon – but they were there in the armies. You will remember in the days of Shaka, Mzilikazi and Lobengula that twins and disabled children were considered taboo. But today they are accepted like anyone else. Today, the world has come of age and people are busy doing things other than war, amongst them improving the education system. Laws set by human rights organisations protect everyone.

There is a Ndebele saying that can be literally translated as: 'that which has horns cannot be hidden' and this is true – homosexuals cannot be hidden and neither can they be ignored. In Zimbabwe, gay people are afraid to come out, as they are vulnerable to violence from others; they are also afraid to be fired from their places of work or arrested by the police. This is sad. I also want people and my family to know who I am in love with. As I write, I have been in a *relationship with a man for the past two years. We moved in together as would married heterosexuals. We are members of GALZ, an organisation that is trying to fight against discrimination of homosexuals. Being a member of GALZ has helped me accept my sexuality like any other person would. Although there are so many issues that need to be dealt with in society, I still wonder why people change their attitudes towards me when they find out about my sexuality, when in fact I am just like any other human being.*

I would like people to know that gay people are not as bad as they are portrayed in the media. We are peace-loving people; we live our lives without bothering anyone. I need my rights just like any other person; there must not be violence against gay people. We need the same jobs as everyone else; we need to be allowed to marry and adopt children if need be and we need political participation.

With these few words I hope you will be able to research into people like me who are gay so that the nation will understand us better. It is important that we all live in harmony and work together as Zimbabweans.

2 • sexuality in ancient African societies

Many Africans today believe that whites introduced homosexuality to the continent during colonialism, abusing their power and wealth to corrupt the traditional African way of life. As we shall see in later chapters, there is a grain of truth in this view. But we also know that Africans knew of, practised and, in some cases, even honoured sexual relations between males or between females long before whites ever arrived. How long before? The archaeologist Peter Garlake found one Bushman painting in a cave in Zimbabwe that shows several males engaging in sex acts together. It dates from at least one thousand, but more probably two thousand, years ago.

Same-sex practices were certainly a part of traditional Bushman and related Khoi societies in southern Africa in more recent times. The German anthropologist Kurt Falk researched this very question in the most remote regions of Namibia and Angola in the 1920s. He found there a variety of same-sex sexual relations and the words to describe them, including cases of women using artificial penises with female partners. Indeed, he found that married Bushmen women were, in his words, 'very devoted' to this kind of sex with each other. Falk did not wonder why this would be. Other historians, however, have noted how the Stone Age Bushman and Khoi were at constant risk of famine. They did not farm but relied on hunting, gathering and to some extent little herds of sheep and goats. The women's sex play with each other may therefore have reflected their awareness of the need to limit pregnancies and avoid births during times of drought or food shortage.

The women's lesbian-like sex play may also have reflected their relative freedom from male authority in these communal societies. Falk discovered that men seemed to accept their wives' decisions with little more than a grumble. They simply masturbated each other or had anal intercourse when they did not have access to the womenfolk. To yet another anthropologist referring to Bushmen in Botswana in the 1930s, intimate same-sex friendships including homosexual acts were considered quite normal and did not bring blame or shame to either the men or women who engaged in them.

The ancient Bushmen of Zimbabwe moved away or intermarried with Bantu-speakers who began to arrive in the region from the north about two thousand years ago. These migrants brought with them iron tools, pottery, livestock and a knowledge of agriculture. Their wealth, however, demanded much more labour to sustain than simple gathering and hunting. Fields had to be prepared for planting, crops had to be weeded and protected from pests, and animals had to be guarded against predators. Labour shortages at key moments in the farming season could lead to hunger and poverty. And so, unlike the Bushmen, Bantu-speakers saw many children as an economic asset in that they increased the labour available to the family for production. The labour of many children, including grown children, also kept the elders alive long past their economically active years. Where the Bushmen had abandoned the aged and feeble to die, Bantu-speaking societies valued elders for their wisdom and political roles. Relations between men and women were therefore defined to a large degree through a culture that emphasised high fertility.

The religious beliefs of these newcomers reinforced the idea that sexual relations were important not just for immediate economic reasons, but also for the spiritual welfare of the people as a whole and for the fertility of the land. The ancestors of the Shona, for example, believed in a hierarchy of spirits ranging from powerful guardians of large territories to local family ancestors. Those ancestors were respected as wise elders. They would be consulted and appeased for their power to influence rains, to improve soil fertility, to resolve family disputes and to offer advice on just about any aspect of community life. So, for a man or woman to have many children did not mean merely acquiring a source of labour and a source of support through to old age. It was also a way of securing descendants. Many descendants meant more people to remember you and to honour you as an ancestral spirit. The most powerful spirits, known as *mhondoro*, were in fact precisely those ancestors who had established the biggest, most geographically widespread lineages through having had the most children in their lifetime.

By contrast, failure to produce children disallowed a person from receiving full burial rites. His or her spirit quickly faded, forgotten by later generations.

Among the ancient Shona, fertility was assured through innumerable rituals, symbolic imagery and day-to-day practices. Many of these still have a hold on the popular imagination today. For example, the anthropologist Herbert Aschwanden found that amongst the Karanga there is a belief that a man's semen 'makes him immortal', that 'the act of procreation is a sacred event' and that the male orgasm is comparable to God descending to the people. The Shona tradition of praise poetry also celebrates sexual intercourse resulting in male orgasm and female pregnancy. A common belief amongst Shona men is that an orgasm without the goal of making children is meaningless. Many women also understand the need to receive sperm vaginally on a regular basis as a crucial part of maintaining their physical and emotional good health.

Shona traditions do recognise some variety within the dominant ideals of fertility for women and virility for men. Men of different totems, for example, were thought to have different sexual abilities and tastes. *Ngara* (porcupine) men had an especially good reputation for their sexual virility, *Mhofu* (eland) for their secretiveness, *Shiri* (bird) for coarseness and so on. Society also recognised variations in female sexuality, mainly according to age and successful pregnancies. Women who had many pregnancies over their fertile years earned almost as much prestige in the eyes of the community as did the virile men. Yet, abstinence in some situations was allowed or even preferred, notably in the late stages of pregnancy and while breast-feeding a child. The wife of a polygamous man would be expected to wait patiently for her turn with him rather than to seek sex outside the marriage. Female sexuality also included knowledge of methods to balance the expectations of the husband and his family with personal health. The discreet use of charms and herbs, for example, could prevent or abort those rare pregnancies that were unwanted for health reasons. At the other extreme, a married woman who could not get pregnant or carry a pregnancy to term became an object of scorn and pity. Failure in this way provided grounds for divorce.

Children had to be taught these expectations and were chastised if they appeared to be straying from the ideals of proper behaviour. The Shona did not have initiation or circumcision schools like many of the other cultures in the region, where the change from childhood to adulthood was marked by rituals, genital cutting and formal lessons. Rather, for Shona girls and boys alike, the main source of education about sexuality and gender roles was observation. Aunts (*vatete*), uncles (*vababa*) and other elders would also offer instruction about particular responsibilities and methods of bringing sexual pleasure or reproductive success. Some societies in the region allowed girls and boys to practise their lessons or to play together sexually as long as no pregnancy resulted. Among the Zulu, thigh sex was called *hlobonga*, also known as *ukumetsha* amongst the Xhosa, and *gangisa* amongst the Shangaan. Homosexual experimentation amongst adolescents also took place as a normal part of this learning process. Boys did the herding. Out in the bush, sexual play with each other was actually expected at the age of puberty in order to prepare for marriage. An intimate friend – *sahwira* – could be trusted with this and other secrets.

Among girls, certain kinds of sex play were also considered a normal and desirable phase that helped to prepare them for marriage. *Kusenga*, for example, was the practice of unmarried girls to manually stretch their *labia majora* through a daily exercise. A girl might spend hours at *kusenga*, alone or with help from a close friend. Not for a moment was this seen as masturbation or lesbian-like behaviour. On the contrary, *kusenga* was thought to be primarily in the interest of pleasing the future husband.

A child's interest in same-sex sex play usually faded away as he or she matured, especially when it brought the mockery of peers and perhaps a talking-to by elders. Yet cases still occurred of individuals straying from the expected heterosexual norms – for example, a boy who preferred to play with girls or a girl who refused marriage. In some cases, however, the strange behaviour continued even after the time had come for marriage. Because this potentially meant harm to the good standing of their families, elders would consult with *n'angas* (diviners) to determine the causes and the level of danger that the behaviour threatened. These varied according to many factors. At a low level of threat were offences thought to be caused by neglect or the frustration of natural sexual needs. Provided the act did not involve a sex act that crossed rank, age and totem (*mutupo*, or incest) lines, then the punishment could be light. Adultery by a neglected wife with a non-kinsman, for example, might require as little as the payment of a few beasts in compensation to the husband. Many forms of adultery by the husband were, meanwhile, not considered an offence at all but rather a man's right. A man could take his wife's younger sister to bed, for example, through the custom of *chiramu*, while a father-in-law could claim the same right to a son's new wife.

By contrast, sex acts that did cross forbidden lines could bring much stronger penalties. A case of adultery that involved incest received punishment as severe as exile. Another offence at this level of danger to the social order was having sex with an animal (bestiality). Such an act was usually linked to witchcraft (*huroyi*, or deliberate evil). The offender, or witch (*muroyi*), could be exiled or even killed if the behaviour was maintained.

As well as *muroyi*, the Shona believed in several types of spirit that could affect sexual conduct. Among the most feared was the avenging spirit, or *ngozi*. Unlike the pure evil of *muroyi*, the evil caused by *ngozi* stemmed from a deceased person's legitimate anger against a past injustice. An innocent victim of war or murder, for example, could return to demand justice. Another common cause for an avenging spirit was a wife who had been neglected or ill-treated in life. Her spirit would come back to haunt the offending husband and the in-laws who had failed in their duties to protect her. *Ngozi* were especially fond of bringing shame upon the family by making people behave in sexually outrageous ways. Girls who suddenly began flirting or kissing in public, or junior wives who openly seduced men, were probably possessed by such a spirit. The only solution was to appease the *ngozi* by offering compensation to the family that had suffered the original offence. Typically this would involve the haunted family giving up a virgin daughter to become a servant or slave in the family that had been harmed. In extreme cases the girl might have to be ritually executed to make the *ngozi* go away.

One type of *ngozi* put particular pressure on families to ensure that their children grew up to marry and have children. When an infertile woman or an impotent man died, a rat was thrown on their grave. The humiliated spirit returned to haunt the family.

Another type of spirit that affected women's sexuality was the *chidhoma*, or *chikwambo*, the Shona equivalent of the *tokoloshi* known throughout southern Africa. A *chidhoma* was an imp with a huge penis that, amongst other mischief, sometimes crept into married women's huts at night to stimulate them sexually. Visits by a *chidhoma* during the night could explain both a woman's unusual lack of sexual modesty and her lack of interest in her husband's attentions. How could she be blamed for either of these if she had been satisfied or over-stimulated by the *chidhoma*? Rather than punishing the woman for these inappropriate behaviours, a cure would therefore be sought by making the *chidhoma* go away through performing the proper rituals and sacrifices.

What about those men who did not or could not fulfil their marriage obligations? If it were a simple case of impotence or dislike of the wife, various methods could save the family from the shame of childlessness. These included aphrodisiacs to stimulate sexual performance. A wife could also turn to a husband-taming herb known as *mupfuhwira* in order to ensure that the husband did not wander far from the marriage bed. Lack of interest in the sexual obligations of marriage might also be associated with stranger spirits known as *mashave* who were simply passing through. Their behaviour often reflected foreign cultures and was thus unpredictable and potentially dangerous. They had to be tolerated and appeased until they eventually wandered off again. This would be known when the husband returned to the wife's hut.

If the problem persisted for a long time, or if it seemed that homosexual desires were present, then witchcraft could be at play. This demanded radical action to protect the whole community. In practice, however, the most extreme punishments were usually avoided. What if the accused witch returned as a *ngozi* to cause even greater havoc? Elders therefore sometimes went to great lengths to avoid finding the proof needed to justify an execution. According to one *n'anga*, 'homosexuals were also regarded as unstable or bewitched or witches themselves. People were afraid that maybe they would be violent because of the assumed instability, or that they [the accusers] might in turn be bewitched. So, basically, the homosexuals were left alone. For them to be killed it would have taken the village elders a long time going to several traditional healers to find out the truth. Sometimes the healers would refuse to find out because they would not have wanted to be the cause of someone's death.'

Same-sex behaviours might also be explained by other factors that removed any hint of blame from an individual. These included rare cases where an individual possessed both male and female sex organs. Same-sex couples were assumed to be of this nature and they lived together as husband and wife without attracting criticism. Similarly, a man who never married or appeared satisfied with a life of celibacy was thought to have *chitsina*, a streak of bad luck that was otherwise impossible to explain. Even in cases involving healthy males beyond the years of acceptable experimentation, same-sex sexual acts were not necessarily taken as serious breaches of morality. They could be mere accidents stemming from physical closeness. After all, bachelors normally slept together, typically in the nude, and huddled together for warmth against the cold winter nights. Who could blame them if such closeness sometimes unavoidably stimulated arousal? This was especially common with individuals under the influence of alcohol.

The punishment in such cases was usually light – a mere token if the accused admitted the accusations, although heavier if the assault involved force. As Headman Mbata from Mazoe (now Mazowe) district explained in a 1921 case, a deliberate attempt at sodomy or indecent assault required compensation of one beast. 'If however it was done while sleeping we would still require reparation but only a small amount.' To put this in context, the compensation for breaking off a promise to marry was normally set at ten to twelve beasts.

All these ways of understanding exceptions to the norm allowed families to accept sometimes quite odd behaviour by their children without blaming or punishing them. The 1927 case of Nomxadana Mazinge provides a good example of this attitude of acceptance. Nomxadana was a young man of about twenty-two when he was discovered in one of Salisbury's posh white suburbs. He was employed as a female nurse who went by the name of Maggie. He wore female clothes, including women's underwear and high heels. The discovery shocked the white community and the case went to court. His father was brought in to explain the young man's behaviour. Mr Slopo Mazinge replied simply, 'I have never noticed anything peculiar about Aced [i.e. the accused, Nomxadana]. I have always though him sound in his mind ... At the kraal Aced used always to dress in female clothes. He has always worked as a nurse. He associated mostly with girls at the kraal. My son has been wearing dresses ever since he was a baby. He has never discarded them although I have often given him males' clothes but he has refused to wear them. I have never thought him mentally affected.'

Another important part of the cultural protection against sexual scandal was that talking publicly about sex was taboo. Polite people turned their eyes away and, if possible, shut their ears and eyes against suspicious behaviour. What this meant was that sexual acts that were forbidden or shameful in theory could take place in practice as long as they remained a secret. For example, the custom of *kupindira* or *kusikira rudzi* (the creation of kin, or the survival of the lineage) allowed families to avoid the shame of a man's inability to make his wife pregnant. By this custom, either the man himself, his parents or his in-laws secretly invited a trusted male relative to fulfil the task, typically a brother. A child conceived in this way would bear the family resemblance so no one would know that the husband had failed in his fundamental duty as a man. Talk and rumours about a shameful sexual failure would be averted, as would the potential *ngozi* in the case of failure.

One case from Hwange district in 1923 illustrates how effective this taboo could be in suppressing knowledge of same-sex relationships. The case involved a middle-aged BaSili, or Bushman, named Mashumba and a youth named Njebe. The first to hear of trouble was the village headman, Maboma, when Mashumba complained that Njebe had beaten him up. Maboma held court to settle the case. At first it seemed like an easy case as Njebe admitted the assault. To Maboma's surprise, however, Njebe went on to explain that he and Mashumba had been having sex together in the open veld three times a week for the previous three years. Njebe further explained that he had lately begun to worry about becoming pregnant as a result of the intercourse and he had therefore requested an end to the relationship. Mashumba agreed without argument. Later, however, the two quarrelled after Mashumba proposed to have another go. According to Njebe: 'I struck Accd [Mashumba] because he said, "Come on, let us mount one another as before."' Mashumba, meanwhile, did not dispute the facts. He just thought Njebe should be punished for beating him up.

Not knowing how to handle such an unusual case, Maboma referred it to the colonial police. For us today, perhaps the most remarkable thing about the story is that the headman of a small village could have been so blind to an openly homosexual relationship that had been taking place within the village for all those years. Gays and lesbians in Zimbabwe today also acknowledge that traditional culture can work in their favour in a similar manner. One lesbian living in a small agricultural village in the mid-1990s put it this way: 'They [the neighbours] don't want to know that I am lesbian, though I bring my girlfriends here. They prefer to think that I'm just a very moral girl when they see

I don't hang around with boys. I don't see how you can really be blind to two people who are lovers, but they are.' Or they choose to be.

⌒ ⌣

Some men and women are more successful at reproduction than others. Over time, this natural difference in fertility contributed to the development of class differences in ancient African societies. These in turn gave rise to sophisticated forms of government and international relations. By around the year 1200, for example, a clear class structure had emerged amongst the Karanga. Elite men possessed huge herds of cattle that they used for paying *roora* (also known as *lobola*, or bride-price) to acquire more wives, for loaning out to their male subjects, and for attracting and rewarding new followers. They then used the tribute labour of their followers to mine for gold, to import luxury goods from as far away as China, and to build monumental houses of stone (*madzimbabwe*) for themselves and their families. By the time the Portuguese arrived in Zimbabwe in the early 16th century, the most important Karanga rulers were said to have dozens or even hundreds of wives of varying status and to enjoy political authority and spiritual prestige over a vast area.

The power of these early states rested upon the show of wealth of the elites, as well as their ability to command a military force. In addition, high state officials maintained an air of mystery around themselves that set them apart from commoners. In this, politics and religion blended and reinforced each other. The king, or *mutapa*, thus did not simply rule on his and his advisers' will; rather, he interpreted and represented the will of the ancestral spirits. Through his mediums he could ensure that those spirits brought rain and fertility, or he could withhold them. As such he needed to be shielded behind walls and curtains from the polluting eyes of mere commoners. The *mutapa* could also not be allowed to die from sickness or accidental causes. When the time neared, he was supposed to die in a ritual suicide, with some assistance if necessary. This was to ensure that the spirit, which protected the health of his people, was passed on without disturbance to his successor.

The *mutapa* placed himself outside normal humanity through yet another powerful symbolic gesture – ritual incest. By marrying his full sister he broke one of society's biggest taboos. The goal was not to produce a child as an heir; rather, it was to 'fortify installation' against rival claimants to the status of *mutapa*. In the case of the Manyika in eastern Zimbabwe, the king, or *chikanga*, was, for the same reason, said to have had sex with his own daughter on the back of a tethered crocodile, that animal being a symbol of the terrible power of the kingship. Such unions were known as *kupinga nyika* (meaning, to protect the land or nation). When practised correctly, *kupinga nyika* increased the fearful mystery and hence the political power of the ruling family, thereby reducing the danger of destructive civil wars.

Another violation of sexual norms that commanded people's respect was expressed in the role of the *mbonga* (guardian) or *mamuna* (female husband) of the chief. The *mbonga* was often the actual sister or aunt of the ruler. The spirit of a powerful male ancestor worked through her in order to provide advice as well as *muti* (protective medicine or magic) to the ruler during hunting expeditions and war. An *mbonga* could not offend the guardian spirit by sleeping with a real man. She was therefore supposed to be a virgin and to remain celibate out of respect to the ancestor, who returned the respect by keeping the *muti* strong.

The dangers of breaking that rule are famously recalled in the oral tradition of VaNyemba. VaNyemba was *mbonga* to the ancestors of the Chihota people who lived in the eastern part of Zimbabwe in the 18th century. On one occasion, she was accompanying her brothers on an elephant-hunting expedition to protect them from danger. The brothers entrusted her to the care of a local headman while they tracked the elephants. That headman broke the trust by raping her. Shamed by this violation, and fearful that her brothers on the hunt were now in mortal danger, VaNyemba killed herself. The brothers survived but raised an army to avenge the headman's crime. In this way, and by keeping the tradition alive through rituals to this very day, they successfully appeased the ancestor and allowed the Chihota people to prosper.

Ritual incest and celibacy may not have been the only forms of sexual inversion that served a political purpose in pre-colonial southern Africa. Evidence from Angola and Namibia from as early as the 16th century refers to a caste of male diviners known as *zvibanda, chibados, quimbanda, gangas* or *kibambaa*. Powerful female spirits worked through these men. They were said to have dressed as women except for a loincloth open at the back to invite anal penetration. The men who penetrated a *chibanda* paid a fee, but in return experienced direct contact with the spirit. That spirit then brought good crops or hunting, good health, or protection from evil spirits. The disapproving Portuguese found that *zvibandas*, in some cases, formally married each other and were well respected as diviners or healers in their societies. Some even turned up in the slave ships bound for the Americas where they may have inspired the cross-dressing cult figures and rituals of slave religions like Candomblé and Santeria. Male African slaves who dressed as women were also found amongst the hundreds of victims persecuted for sodomy during the Catholic Inquisition in both the Americas and Spain itself.

There is little evidence of a caste equivalent to *zvibanda* in ancient Zimbabwe. Symbolic gender and sexual inversion amongst the elites, however, was known. The main war chiefs to the *mutapa* in the 16th and 17th centuries, for example, were called *sono*, meaning 'women'. Below them were advisers known as *karanga*, literally meaning 'the junior wife' of *mutapa*. Gender inversion could also emerge amongst the general population when a spirit of the opposite sex possessed a child to prepare it for the role of spirit medium (*n'anga, sangoma* or *sanusi*). A child showing signs of this who did not respond to medicine to correct its behaviour would then most likely be apprenticed to learn the arts of divination. A boy who liked to play with girls instead of boys would be an example. As time went on, the female spirit who occupied a male body would show itself in increasingly feminine characteristics in the man, even to the point of insisting that the man wear women's clothing. The same would apply to a woman possessed by, for example, a male *njuzu*. Aschwanden describes such a case amongst the Karanga where an *njuzu* inhabited a woman named Angela. Its increasingly violent possessions made it impossible for Angela to have sex with her husband. Eventually, even thinking about sex with men began to make her ill.

Ritual gender inversion also appears amongst the Venda people in southern Zimbabwe and northern Transvaal (now Limpopo). Venda women in charge of initiation schools were called 'masters' (*nematei*) while the senior men who instructed boys were known as 'mistresses' (*nyamungozwa*). Among the Lovedu, another Karanga offshoot that migrated southwards from around 1600, the inversion involved women rather than men. The Lovedu 'Rain Queen' achieved the status of king by maintaining her virginity and by marriage to girls. The young girls served her in the same way that a regular wife would serve a husband, only to be replaced once they reached puberty when they were married off to men in the proper fashion. Another remarkable case of gender inversion for political reasons was that of Nzinga (also sometimes spelled Njinga or Zingha), ruler of the Ndongo (later Matamba) state for nearly forty years in the 17th century in what is now Angola. While Nzinga herself dressed and was addressed as a man, she reportedly had her male advisers dress in women's clothing.

Other forms of woman–woman marriage were also found and regarded with respect in many African societies. Typically this involved a senior woman, often a widow, who paid *lobola* to acquire a young wife. The wife then got pregnant by an invited man who had no claims upon the offspring. In this way, a widow who preferred not to remarry into her deceased husband's family could build up a family that belonged to her own household. Cases are recorded of women who became independently wealthy in this way as their daughters were in turn married off and brought in *lobola*.

Of course, none of this tells us about actual sexual orientation or conduct. A man may be a *sono* or *karanga* in title but still be a husband in sexual terms. A woman who becomes a husband by virtue of paying *lobola* may likewise continue to enjoy sexual relations with men. Nonetheless, we can reasonably speculate that some of the people who fulfilled these unusual gender roles did so in part because they offered a respectable cover for unusual sexual tastes. It certainly remains the case today that many African gays and lesbians actually prefer traditional means of enjoying their sexuality as compared to the western gay rights approach. By becoming a *n'anga* or *sangoma* they are excused from marriage or perhaps may even marry into their own sex while continuing to enjoy the blessing of family and community.

We also know from oral testimony that even outside these unusual gender roles, traditional culture recognised that intentional male–male sexual acts could take place as a form of *muti*. This had its own term in Shona to distinguish it from witchcraft: *divisi rakaipa* (bad medicine). By most accounts, bad *divisi* amongst the Shona involved incest with a female relative for the purpose of curing an otherwise incurable disease or persistent misfortune. As one Shona scholar expressed it, 'for medicinal purposes a brother and sister may mate'. But male–male *divisi rakaipa* was even more fearfully powerful. It could be used to cure impotence, to improve soil fertility, or to advance political ambitions. It would only work, however, if the act were kept in utter secrecy. A man willing to try such terrible *muti* would thus typically do so upon a young relative, pawn or slave. For the victim to report the crime he would need to overcome both his fear of the *divisi rakaipa* itself and the man's direct power over him.

⁓ ⌣

The Shona began to trade with Arabs, Persians, Indians and mixed-race Swahili from about a thousand years ago. Many of those Muslim traders came from highly urbanised societies with long traditions of tolerance for more or less open homosexual behaviour. While it is possible that Shona men learned new ideas about sexuality at the coastal trading centres, they do not seem to have carried them home to Zimbabwe. Even those Shona who converted to Islam, the Varemba, do not seem to have adopted Arab/Swahili notions about gender or sexuality. With the exception of practising male circumcision and marriage within the clan, the sexual and marital customs of the Varemba remained the same as they were in wider Shona society.

Similarly, we know that the Portuguese who arrived in Zimbabwe in the early 1500s came from a society where homosexual behaviour was relatively tolerated. Even one of their kings in the mid-1600s (Affonso VI) was notorious for his active homosexuality. But there is no evidence to suggest that the Portuguese exported such behaviour to their colonial empire. On the contrary, the Portuguese were better known for their lusty behaviour with African women. The Pope himself intervened again and again to try to prevent Portuguese men from entering into relations with African women. This had little effect. In the case of their colony in Mozambique, the tendency was for each generation of Portuguese to become more and more African in their appearance and behaviour. By the end of the 19th century, many so-called Portuguese in the Zambezi valley not only had African physical features but had also adopted aspects of African culture such as polygamy and *lobola*.

A much bigger cultural influence upon Zimbabwe in the pre-colonial era came from other Africans. This became apparent in the early 19th century during a period of upheaval known as the *mfecane* or *lifaqane*. A new style of leader and a new style of state had first emerged during the early 1800s in what is now KwaZulu-Natal. Shaka of the Zulu is the most famous of these leaders. He sought to harness the sexual energy of young men to the cause of military and political expansion. For instance, he abolished the ancient custom whereby boys spent several months at circumcision schools learning to become men under the supervision of local elders. In its place he initiated regiments where young men went for year-round military training. Warriors were then not allowed to marry or even to have thigh sex with girls until they had completed their military service to Shaka's satisfaction. This provided an incentive to bravery that helped turn the Zulu army into the most successful in the region. Zulu methods were then copied or adapted by others such as the Swazi, the Kololo (later Lozi) and the Ngoni who imposed their own new states as far and wide as modern-day Zambia and Tanzania.

Zulu-style controls over sexuality were introduced into Zimbabwe by groups of warriors and followers who migrated there from the mid-1830s. The most influential of these were the Ndebele and the Gaza-Ngoni (later known as the Shangaan). These two groups settled in southern Zimbabwe where they absorbed large numbers of Shona into their respective kingdoms. Both employed the regimental system to maintain highly disciplined armies that raided far and wide for cattle, wives and other tributes. For young men, this military service meant delaying marriage for five to ten years. But even after marriage the men were not free from the demands of the state. The first Ndebele king, Mzilikazi, punished older men who allowed themselves to be charmed into cowardice by married life by banishing them from their families. The missionary Robert Moffat observed this when he visited an Ndebele town populated exclusively by women and children. All contact between them and the men's village eight miles away was forbidden on pain of death until the men redeemed themselves in battle.

Like the Shona states that they conquered, the Ndebele and Ngoni invaders drew upon religious symbols as well as military force in order to demonstrate their power. As with the Shona, this included cases of gender and sexual inversion that expressed spiritual authority. Hence, the most effective Ndebele healers and diviners were men with the most exaggerated feminine (or masculine in the case of women) behaviour and dress. Shaka himself was said to have had this trait of effeminate characteristics, even to the point of claiming to have menstrual cramps. The Ndebele also adopted the role of *mbonga*. Lozikeyi was such a guardian, and reputedly the most powerful of the wives of Lobengula, the second Ndebele king. Lozikeyi had her own wife as well, both to keep her company and to bear children from Lobengula on her behalf.

Among the Ndebele and Ngoni warriors, it was believed that abstaining from sexual intercourse immediately prior to battle would heighten their preparedness for combat and hence improve their chances of victory. Battle preparations could also entail sex with males, not just amongst the warriors going into the fray but right up to the highest level of command. This followed the model of *divisi rakaipa*, that is, the warrior (the man in need of protection) taking his satisfaction on a passive younger servant. Of course, this was supposed to be kept secret in order to make it work, but evidence from similar militaristic states elsewhere in Africa, such as the Azande (Sudan, DR Congo), Nupe (Nigeria), and Tutsi (Rwanda, Burundi), suggests that it was probably an open secret.

Some Shona joined the Ndebele and Ngoni states, although as low-caste clients or as slaves. Others, however, maintained a steady resistance throughout the 19th century. Some of these adopted Ndebele customs that they believed would improve their military skills and fortunes. What was probably once rare and greatly feared thus gradually became more commonplace. As one elderly Karanga informant told us:

> I know the *ngochani* was traditionally done by chiefs and the leaders of soldiers here in Zimbabwe. The chiefs here were given strong medicines by the Ndebele and Zulu [Gaza-Ngoni] *n'angas* ... I also know that even the Ndebele and Shona when they were fighting, the soldiers they were made to have sex with other men for the whole group to be powerful. You see the Ndebele and Zulus were practising it since long back. But due to friendship, we Shona people have learned about that medicine from them and we are also doing it.

Whether the *ngochani* described above was really introduced by the Ndebele and Ngoni invaders or was a revival of ancient indigenous customs is impossible to know for sure. But whatever the case, the colonial conquest of Zimbabwe by whites between 1890 and 1897 only inflamed the stress and turmoil that African societies were under and increased the need for powerful *muti* to restore independence and social harmony. This seems to have encouraged even more male–male *divisi rakaipa*. One European missionary who was present during that time gives a hint of this. He observed in 1896 that sodomy was, in his words, 'simply common' in the villages of the Zezuru people around Fort Salisbury (Harare). This he assumed was a sign of the general moral corruption of Africans and further proof of the need for more Christian missionaries. Yet, unknown to him, the Zezuru at that very moment were preparing to join other Ndebele and Shona groups in a war to drive the whites out of the country once and for all. Could it be that the rumours of sodomy that the missionary was hearing reflected not everyday moral corruption amongst Africans, but the spiritual rearmament of the people in preparation for the first *chimurenga,* or war of liberation?

⌒ ⌣

The ancestors of the Shona and Ndebele of today, like most Africans, clearly placed great emphasis on sex as a means to reproduction. Sex done properly (with procreation in mind) connected the individual to the family, to ancestors and ultimately to God. Sex done properly brought children, with direct material benefits to the individual, the extended family and the state. It was a means to good standing in the community and was understood as essential to good health.

But sexuality in ancient Zimbabwe, as elsewhere in Africa, was clearly more complicated than the idealised heterosexuality that contemporary African leaders now claim as African tradition. For example, so strong were the social expectations to do sex properly that breaking from the norm acquired special symbolic power. The deliberate transgression of sexual norms could in fact generate powerful *muti* for good or evil in the eyes of the community. The need, or the desire, for such *muti* was greater or lesser depending on the stress a community was experiencing at any given time, notably, stress from drought, pestilence or war. Those conditions applied in Zimbabwe, as they did in much of southern Africa, as the 19th century drew to a close.

In short, we can say that sexuality in Zimbabwe on the eve of European conquest was both more varied than has usually been recognised, and in a state of change. As we shall see in the next few chapters, a striking irony behind the accusation that sexual immorality and homosexuality are western imports into Africa is that many of the first Europeans to observe African cultures closely were shocked by African willingness to bend the supposed natural laws of sexuality.

41

A cave painting, near Guruve, Zimbabwe
(Photo courtesy of Peter Garlake)

The cave paintings of the ancient San peoples or Bushmen are not always easy for the modern eye to make sense of. Experts, however, have concluded that they sometimes show sexual acts that contradict the stereotypes about Africa as a place where sex was historically only reproduction-oriented.

For example, the archeologist Peter Garlake described the painting above as a 'common San healing action'. The pale (sick?) man on the bottom left appears to be anally penetrating the healer, who holds ritual objects in his hands. The best estimates date such paintings as being from 1,000 to 11,000 years old.

Unyankwabe: A wife for Zodwa's ancestors

Nkunzi Nkabinde and Ruth Morgan of the Gay and Lesbian Archives, South Africa, have been conducting oral interviews with female traditional healers, or *sangomas*, for several years. Among other things, they have been trying to find out whether there could be an element of lesbian sexuality amongst these women or within traditional forms of woman–woman marriage. This is a claim that western anthropologists and African LGBT activists have long thought possible but which has brought angry denials from a number of African scholars. We hope that the story that follows puts an end to those denials. It is a shortened version of an actual interview with a Zulu *sangoma*.

My name is Zodwa. I was born in a small village in South Africa. My father had twelve wives of whom my mother was the fifth. I had to get married to the man that was chosen for me when I was fifteen. The Dlamini family brought 18 cattle for my lobola: *amongst them were two bulls and sixteen cows, as I was a virgin.*

Two weeks after the lobola *was paid we got married. Two cows and two goats were slaughtered from my family's side and even the Dlamini family slaughtered two cows and two goats. They did this as they combined our family ancestors. After that I had to go and live with him. When I arrived there I found that he had three wives. I was going to be wife number four. He didn't have any children with any of his wives.*

43

Because I am not a talkative person I would sit in my room and listen to my thoughts. I stayed with this man for four months. Throughout these four months he never came to my room at night. I would only see him in the morning, when he came to say good morning.

One day he came at night. As I was fast asleep, I didn't hear him when he came inside the door. I just heard him when he started to kiss me and I didn't know what to do because that was the first time I was having a man next to me. My body started to shiver and my heart was beating so fast. He told me to relax, that everything was going to be all right and then he undressed me. A part of me wanted to cry; another part of me wanted to run away. Inside my heart I know I didn't want this man and I didn't have feelings for him. During that moment I felt something sitting on top of my stomach and then when he tried to get on top of me, I thought that surely it was a snake. Then he just jumped off me and yelled 'there is a snake on top of you on your stomach'. I sat up straight and the snake kept on playing around my naked body. The snake crawled down from my bed to the floor and out my bedroom. Then he said to me 'your ancestors are strong'. I went back to sleep. He slept in my bedroom but he didn't do what he wanted. In the morning when we woke up he told me that he had dreamed of his great grandfathers. They told him not to touch me until I was eighteen years old.

When I was eighteen, I was already grown up. One day when I went to fetch water, I saw the face of an old man. I looked behind me thinking maybe he was standing behind me but, to my surprise, he was not there. Quickly, I turned and looked right into the water. The old man's face was there. Then he said: 'I am your great grandfather-in-law. I am the one who sent your husband to pay lobola for you. I want you to go and take the divination bag of bones which were mine when I was a sangoma there in the cave. Don't be afraid. I will tell the family where you are. I want you to go now. Don't look back.'

I found myself going to that cave that the old man was

telling me about. On the way I kept on hearing the voice of this old man saying: 'Don't look back', but in my heart I wanted to look back. When I arrived at the cave it was late and dark. When I got there I found an old lady standing outside the cave. She said to me: 'I have been waiting here for you. Your ancestors told me you were going to come.' She took me inside, dressed me in amabhayi (wrap-around cloths), put this white muthi (medicine) on my face and all over my body. My hair was twisted by this old lady. She taught me how to grind muthi and how to use it. I started my training to become a sangoma when I got there. I stayed there for two years, continuing with my training. Sometimes I went to live under the water to learn from the ancestors who live there for a month at a time and after that I would come back to the cave.

One day on my 20th birthday, I was sitting with my trainer. She asked me if I had ever slept with a man. When I replied: 'No,' she asked: 'What about a woman?' I replied: 'No, how can I sleep with a woman while I am woman?' She said: 'You can because I know inside of you there is a part that wants another woman.' I couldn't disagree with her because I knew she was telling the truth. There is a part of me which I choose to ignore. When I was staying with my half-sisters, sometimes I wanted more from them; I wanted to kiss their lips and touch them. But I couldn't tell anyone because I knew I would be beaten if I spoke about that kind of thing in my family.

She told me to get undressed and be naked. As she was my trainer, I didn't argue and she instructed me to go and swim in the lake. I did as I was instructed and after 20 minutes I came back naked to the cave. It was dark. After I returned I found out that she had put icansi (grass mat) on the floor for me to lie down on. Then she told me to lie down on my back and relax. I did as she said. As I was lying down, she came naked and knelt down next to me and started to caress me, kissing my body all over. I was nervous; my body was trembling. Then she said: 'Do you want to have a woman or not?' Then I found myself giving in. I started then to sleep with a woman and was able to be free.

When my husband found out that he couldn't have children, although he had four wives, he asked me to plead with him to the ancestors because he had spent money going to the medical doctors without success. He respected the fact that I didn't belong to him as I belonged to the ancestors. Then we made a plea by slaughtering a goat. We made a ceremony for the ancestors. After a week had passed since the ceremony, my husband came to me and told me that the ancestors had given him an answer. They had shown him in a dream that if he wanted to have a child, he firstly had to go and marry a girl who must stay here with me. I didn't disagree with him. I told him that if his grandfather wanted him to do this, he shouldn't wait. Then we agreed that he would go and pay the lobola for the ancestors but the girl was going to stay with me. She would be my unyankwabe, my ancestral wife. Unyankwabe is a person you are given by the ancestors: if you are a sangoma you have to have someone to look after you. It may be your husband, your sister or your uncle, anyone that the ancestors will choose for you to trust and believe in. That is unyankwabe.

He went to look for the family because he knew the girl, Busisiwe, and the place the ancestors had shown him in his dream. Then he came back two days after that and told me that they had found the family of the girl. Then I said they could bring her to see me.

We went into my house, closed the door, sat down and started to talk. I just looked deep inside Busisiwe's eyes and she was looking into mine. There was a vibration that happened between us and then I started to have those feelings that I had when I was with my trainer. Those were the feelings that I had never told anyone about. She told me that my husband had explained everything to her, but she didn't understand how she could marry an ancestor who is a man while she doesn't want to be with a man. Then I had to tell her that the ancestor that she is going to marry is in me: she will never have to be with a man if she doesn't want to. She said if she was going to be forced to accept the proposal she would do so. Otherwise she didn't want to accept this. I had to explain to her that she was going to be free and that no one was going to take her freedom away. She asked me if I was a same-sex oriented sangoma using the isiZulu words 'ngabe uyinkonkoni yesangoma?'. I told her that I didn't understand the words. It was a question I didn't know to answer, because it never came that way to me. I never saw myself as anything. I just saw myself as a sangoma and a woman who has feelings for another woman.

Although I never expressed my feelings to anyone else it was something that had happened to me with my trainer and a kiss once with a child at school. I never had anyone in my life to love me or share my feelings with. I have been alone all my life and then I said: 'I don't know but I have feelings which I never told anyone about them. I feel more attracted to women than to men.' Then she smiled at me. She said: 'Your secret is safe with me. Tell your husband that I said it's okay he can come and pay the lobola for me.' After that she left and I told my husband that she had agreed to marry my ancestor and my husband went back to her place with his family members to pay the lobola and she came to join the family.

After they paid lobola for her she didn't waste any time moving in with me. After two weeks, during the day, we were alone when my amathwasa (trainees) had gone to the fields to look for muthi. She started to ask me why I had married. Then, during our lovely conversation, she asked me how I felt about her. She wanted to know if I felt attracted to her. I just didn't know what to say. Then my heart started to beat so fast I found myself mumbling. She kissed me and said that we had to hide our feelings. Then we kissed and we never told everybody.

We sleep together staying in the same house. She helps me inside the house. She even helps me to teach amathwasa. She has learned to beat the drums and the trainees take her as their mother as they love her so much. Although they don't know that we are lovers: it is just between me and her.

In the month that she was living with the family, my

husband's first wife announced that she was pregnant and after that all of his wives fell pregnant. That's how I came to stay with her and how I got to show my feelings to her. Because I'm secretive, I never told anyone a thing. But when she started to stay here, we became so close until we became intermingled. Even my husband is dying of old age and he has never suspected a thing.

3 • early european influences on African sexualities

No one disputes that Europeans had a huge influence on African societies once they began their colonisation of the continent in earnest. This included the spread of epidemic diseases such as syphilis amongst humans and rinderpest amongst cattle. Europeans also introduced new ideas (salvation, guilt, hellfire ...), new technologies (guns, railways, whisky ...) and new relations of production (wage labour, chattel slavery, deferred pay ...) that struck at the heart of traditional society and values. New institutions and ways of organising people and property, such as title deeds to land, prisons, taxation, *chefs de cercle* and other kinds of bureaucratic chiefs, all combined to impose further, often violent, change to the ways that Africans lived.

Change for Africans extended to sexuality and gender relations in ways, and with a speed, that often created confusion and anger in the process. It was, and remains, tempting to blame the Europeans for the breakdown of the old moral order that allowed these changes to occur, whether it be prostitution or elopement or homosexuality. But is it really fair to blame Europeans when many Africans in fact eagerly took advantage of the new conditions and opportunities created by Christianity, capitalism and colonial rule? Is it fair to blame Europeans for the breakdown of the old order when, in fact, Europeans sometimes openly admired and actively supported the patriarchal ideals of traditional society through a policy known as Indirect Rule? The history of rapidly changing sexualities and gender roles in Africa is without doubt far more complicated than a simple corruption of Africa by decadent Europeans.

The task of the next three chapters is to explore this history as it played out in southern Africa, beginning from the very first European nibbles around the fringes of the region in the 16th and 17th centuries. The major focus in the first of these chapters, however, will be on the period that witnessed the establishment of a vast industrial empire centred upon Johannesburg, that is, the late 19th and early 20th centuries. The picture that emerges is that Africans were not passive victims of the new regime. On the contrary, they were active, complicated personalities who helped to shape the ways that changes in sexuality and society unfolded. The homosexual practices and identities that we see in Africa today are thus not mere imitations of western gay life, or learned from depraved priests, abusive colonial officials and perverted tourists. Such people undoubtedly existed here and there and they too had their impacts upon individual Africans; but, overall, modern African gay identities can be traced back to much broader changes in society. They are rooted in the struggles and debates about proper sexuality between Africans and Europeans over many years, debates that Europeans often could not control.

~ ⌣

The first European attempts to colonise central and southern Africa were made by the Portuguese, beginning in 1491 with their mission to the Kongo kingdom. By 1568, this mission had collapsed from the effects of civil war and slave trading. Outposts along the Angola coast, meanwhile, hardly grew beyond points for the export of slaves and for the marshalling of small armies to stir up trouble in the interior whenever the supply of slaves threatened to run dry. Portuguese colonialism thus had little direct impact on Africans in Angola in the pre-industrial period. The chaotic violence caused by their slave trading, however, did have indirect effects. In particular, it gave rise to wandering bands of brutalised men known as the Jagas, or Imbangala. These bands were said to have practised cannibalism, ritual child-killing and male–male sex or gender inversion to terrify their prey or to build up their awesome reputation.

Anna Nzinga was the most famous case of that. In the 1620s she took advantage of the political turmoil of the time, forging an alliance with the Jagas to secure her unusual claim to rule the Ndongo state. Sometime in the 1640s she decided to become a man, as the historian John Thornton phrased it, wearing men's clothes and taking male concubines, who were forbidden by her, on pain of death, to have sexual relations with women of the court. Nzinga was also said to excel at 'manly arts', such as the use of guns, and she personally led her warriors into battle against various enemies, including the Portuguese. She never gave birth to an heir but, after her death, was succeeded in the role of king by her sister. These events were regarded by the Portuguese and other Europeans of the time as scandalous and, indeed, were often taken as one more sign of African savagery.

Portuguese colonialism was better established on the eastern side of the continent, including through feudal landholdings in the Zambezi valley. In the 16th century, Portuguese traders and missionaries reached as far as the north-eastern part of present-day Zimbabwe, where they set up trading posts and made some converts to Christianity. There is little evidence, however, of any long-term cultural impact. Even in the lower Zambezi valley, Portuguese cultural influences remained extremely weak well into the 20th century. Far from corrupting African morals, Portuguese men tended to become Africanised in behaviour and appearance over time, through intermarriage with the families of local African elites and by adopting such practices as *lobola*. The disruptive effects of the slave trade were meanwhile much less than on the west coast, although here too there is some evidence of roving bands of cannibals and gender inversion that may be indirectly linked to the violence of Portuguese interventions.

The Dutch were the second group of Europeans to arrive in southern Africa and their impact upon African societies was ultimately much more profound. Their first outpost of Kaapstadt (Cape Town) was established in 1652. It was only a small part of a vast global trading empire rather than part of a campaign of territorial conquest or a religious crusade. The Dutch, nonetheless, brought a set of laws and social relations that grew from the Cape into a sprawling agricultural, slave-based colony. That code of law was then adopted by the British when they took over the colony in the early 19th century. Under British rule, so-called Roman-Dutch law was extended over an ever-widening area, including new colonies like Natal and Basutoland. It reached Zimbabwe when the Pioneer Column claimed Mashonaland as British territory in 1890. Roman-Dutch law, and the sexuality that it defines as proper, remains the basis of Zimbabwean law to this day.

Today, of course, the Netherlands is one of the most liberal societies in the world: even some of their right-wing politicians are gay. But it was not always so. In the 17th and 18th centuries, most Dutch practised a very devout and intolerant form of Protestant belief called Calvinism. They understood sensual pleasures of all kinds to interfere with or corrupt healthy spirituality, which in turn interfered with God's plan for material prosperity for the elect. Those sex acts that deviated from God's supposed intention (that is, reproduction between legally married Christians) were especially despised. Such acts were termed *venus monstrosa* or monstrous lust and those found guilty of it could face the death penalty. Monstrous lust included heterosexual intercourse between a Christian and a Jew, adultery, self-masturbation, female–female sexual affairs and male–male sodomy. 1730 was a particularly harsh year for repression of the latter in the Netherlands, when as many as eighty men were sentenced to death for having sex with males.

Cases of male–male sexuality also occurred in the isolated outpost of Kaapstadt. Who could be surprised by this? Men arrived there after weeks, sometimes months, at sea. They remained in port until the weather permitted, the cargo was loaded and the men felt refreshed. This could take several months. Meanwhile, unlike at other ports of call on the long journey from Europe to Asia, there were few women to assist the men towards that refreshed feeling. The local Khoisan population was sparse, and in any case the Dutch East India Company that administered the outpost prohibited its employees from taking local concubines. Among imported slaves at the Cape, males outnumbered females by as many as eight to one. Meanwhile, the few Dutch women there tended to be of the respectable or officer classes, married to company officials. In other words, for the majority of men who desired sexual relations during shore leave this left only 'monstrous' options. The fact that same-sex practices were not uncommon amongst local Khoi peoples, and that, likewise, most of the imported male slaves came from societies in Asia where same-sex relations were well known and relatively tolerated, made it easier for the sailors to find male partners for quick sex. The earliest case where we know the names of men involved in such affairs was that of the Dutch sailor Rijkaart Jacobse and the 'Hottentot' (Khoi) Claas Blank in 1735.

As in the Netherlands, punishments for such behaviour were severe. Sometimes the guilty were banished to a prison colony on Robben Island; others faced torture and execution by drowning. In a case from 1753, for instance, three men of different races were found guilty of consensual anal sex. They were tied together and then thrown to their deaths in the harbour. Up to five cases of sodomy were tried every year throughout the Dutch period, many of them involving slaves.

The British took over the Cape Colony in 1806 and they maintained the laws that cruelly punished so-called unnatural behaviour. In practice, however, the number of cases of reported male–male sexual crimes declined rapidly, reflecting the changing political and social situation. For one thing, Cape Town under British rule developed quickly into a small city. As the 'tavern of the seas', it attracted an ample supply of female prostitutes to its brothels from all around the empire. Sodomy with a male was no longer the only option for sex-starved seamen on shore-leave. For another thing, the British worried about provoking the conquered Dutch farmers, the Boers. It was a delicate political situation that could easily be upset if the new government started punishing the Boers' property (that is, slaves who were caught misbehaving). The British therefore tended to stay out of the business of policing slaves' and other private employees' morality, satisfied that the Boers generally took care of such matters themselves, with whips, chains and stern lectures from the Bible.

Punishments for those who were caught and tried for same-sex crimes also grew lighter over time. In fact, only a handful of convicted sodomists were ever executed under British rule. The very last man to be hanged in the Cape Colony for that crime was described as a Bastard Hottentot (meaning a mixed-race Khoi) named Adam January. January was hanged in 1852 for sexually assaulting another labourer, although the Governor later expressed regret about this. By the 1870s, the government effectively promised that there would be no more executions for sodomy.

Complicating matters after 1840 was the fact that the colony began to expand rapidly to include more and more Bantu-speaking peoples along the frontier. Societies such as the Xhosa and Fingo, and later the Zulu, Basotho and others, shared much in common with the Shona and Ndebele in their cultural understanding and practices around sexuality. They all placed high emphasis on sex for procreation, good health and spiritual meaning. They did not hide all this from the children; rather, children were taught the importance of proper sexuality to achieve social adulthood and community harmony, typically through initiation or circumcision school. Adolescents were also encouraged to practise their sexual skills or develop their sexual self-confidence in ways that did not threaten social harmony or family reputation by producing illegitimate children – for example, by thigh sex (sexual 'outercourse') and, for girls, through repeated stretching of the *labia majora*.

The first European missionaries tended to interpret African attitudes and customs as lasciviousness, in other words, an immoral fascination with sex. About the only thing good they saw in it was that there was apparently no or very little homosexuality. Otherwise, they campaigned relentlessly against African customs and, in some cases, even supported the use of force to impose European ideals of sexual morality. Colonial officials in the region were often privately sympathetic to this view but they tended to be more cautious in their public role about interfering too much with African gender and sexual relations. They quickly realised that such interference could be a recipe for political disaster were it to spark rebelliousness amongst the chiefs and senior men whom colonial governments relied upon to maintain social order and to collect taxes in the rural areas. As the frontier expanded, therefore, those Africans who remained in the rural areas were, for the most part, allowed to keep their customary laws and courts, a principle later called Indirect Rule. Roman-Dutch law applied only to those Africans who found themselves on lands claimed by the European settlers or who migrated to look for work in the growing towns.

The number of Africans in that second category grew rapidly as the colonial economy started to prosper. It began with young men during the idle phase of the agricultural season who took advantage of the time on their hands to travel to the commercial and industrial centres of the Cape and Natal. There they sought to earn cash to buy guns, ploughs, and other consumer items, and to pay the taxes that had been imposed upon them. At first, very few women either wanted or were able to make the same journey, with the result that the African population in towns was overwhelmingly male. Far from home and without the chance of *hlobonga* with girls, let alone marriage, some African men began to experiment with same-sex *hlobonga.* The first such case took place in 1860 in Pietermaritzburg when a certain Udelela was found guilty of attempted sodomy. The Natal courts took a very harsh view. For his crime, Udelela received fifty lashes followed by eighteen months of imprisonment with hard labour. In April of 1867, Mxakaza in Greytown was given five years and thirty lashes. Hogoza, also known as Ndhlebekanyilanga, paid an even higher price the following year. A Zulu youth who was just eighteen years old, Hogoza had been one of five young men sharing a hut in the Durban area. He assaulted Ziswana, who was only thirteen or fourteen years old, and then ran away. When caught, he defended himself by saying that there had been no actual penetration but then compounded his crime by attempting to bribe the other witnesses and the police. Hogoza became the last known male under British rule in southern Africa to be condemned to hang for having had sex with a male.

Over the years there were also reports of male–male sex in and around military camps, particularly between 1900 and 1902 when large numbers of soldiers from around the British Empire arrived in South Africa for the war against Boer independence. The number of such cases involving Africans is notably small, although the camp at Ladysmith may have been an exception. Two Zulu men, Ndukwana kaMbengwana and Qalizwe, later told the missionary James Stuart that, during the war, 'some natives in Ladysmith allow soldiers to commit sodomy by kneeling and presenting the buttocks (*dunuzaing*), the soldier having connection by the anus'. They were in effect prostitutes who charged ten shillings for the act. Others, according to Qalizwe, both young and old men, were victims of rape in the area around Howick military hospital.

These were isolated cases, to be sure, and the large majority of African migrants continued to hold to traditional practices while away from home, including celibacy. Indeed, not even the discovery of diamonds near Kimberley in 1867 and the emergence of a boom town in the northern Cape had an immediate impact upon African sexuality. Kimberley was in fact unusual for the time in that it attracted hundreds of female prostitutes of all races who catered to clients with cash, irrespective of race. In the early days of the diamond rush, when Africans could independently stake claims to dig and to own diamond mines, they possessed the means to visit the brothels and even to bring their families to stay with them. It was likely that it was this hot-blooded heterosexual atmosphere that gave rise to Kimberley's reputation as *Sotoma* (Sodom), as it came to be known amongst the Basotho.

The meaning of *Sotoma* in popular culture changed over time, however, as the diamond boom created the conditions that gave rise to a distinctively African form of male–male sexual relationship. *Inkotshane* (or *izinkotshane* referring to the plural 'wives') had its origins in the closed compound system that was introduced in 1879. By that time, small diggers had mostly been squeezed out from independent ownership of property by the big companies such as De Beers. Thousands of unemployed Africans lived in unregulated camps around the mines, hoping to find jobs or, better still, somehow tap into the growing trade in smuggled diamonds. The closed compound system was introduced primarily to control that illegal trade. The closed compounds also enabled the mining companies to cut the wages and other costs needed to maintain their workforce. By this system, African men were virtually imprisoned for the length of their contracts within fenced areas where they were fed on cheap, mass-produced rations. Outside the daily routine of work, they bathed, passed the time, and slept together in huge barrack-like buildings, typically divided into dormitories of eight to sixteen bunk beds. No women were allowed within the compound.

By 1885, over 25,000 men were locked up in such conditions. That was the year the first inklings emerged that the old practice of unmarried young men having thigh sex with girls (*hlobonga, ukumetsha,* or *gangisa*) was being adapted to the new situation. The pioneers in this respect were, by all accounts, the Tsonga or Shangaan. They often walked all the way from southern Mozambique, through Natal and the Orange Free State, and finally to Kimberley, where they made up the majority of mine labourers. Far from home for long periods of time, fenced off from the surrounding community and, accompanied by young boys as their servants, the men sought sexual release by *gangisa* with the boys. Whether they invented the word *inkotshane* out of an existing Tsonga word that mocked sexually loose girls, or whether they picked it up from Zulu, is impossible to know for certain. We do know, however, that, within two decades, the word and the practice it described was understood in many African languages far and wide throughout the region.

Gold rather than diamonds was the engine driving the rise of this new subculture. Gold was discovered on the Witwatersrand in 1886. Even more than the mines at Kimberley, it needed an army of cheap labour. Despite the hardships of the working conditions, African men streamed in from the surrounding countries in their hundreds and thousands to provide that army. Many were attracted by the prospect of relatively good wages and adventure; some were tricked by corrupt recruiters and liquor-sellers; others were fleeing crushing poverty or civil conflicts at home. They found accommodation in massive compounds that sprang up around the mines. Meanwhile, police and native administrators took often ruthless action to keep women and children away. A measure of their success can be judged by the fact that there were 90 known Tsonga women in the Johannesburg area in 1896 compared to 30,000 Tsonga men.

The practice of taking boys or youth as temporary wives quickly became the norm, or at least unremarkable in this context. But people often like to put a name and a face to big changes to help understand them better. And so it is that oral history refers to one man in particular who popularised the practice – Sokisi or *Ishe* (Lord) Socks. Sokisi was a Tsonga migrant working at Brakpan mine in the early 1890s. He so preferred *izinkotshane* that a new expression entered the language in his honour. *Umteto ka Sokisi*, meaning 'Sokisi rules' or 'the rules of mine marriage', was a code of conduct that defined precise kinds of behaviour that were allowed between males in a sexual relationship in the mine hostels. They prohibited anal penetration, for example, in favour of between-the-thighs sex. As in male–female *hlobonga*, the rules stated that the *inkotshane* had to remain passive and could not reciprocate the sex act; in other words, only the husband could enjoy an orgasm. The wife, sometimes called *nsati* (which literally meant woman or wife) or *umfaan* (young boy), also performed other feminine duties such as cooking and fetching water and firewood. Over time, the males who filled this role even became feminised in appearance, for example, by adopting feminine dress, wearing false breasts made of coconut shells, putting on scent and keeping well shaven.

For some years these practices remained largely hidden, even from mine management. By 1902, however, rumours had travelled back to Mozambique and it was the Portuguese Governor General himself who protested to the British authorities about the suspected sexual exploitation of African boys at the mines. He was diplomatically told not to worry. It was not that the British could fully deny the accusations, they were simply unwilling to do anything that might disturb the smooth flow of labour into the mines, even to talk publicly about the issue. In the aftermath of the Anglo-Boer war, the shortage of labour was so desperate that they dared not risk losing any workers by interfering too closely, or by publicly discussing the workers' private lives.

Ironically, this very shortage of labour is what eventually brought the secret out into open public debate. Between 1904 and 1906 over 60,000 Chinese men were brought into South Africa to ease the labour shortage and get the mines back into full production. They were under contracts that required them to go home at the end and that specified that they were to do only unskilled labour. Nonetheless, white workers feared that the companies might eventually use the Chinese either to replace whites or to force wage cuts. The white workers therefore staged a number of violent and openly racist anti-Chinese campaigns. When this did not work, they tried another tactic to pressure the government to send the Chinese home. In 1905, whites spread a rumour that the Chinese used 'catamites' (or passive sodomists) and were teaching the African workers 'unnatural vice'. A huge scandal erupted that caused major embarrassment to the imperial government back in London. A public enquiry identified a small number of alleged catamites who were promptly deported back to China. On the whole, however, it proved the accusations false. The government must have hoped that that was the end of the story.

It wasn't. The catamite scandal encouraged missionaries to speak out about another secret which they knew had more basis in fact. The American missionary, Albert Baker, came forward with the claim that homosexual relations amongst Africans were much more widespread than they had ever been amongst the Chinese. They were also worse, he wrote, in that male–male sexual relations amongst African workers often involved child abuse, improper use of authority and violence up to and including kidnapping, rape and even murder. So shocking were his allegations that the government had no choice but to order another public enquiry. It appointed two men to investigate the problem and propose solutions: a magistrate named J. Glenn Leary, and Henry M. Taberer, a fluent Xhosa-speaker then working in the Native Affairs Department.

Leary and Taberer began by interviewing a wide range of missionaries, mine overseers and African men and youths on mine compounds around Johannesburg. From the information they gathered about 'unnatural vice', as they phrased it, they prepared a report in early 1907.

This concluded that Baker's claims were basically correct and that the practice of *inkotshane* was widespread and popular amongst African workers. How much so? One witness claimed that out of eleven new recruits to his mine one day, eight were taken as wives by the next. Others claimed that 'no one' was without an *inkotshane*. Leary and Taberer disagreed with Baker's claim that the men formally married with *lobola*. They also found little evidence that violence or child abuse was rampant. In some ways, however, this last finding almost made matters worse. The wives, it seems, did not have to be forced but actually accepted, profited from and perhaps even enjoyed the relationship. It was a potentially big blow to the British view of themselves as a civilising influence upon African morals.

Leary and Taberer made a reasonable effort to try to understand why obviously heterosexual men were choosing to have sex with younger males. After all, the cultures they came from had no category of homosexual and they stressed the importance of virility and fertility to masculine and feminine identities. Many of the men actually had female wives and children back home in the rural areas. So why did they do it?

Leary and Taberer concluded that the men behaved as they did in part because of sexual frustration caused by the compound system, where they were housed in male-only hostels for long contracts away from home. The men themselves explained it in part as a reaction to fears about going to female prostitutes in the surrounding farms and townships because, unlike in Kimberley, the Johannesburg compounds were open for the men to move in and out. Their fears included sexually transmitted diseases such as syphilis, which, in the days before penicillin, was known amongst the men as a slow, humiliating death sentence. There was also the fear of losing hard-earned wages to a town woman and thereby being unable to provide for the real family back home. Finally, there was the very sensible fear of the criminal gangs that patrolled the townships from the earliest days of the Johannesburg gold-rush. Safer by far for the men to stay within the compound and pretend that boys were girls.

The wives, meanwhile, submitted to being 'breathed upon' by men because, in the first place, they were from cultures where young people showed respect and obedience to elders. Secondly, the men gave them gifts, money and protection in return. This was worth a lot considering the low pay and the high danger in mine work. A male wife in this situation could also count upon the fact that, as he grew more mature and acquired some savings of his own, he could graduate from the wife role to become a husband. In other words, it was a phase of life to be passed through, building character towards full manhood. Neither the men nor the wives regarded the affairs as real sex but simply as play or a harmless pastime. Even the women back home do not seem to have been greatly upset by the rumours they began to hear about their men's behaviour at the mines. After all, it was far better that a husband take a sexual partner who did not give him a disease or get pregnant than to go to a town prostitute who did. On both counts, a town wife was far more threatening to a rural wife than a boy wife at the mines would ever be.

Later reports and the recollections of the men themselves have complicated this picture by offering other explanations of *inkotshane* as well, including fun, desire and rebellion against traditional authority. Some old men who have recalled those days thought that taking male sexual partners was in fact the majority practice, not a rare or secretive one. Dances, feasts and wedding processions added to the sense of fun that was otherwise so lacking in the bleak environment of the industrial compounds. They expressed that they got emotional, not just sexual, satisfaction out of the relationship. It is not that the men considered themselves gay, but they admitted to feeling affection or even love towards their *umfaans*. One story about Sokisi also suggests that taking *izinkotshane* was a way for young men to stand up against the interference of elders. Apparently, King Gungunyana had heard about Sokisi and ordered him to return to Mozambique to be punished. Sokisi not only remained in Transvaal in defiance of his king, he cheekily renamed his principal *inkotshane* Sonile, after Gungunyana's chief wife.

Leary and Taberer tried to reassure the government that the problem was not necessarily as bad as it first seemed. For one thing, they claimed, *inkotshane* was limited to Africans from Mozambique and that therefore some of the blame could be passed on to the Portuguese. In fact, African witnesses did not fully support this notion, as they mentioned other ethnic groups such as the Nyanja (Malawi) and even the Shona as taking part. James Ngonyana was a witness from Melsetter (now Chimanimani, in south-east Zimbabwe). He explained that the practice may have originated amongst the Shangaan but now 'the men take boys from any tribe'.

There was also some debate about the kind of sex that took place. Most people thought it was *hlobonga* only and they claimed that no 'actual sodomy' took place. Of course, since no African words were ever recorded for this concept during the inquiry, it is hard to know how accurately it was translated. But at least one witness clearly understood and strongly disagreed with the no-sodomy rule. Phillip Nyampule, a Chopi from Mozambique, told the inquiry that, in his experience, anal penetration was also practised. He further disagreed with one of Leary and Taberer's ideas to discourage it. 'I do not think the separation of the boys from the men would have any effect because the grown-up men do it themselves, with each other. Because the men practise it amongst themselves, the little boys also practise it with each other.'

After listening to all this testimony, Leary and Taberer had to come up with recommendations for the government. They considered a number of strategies to try to put an end to *inkotshane*, including firing men found doing it and publicly shaming them in front of their families back in the home villages. They concluded that these ideas were not practical. In fact, drastic measures to repress such a widespread and apparently popular practice would be likely to backfire and might lead large numbers of men to desert their work altogether. Leary and Taberer therefore favoured a gradual approach to encourage the men to change their ways. For starters, they recommended that curtains be removed from around the men's beds so that no sexual activity could take place in secrecy. They also supported the idea of allowing more missionaries into the compounds to increase their direct propaganda against homosexuality. The practice of men bringing very young boys with them from Mozambique was to be discouraged.

Most of these recommendations were accepted by the government and passed into law in 1907. The mine-owners themselves, however, made no secret of their lack of enthusiasm. Their business was to make money, not to judge sexual morality. They worried that even such mild steps as removing curtains would either drive their precious cheap labour away from the mines, or would lead to increased recruiting costs. In other words, if *inkotshane* were suppressed and the men turned to female prostitutes instead, they would get sick from sexually transmitted diseases and would need to be replaced. Despite the new law, therefore, and despite Bible-thumping campaigns by the missionaries, *inkotshane* did not noticeably decrease in the following years. On the contrary, it seems to have grown even more commonplace in line with the growing numbers of migrant labourers housed in mine compounds and male-only hostels.

The war years, 1914 to 1918, were especially rich in missionary complaints about *inkotshane,* perhaps because the pressures to increase production for the war led government and companies to relax even their limited monitoring of the workers' social lives. But the practice also continued to grow from the 1920s to the 1950s, years that saw the number of women in town increase dramatically. By the early 1960s, blaming *inkotshane* on the shortage of women no longer applied, if it ever truly did. Instead, being and taking an *inkotshane* had become a part of mass working-class culture, an initiation from boyhood to manhood that proved a man's worth to himself and his community.

And so, the issue of *inkotshane* kept resurfacing. To avoid embarrassment, the government sometimes found itself having to cover up the facts from nosey questioners who might disturb the labour situation. When Mpondo chiefs in Transkei complained about it in 1928, for example, the government scrambled to assure them that the rumours they had heard were blown out of proportion. When a Catholic priest in Basutoland complained about it in 1947, he was deported from the colony. Even in the 1950s and 1960s, when male homosexuality began to be mentioned in African fiction and in letters to the African press, it almost seemed as if a censor were at work to stop full and honest investigation from taking place. It was not until the 1970s that the mine companies and the mine-workers' union began to take decisive steps towards destroying the mine marriage system, by which time probably millions of African men had passed through it.

~ ⌣

Kimberley and Johannesburg were by no means the only industrial or administrative centres in Africa to experience something like the mine marriage phenomenon. French officials noted it in some of their Central African colonies as well, while Michael Davison, a gay man himself, described a well-established drag and homosexual scene in the African slums of Dakar when he visited it in 1949. It seems likely that further research will uncover similar kinds of relationships in other places where the economic system depended on long-term male migration and restricted female urbanisation.

In the chapters that follow we will look at how this may have affected African societies as a whole. For now, however, a fair conclusion we can make is that Europeans clearly did not introduce male–male sexuality to Africa, or teach Africans their homosexual ways. What they did do was to create a particularly brutal form of racist capitalism that effectively encouraged African men to invent their own new type of male–male sexual relationship. There certainly were instances where boys and young men were raped or kidnapped or threatened or pressurised against their will into abusive and humiliating sexual relations. The majority of evidence, however, suggests that such cases were relatively rare and that participants understood and appreciated the advantages. In the context, and surprising as this may sound to the modern ear, the new relationship had some quite positive elements for the physical and emotional health of Africans.

A difference of opinion

The following is an adaptation of the actual testimony given by two African men at the City and Suburban Gold Mine, Johannesburg on 18 January 1907. The interviews were part of the government enquiry into 'alleged prevalence of unnatural vice amongst Natives in mine compounds'. They give a good sense of the conflicting views and the different prejudices that Europeans and Africans brought to the question. Of particular interest is the way that racism and homophobia worked together in the minds of the colonial officials.

Picture the scene: a low-slung, barracks-like building; a bare light bulb hanging from the rafters; two distinguished-looking white men behind a wide oak desk; an African clerk poised at a side table. The first witness enters, trying to look respectable in his faded jacket, black cotton tie and starched, threadbare shirt. His neatly pressed trousers ride just about an inch too high above his ankles as he takes his seat on a stool in front of the commissioners. They acknowledge him and then each other with a nod. Mr Henry Taberer, glancing over his notes, begins:

'Mr James Ngonyana?'

'Yes, baas.'

'Do you need an interpreter?'

'No, baas'.

'Well done. Shall we, Mr Leary?'

Leary takes the cue. A magistrate, he wastes no time in getting to the point. 'What are you?' he asks.

'A Shangaan, my baas.'

'Where is your kraal?'

'At Melsetter, baas, in Southern Rhodesia.'

'Who is your chief?'

'Tshomo. He is beyond the Sabi River.'

'How long have you been here?'

'Twelve years on the fields, baas. At first I worked in the City and Suburban and afterwards I worked for the missionary, Mr Baker. I am now teaching at the Wolhuter School Compounds and Interior Mission.'

'What tribes are represented there?'

'Practically all tribes.'

Leary narrows his gaze and takes the witness's soft brown eyes directly into his own. 'James,' he says gravely, 'I believe you are aware of the nature of this inquiry. Your employer, Mr Baker, kindly gave your name to us. I want you to be an honest African and tell us everything you know. There is no reason to be afraid. Do you understand?'

Ngonyana nods, adjusting his tie. 'Yes, baas.'

'Do you know this practice, inkotshane?'

The suddenness of the question takes Ngonyana by surprise. He pauses. After drawing a deep breath, he continues in a measured tone. 'Yes, baas. It is a custom whereby the men make love to the younger boys. They sleep with them and use them as wives, lying with them from the front, between the thighs.'

Leary purses his lips, shifts his papers, and casts a frown towards Taberer. 'Between the thighs, you say? Not, erm, not ... '

'I have never heard that there has been the other ... '

'I see. I see. And when precisely did you first hear of this revolting practice?'

'At the City and Suburban at the end of 1895. It is not a practice in our own country and anybody caught doing it would be killed. I am talking about the Shangaan. There was a good deal of it here in 1895 but it is much worse

now. I have seen this thing done myself when I was living in the compounds. The principal people who do it are the Shangaan, Inhambanes and M'chopi.'

Leary and Taberer turn to each other with a brief, knowing smirk. 'In other words, all Natives from Portuguese territory. Any others?'

'I have not seen it amongst the Xoxa nor the Pondo. The Swazi are about the same as the Zulu, I think. I have seen none amongst either the Basutoland Basuto or the Transvaal Basuto. But I think that the tribes do not specialise; the men take boys from any tribe.'

'Explain exactly what you mean by "take",' says Taberer. 'Are you saying they kidnap the boys? Do they use force?'

'No, baas. The people who practise this pay for the boys to the relatives in the country they come from.'

'Pay? Are you saying that they pay lobola?'

'Not lobola as such. In fact, I do not know what amount of money they pay; it is according to agreement. I know it is the custom that sometimes the relatives leave the boys here and go home with the money that has been paid for the boy. Boys have come to me and complained that they have been prevented by the mine guards from coming to school, and threatened with a thrashing.'

'Go on ...'

'The mine guards are the worst offenders, baas. Some of these boys are kept by several men: others are simply recognised as inkotshanes and used by anybody, even strangers. Their payment is sometimes in the shape of a handkerchief or a waist cloth and sometimes in money.'

'Tell us, James, why did you not report this thing to the authorities when you first heard of it?'

'I did not know it was a crime according to the laws of white people. That is because when some boys who refused to be practised on complained to the Compound Manager nothing was done.'

'I see. Did many of the boys complain?'

'In fact, not. The boys like being inkotshane because of the pay they receive and the money their fathers are given.'

After a moment of silence, Leary pushes himself back from the desk and turns to his colleague. 'Mr Taberer, do you wish to pursue any further questions?'

'None at this time, Mr Leary. Thank you, Mr Ngonyana. You are a courageous African to speak to us so honestly about these most distasteful matters. You may step down.'

'Yes, baas.'

The first witness withdraws from the room. The next enters with calm dignity, his shoes pattering softly as they cross the polished cement floor. An older man, flecks of white in his hair, he slowly takes his seat upon the bare stool as directed. 'Do you speak English?' Leary addresses him.

'Yes, your Worships.'

'You are a Christian?'

'I am proud to be so, your Worships.'

'Very good. Tell us now your name, and what are you?'

'I am called Phillip Nyampule. I am a M'Chopi, from Portuguese East Africa. My chief is three days north of Delagoa Bay.'

'How long have you been here?'

'I have been on the Rand about 15 years. When I first came I worked on the Wemmer mine. I left the mine in 1902 and am employed under Mr Baker on mission work. Before working at the Wemmer, I worked at the Glencairn and at the Crown Reef. I am now a teacher at the Ferreira mine.'

'Tell us what you know about inkotshane.*'*

Silence, save for the busy scratching of the clerk's quill on paper. Nyampule casts a quick glance over to the clerk, who refuses to meet his eye. After a cough to clear his throat, Nyampule admits, 'I know of this practice. When I was in the compounds I was one of the subjects. I was an inkotshane. *The guards and other natives used to make use of us as wives.'*

'Did you consent to be a wife in this fashion?'

'I consented to be one of them. I was forced to consent to this because I was under these guards and they used threats against us. They also used to give me presents; sometimes

five shillings and sometimes two. I also used to make presents in return.'

'You will pardon us, I trust, should we offend decency by asking such questions, but Mr Nyampule, how is it possible for one male to make a wife of another male?'

'The custom is to sleep with a man from in front or from behind. They do it through the thighs but there are some who enter the behind of the other.'

'Actual sodomy?'

'Yes. I was subjected to both forms. I was inkotshane with two men at different times.'

'Is this a custom amongst the pagans of your country?'

'This practice does not prevail there.'

Taberer interjects, 'I have heard that the Portuguese soldiers practise this with your people.'

'I have heard so, yes, but I have not seen it to my knowledge.'

'Where then do you suppose that it first started?'

'It was started by a Shangaan at Springs. This man collected a number of boys. He told us that they were his wives and that we should do the same. That was many years ago. The Shangaan, M'Chopi and Inhambane are the principal offenders. I have never heard of Xoxa or Basuto practising it.'

'And are the men not ashamed? Why do they do this when I understand that there are women on some of the farms in the area?'

'Men can get women, your Worship, but they are afraid of becoming sick, especially in the penis. The women are loose, and after some time with them, the penis can fall off. I think some of the men also prefer the boys because of the enjoyment. There is a practice of men going from compound to compound competing in dancing and thereby attracting boys who select them as their keepers.'

'So, are we to understand from this that it is not only the gold mines that are affected?'

'Yes, your Worships. This practice existed on the coal mines at Vereeniging where I was teaching in 1903 and 1904.

I know this existed because one of my boys confessed to me and I also heard them quarrelling about inkotshane money. At the Ferreira, where I am now teaching, the practice is very common.'

'It has been said that some natives lobola the inkotshane. Is this the case?'

'Yes. They pay money to the elder relatives. They pay two or three pounds. Some of the boys object and others do not. Those who object are forced.'

'And when the boys grow older, do they still remain as wives?'

Nyampule looks down at the floor for a moment, gathering his strength. He then addresses the magistrate boldly. 'To speak for myself', he says, 'when I grew up I ceased to be inkotshane but I took an inkotshane in my own turn. I practised the thing both ways upon him, from the front and from behind. I also practised actual sodomy.'

'Good God, man, what did the Compound Managers have to say about all this?' There is an anxious pause. 'Come on, now, speak up.'

'Your Worship, this practice prevailed when I arrived here. It has gone on increasingly and it is worse now. I never complained about it to the Compound Manager or anybody, nor do I know of any case where a boy complained to him. I have seen the Compound Manager at the Wemmer strike a man that he caught in the act. But otherwise it is not talked about by the whites. I did not even know that a man could be legally punished for this offence when I first came here.'

Taberer shakes his head in dismay. Leary, however, presses on. 'Now, of course, you are aware of the evil of this practice. What remedy do you then suggest?'

'The remedy I suggest is to make the European Managers responsible for reporting any cases which come to their notice, not the indunas. The guilty ones can then be punished. Now, the guilty are often the very ones who are responsible to report.'

'And if this cannot be done? Shall we tell their wives? Shall we separate the boys from the men?'

'I do not think the separation of the boys from the men would have any effect because the grown-up men do it themselves, with each other. Because the men practise it amongst themselves the little boys also practise it with each other.'

'I see ... Well, thank you, Mr Nyampule, that will be all.'

'Begging your pardon, your Worships, but if the men could be provided with proper houses and they could bring their wives ... '

'Thank you, Mr Nyampule. As I said, that will be all.'

4 • sex behind bars

A common belief at the time of the Leary and Taberer enquiry was that *inkotshane* relationships first appeared not in the mine compounds but in prisons and amongst criminal gangs. Gangsters who graduated from the prisons then taught or forced men and boys at the mines to engage in this kind of sex, sometimes by initiating them through gang rape. Even today, people commonly assume that prison sex and male–male sexuality in industrial hostels are basically the same thing and that rape in both places is amongst the main reasons for homosexuality appearing in wider society. This view holds for females as well as males. One study from South Africa in the 1990s, for example, talks about lesbians in prison as tough, fearless and almost as fearsome as the male gangs. In Zimbabwe, articles in the state-controlled press have hinted that 'known lesbians' in the city of Harare (probably meaning GALZ members) could be traced back to a culture of rape, threats and sexual humiliation in prison.

Personal accounts of prison sex paint a more complicated picture. One gang leader, who spoke at length about this very issue in 1912, went so far as to deny that his gang's system of homosexuality had started in prison. On the contrary, explained Nongoloza Mathebula, it dated from when they still moved freely in the hills south of Johannesburg and when gang members could choose equally between taking male or female 'wives'. To give another example, Moses Dlamini spent time as a political prisoner on Robben Island in the mid-1960s. He recalled cases of both horrible gang rapes and loving homosexual relationships. He even described his surprise at meeting a devoted couple of men there who had 'married' many years before at the mines and who desired to maintain their relationship in prison despite angry opposition from the other inmates.

Another anti-apartheid activist who wrote about his time in prison was Zackie Achmat, a slightly-built, gay, coloured youth at the time of his arrest in the 1980s. He had good reason to fear what awaited him behind bars. Yet what happened on his first night in jail was an erotic, almost tender sexual and emotional encounter with a hardened criminal, which forces us to question the stereotypes of homophobia and rape in prison. Two young Zimbabwean men who were interviewed for this research made an even more surprising claim about their time in prison. They would not mind going back, they told us, since their lives as 'wives' had been better in many ways than the poverty and loneliness that they currently experienced as free men in a resettlement village.

In this chapter, we look at different types of same-sex relationships that developed in the prisons of South Africa and how governments in that country tried to deal with them or, in some cases, to exploit them. This history is not just one piece in the larger puzzle of LGBT history. It also speaks to issues that affect the whole of society. For example, prisons have been identified around the world as key contributors to the spread of HIV, particularly when they are overcrowded, understaffed and underfunded to the extent that inmates experience malnutrition and other hardships. Those conditions apply in much of Africa today, creating a high-risk environment that acts like a carburettor to the fuel of HIV/AIDS. Some of the heightened risk in prisons is caused by injection drug use and tattooing, which transmit the virus from blood to blood on dirty needles. But some of it can be linked to sex. If we can therefore separate truths from stereotypes about prison sex, it may help us to imagine creative ways in which to deal with the prison-health crisis.

～〰

Prisons were one of the cornerstones of the colonial system in Africa from the very beginning. South Africa's first penal colony goes back to the 17th century when the Dutch began dumping law-breakers on adesolate pile of rocks a few miles off the coast of Cape Town (Robben Island). Various forms of lock-up, work house, convict station and juvenile reformatory followed as the frontier of white settlement expanded and as unruly new towns sprang up. Social tensions arising from the racism, sexism and economic inequalities of early colonial rule were often inflamed by alcohol to produce a constant human stream through the prison system.

These institutions shared the obvious objective of controlling and punishing law-breakers. There was an element of reform or moral re-education sometimes tacked on, but the ruling assumption in these early days was that people who had broken the law had given up any rights to humane treatment. Prisons, and even supposed reformatories for youths, consequently shared a culture that seemed almost designed to attack the basic human dignity of the inmates. Hunger, terrible cold, excessive heat, beatings, torture, loneliness, boredom, humiliation, hopelessness and warder corruption were all built deeply into the ways that the institutions were organised. After all, the thinking went, if word got out that inmates were treated decently in prison, people might commit more crimes simply in order to avoid work or poverty on the outside.

Under such conditions inmates had to stick together to survive and develop their own codes of honour to keep up their spirits. They also, and almost unavoidably, struck up close physical relationships, whether this be huddling together against the cold, or trading sex in exchange for food and smokes. Some, humiliated by the treatment they received at the hands of warders, took out their rage on other inmates who were weaker than they were.

Isolated cases of sex between prisoners were reported on Robben Island throughout the 18th century. Men caught in the act were usually flogged and given extended sentences. Yet, on the whole, it seems that prison officials largely turned a blind eye. They certainly did not go to extra lengths to uncover secrets amongst the men. How else to explain the case of Claas Blank and Rijkhart Jacobz, two inmates who maintained a homosexual affair for over a decade (1724–35) before they were caught and punished. The British, too, after they took over the Cape, seemed to regard same-sex affairs in prison as basically harmless and perhaps even beneficial. If the prisoners were secretive about it and it kept them quiet, despite the bad living conditions in prison, then it might actually help in the smooth operation of the place.

Concerns did arise once in a while to disturb this attitude: concerns about the men's morality or about possible political embarrassment if the general public were to get to know too much. But almost nothing ever came of these concerns. For example, the imperial government in London in 1872 questioned the slack attitude of prison officials in the Cape Colony and ordered that drastic, immediate steps be taken to stamp out sodomy in the prisons there. They never made clear what precise steps had to be taken, however, and no new funds were provided to help. The Cape Colony, meanwhile, gained self-govern-ing status soon after and no longer had to worry about interference from London. The issue, much like the prisoners themselves, became largely forgotten.

Prison sex next came to public attention shortly after the Chinese catamite scandal in 1906 and the start of the missionary campaigns against *inkotshane* on the mines. By then it was obvious that the prob-lem had not only grown worse since the criticisms of the 1870s, it had also become a potential threat to a very delicate political situation. A bitter and hugely destructive war had just been fought and much of the country had yet to recover economically. The diverse colonies of British southern Africa were moving towards self-government and union, a process of negotiation that involved repressing African rebel-lions and political expectations. The population of the colonies had meanwhile changed dramatically, with more black Africans living in towns than ever before. So, where previously cases of male–male sex in prison involved mostly white or mixed-race inmates, by 1908 there were greatly increased numbers of black African men to deal with as well. The government feared that these men, crowded into brutalising conditions, were learning behaviours that they would eventually carry from prison out into wider society. A growing, criminalised African population was then bound to upset relations with the poor, disgruntled whites and complicate the negotiations for political union.

The Minister of Native Affairs at the time believed that the root of the problem was that large numbers of African men were being convicted of minor crimes such as drunkenness or petty theft. They were then being thrown into jail together with hardened criminals. This practice, he concluded, was 'not only calculated to spread but is actually spreading the evil of sodomy'. Another investigation in 1912 alarmed officials even more when they discovered that sodomy in prisons was taking place in an organised fashion. Homosexual prison gangs not only preyed upon African men, robbing, beating, raping and killing to produce a new generation of hardened criminals: worse, these gangs also held anti-white and anti-colonial feelings. They were a direct threat to the prison guards, with frightening potential to spill out and terrorise the wider society.

The main source of information about the homosexual gang system was a Zulu man named Nongoloza Mathebula. Nongoloza had been one of the founders of the Ninevite gang back in the 1890s. By 1912 he had come to regret his criminal ways and gave evidence to the state about his old gang (later also known as the 28s). He described how the Ninevites were organised with a king or general at the top and with disciplined ranks of officers and soldiers or warriors descending from there. At the very bottom were men who acted as wives, or *wyfies*, sometimes also called *umfaans*, to the higher ranks.

This practice obviously allowed the higher ranks a means to gain sexual release in a male-only environment. But it was also a way for the higher ranks to demonstrate their power and to gain prestige in a place that was otherwise designed to deny men any power and dignity at all. To non-gang members, the open display of homosexual preference was a powerful sign of the gang's willingness not just to break the law but also to mock even the strongest taboos of respectable society. According to Nongoloza, homosexuality and fearlessness made the Ninevites similar to the rebels against God named in the Bible.

The Ninevites did in fact quickly earn a reputation for extreme violence as well as homosexuality. According to one account: 'These organisations hold trials and decree punishments in some cases even sentencing to death by stabbing with a sharpened nail through the shoulders, or strangling with a wet towel, or by putting powdered glass into the victim's food. The more usual punishments, however, are '*tshaya sigubu*' or striking in the ribs, the balloon punishment or throwing into the air, and the knocking out of the front teeth in the case of police informers'. Later accounts also refer to gang rape as a strategy to punish enemies or other prisoners who broke the gang's code of honour. In one case from Durban in 1929, a gang member smashed in the head of another prisoner who had taken his *umfaan*. When asked why he had done it, Dhlamini said simply: '*Kungo mteto loko umfowetu* (that is the law, brother)'.

Violence played an important role in turning men into *wyfies* when they first arrived in prison. In some cases, the new arrivals were obviously womanly in the eyes of the other inmates. This could be due to their physical appearance or beauty (youthful face, full buttocks, small size), or their feminine-like personality (that is, quiet, shy, trusting and respectful in attitude, as a woman was supposed to be in traditional terms). Such men or youths were snatched up as *wyfies* right away. Often this was achieved by the simple trick of offering them food or tobacco in a seeming act of kindness only to demand repayment in the form of sex later that night. In other cases it was a simple matter of rape or the threat of rape.

Many men, however, did not easily fit the ideal of feminine beauty or character. In such cases the gang leadership would have to decide what gender identity should be applied to the newcomer: should he be a soldier or a *wyfie*? That task was mainly the responsibility of an officer called the *ngaka* (Medical Doctor), the Chief Justice, or the Blacksmith. The *ngaka* put the new inmate through various tests to determine what his gender and rank should be. As a rule of thumb, a man who was not willing to commit murder or a stabbing as a test of his bravery was not a real man and therefore should be turned into a wife. Once labelled a *wyfie*, it was then difficult for the man to become a soldier except by committing an act of extreme violence. This was risky though, since committing the necessary manly act could easily result in getting a longer sentence in prison.

It was also quite possible to go the other way, that is, to move from a soldier identity to a *wyfie*. Moses Dlamini vividly describes such a case in his account of a battle between two rival gangs on Robben Island. During the battle, the Big Fives captured the President of the Big Sixes. All that night they subjected him to merciless gang rape. When he emerged the next morning, he was formally removed from the rank of president in a public ceremony before all the members of his gang. The Big Six *ngaka* also formally removed his masculine status by renaming him with a feminine name.

The *ngaka*'s opinion was needed as well to decide which men should be given as *wyfie* to which warrior. The danger of revenge attacks once they were out of prison was high and so it would not help the system to assign men together if they came from the same village. A *ngaka* could probably help as well in determining if the *wyfie* might be either a 'real homosexual' or legitimately possessed in traditional terms. Real (out) gays were not an issue in Nongoloza's days, but closeted gays, or people with repressed homosexual desires, almost certainly were. Indeed, they tended to be imprisoned at least as much and perhaps even more than non-gays. Prison might then actually be nicer for them in some ways than the outside world, something the gangsters could not tolerate. A person who really preferred homosexual sex could in fact cause trouble for the majority by seducing them into forbidden acts or by inflaming rivalry between the gangsters. Real gays were also not desirable as *wyfies* because they did not represent a conquest or triumph for the warrior. They might actually make the warrior look weak since it showed he lacked the power to turn a heterosexual man into a *wyfie*.

A small number of men who preferred sex with men – perhaps even the *ngaka* himself – could protect themselves from suspicion and hostility by using the traditional explanation of spirit possession. Probably the same applied for lesbians in women's prisons as well. Real gays, however, whether out or closeted, were more often the victims of the most extreme violence, including gang rapes. The best way to avoid that fate was to hide real homosexual tendencies or desires. How could anyone ever suspect you of enjoying homosexual sex in prison if you led the most brutal attacks on suspected real gays? Another common strategy was to hide all sex and affection behind endless talk of heterosexual lust. Even shows of simple friendship that would be considered normal between men or between women on the outside, such as holding hands, had to be suppressed. Stanley Nyamfukudza paints a picture of this in a 1991 short story from Zimbabwe called 'Posters on the Wall'. In it, his narrator complains about how the men made a constant fuss over photographs of their girlfriends on the outside and spoke continuously about girls even while they maintained homosexual affairs. 'He didn't give a damn about it,' thinks the narrator. 'He didn't even dislike the fact they fucked each other's bums. He just wished they were more open about it. So he talked about it, asked them why didn't they hold hands and kiss. Were they really in love? He angered them because they much preferred to talk about the females in their photographs.'

Violence against real gays may have been exaggerated in prison but it was not in principle very different from the kind of gender violence that increasingly affected male–female relations in the outside world. In many other ways as well, these prison relationships closely resembled customary marriages on the outside. It was possible, for example, for high-ranking officers to have several wives. Most men, though, could afford only one wife as they were expected to keep 'her' properly with food and presents. *Wyfies,* for their part, were not just sexual servants but also did other tasks for their husbands in the same way that a traditional female wife would, including fetching things, sending messages and doing small domestic chores. *Wyfies* could plead for mercy in disciplinary trials for both *wyfies* and low-ranking soldiers. The main *wyfie* of the general or king could act as the Great Wife of a chief might act back in the villages, settling disputes amongst the other wives. The other *wyfies* could rise or fall in rank depending on their loyal service and how well they fulfilled their womanly role. This included main-taining an effeminate physical appearance such as by shaving closely and not by complaining to or nagging their 'husbands'.

Also, as in traditional marriage, the penalties for adultery could be high. One report from the 1920s refers to an *umfaan* who betrayed his husband and was disembowelled (his guts ripped open) by the gang in punishment. A *wyfie* who reported unwanted intercourse from another man put that man in grave danger. There were also rules regarding exactly what kind of sex was allowed to take place. For example, the 28s in South Africa today are the only gang existing whose code of honour allows the husband to have anal intercourse with the *wyfie*. The other gangs ban it on pain of extreme punishment, including ban-ishment or being turned into a *wyfie*. The fears were that to penetrate a man in this way was to weaken the warrior's strength, while to be penetrated was to take the poison of semen into one's body.

To guard against these dangers, the Big Five gang today even has a rank of spy. Every morning, the spies check the anuses of all the *wyfies* to ensure that they have not allowed the forbidden act during the night. Other sex acts such as oral sex and masturbation were also traditionally banned as being against the dignity of the gang's mascu-line identity. They were also understood to be a danger to health and survival in the belief that, during orgasm, the penis takes in from its surroundings. Would you want to take air bubbles into your blood by masturbating? Between the thighs offered small protection.

Amazingly, even in such a violent, controlling, superstitious and dehumanising system as prison, some men managed to escape sexual relations altogether, or to negotiate the type of relationship that they preferred. This could include secretly engaging in anal sex even if it went against the gang constitution. As one prisoner told researchers Sasha Gear and Kindiza Ngubeni: 'A lot of people are used to doing a boiler. A "boiler" is the old way and that's what they always do.' Another former inmate in a Zimbabwean prison put it this way: 'I know that they generally had sex between the thighs but could also do it through the anus if that was what they agreed beforehand.'

Negotiating such an agreement could also include developing caring or mutual relationships. The most common type of the latter was known in South Africa as *uchincha ipondo* (to exchange money). The exchange could be actual money or food, or it could be taking turns in the active role in the sex act. The exchange might happen between *wyfies*, it might happen between warriors who had not yet established their 'right' to a wife by carrying out an act of violence, or it might happen between non-gang members.

⌒ ⌣

The 28s did not confine their activities to prison. They also robbed, murdered, extorted and kidnapped once they got out. African men in the mine hostels and townships organised themselves into new gangs for defence, often along ethnic or tribal lines. Each of these new gangs established its own rules and structures. The Scotland gang, or 27s, was one of the first, formed sometime in the early 1900s by a man named Kikilijaan. He and his followers left the 28s precisely to escape from the homosexuality there. Mpondo gangs known as *isitshozi*, by contrast, kept up the 28 tradition of kidnapping male wives. The Russians or *MaRashea* were established by Basotho migrant workers in part to protect themselves against the *isitshozi*.

Nongoloza made it clear that he was not afraid of the police or warders and that in fact they were probably afraid of him. An investigation in 1921 revealed another possibility in warder/prisoner relations as well. This came during a trial of two young men accused of sodomy at the Porter Reformatory in Tokai near Cape Town. One of their victims told the court that the term they used for wives was 'canaries' and that the relationship was prevalent. He estimated that no less than fifteen of the thirty-eight boys in a dormitory together were canaries. In other words, nearly everyone was paired off. The canaries did not join together in rebellion against their exploitation nor even report their abuse to the authorities. Why not? Mainly because they believed that the warders were already well aware of the situation and would not assist them. It seems that the warders were either not interested in protecting the canaries or actively corrupt in allowing the senior boys to exploit the younger ones.

The feeble excuses the warders sometimes gave to explain their lack of action only reinforces the impression that they did not care. For example, one of the victims in the case above explained how a warder had come into the room just after the victim had been raped. The rapist was exposed and had obviously committed an assault. No charges were laid, however, on the grounds that his penis was not erect. In another case from Durban in 1929, officials justified themselves against criticisms with a range of arguments. The situation in Durban was no worse than in other prisons in the country, they claimed, the *umfaans* were not always used for sex, the *umfaan* themselves were partly to blame since they did not complain enough and the guilty parties were in fact punished when they were caught. In other words, there was no need to spend money or for the officials to change their attitudes.

Yet as bad as it was in the 1920s, the situation worsened in the 1930s and 1940s. First came the Great Depression, with more people driven to crime by poverty and desperation but fewer government funds to provide for decent conditions in prison. This period also saw ever-growing numbers of Afrikaner and African women abandon their farms and families in the countryside to try their luck at finding employment in town. Often they ended up turning to prostitution or brewing beer to survive and it was not long before some of them acquired the same habits as the men in town, including forming gangs. Gertie Williams's story of her experiences from this time actually mirrors the male–male sexual relationships in male prisons. She told how, when she first arrived in a reformatory for girls in the Cape Province, female 'men' tried to capture her as a wife. Once she resisted and showed that she too was a man, she was allowed to pick a wife of her own. The women who became wives fulfilled traditional roles of women. They were forbidden to eat, to shower, or to smoke *dagga* (marijuana) with the 'men'. Also, as in the men's prisons, violence might be resorted to in order to enforce the gender roles. When a girl teased Williams about her masculine appearance, for example, Williams responded sharply: 'One blow to her face was enough to shut her up, and also anybody else who would speak about me.'

Yet, as with the men, not all female–female relationships followed the husband/wife model or involved violence. Often they did not even involve sex, at least not in the sense of its being genital and orgasm-focused. Female–female sexuality was also often expressed through hugging, kissing, non-genital caressing and intensely close emotional attachment. The women would deny that these were sexual activities but rather something almost traditional, like the *setsoalle* relationship of intimate friendship amongst the Basotho. There were also relationships that were not strictly forced but were driven by the desire for food or other scarce items. The fact is that, as late as the 1970s, black women were not even provided with sanitary pads in many South African prisons. To trade a few moments of physical intimacy in order to acquire them would have seemed like a good deal to many women fearing the indignity of public menstruation.

When the authoritarian and openly racist National Party came to power in South Africa in 1948, the possibilities of reforming the penal system were greatly reduced. The apartheid regime actually introduced new elements of abuse into the system, including the deliberate use of homosexual rape to terrorise political opponents. So far, there is no evidence to suggest that the wardens did this themselves: rather, they encouraged the criminal gangs to do their dirty work. Pan-African Congress activist, Moses Dlamini, gives a terrifying account of this from his time on Robben Island in the early 1960s. Among other things, he describes wardens who actively teamed up with the Big Five gang in choosing wives from incoming prisoners. The idea was to humiliate the political prisoners so that they would never again feel self-confident or manly enough to engage in the anti-apartheid struggle. On his very first night in prison, Dlamini claims to have witnessed twenty of his comrades being taken away to be raped in this way. From female prisons as well there are reports of outright warfare amongst lesbian gangs in the 1980s and that the political prisoners lived with the same fears of victimisation by the gangs that Dlamini described.

We do not yet have first-hand accounts of such abuses from other oppressive racist regimes such as those in Rhodesia or Portuguese-ruled Mozambique. Still, it is easy to imagine that the colonialists there used similar tactics to break the will of African nationalist fighters.

Independence theoretically brought an end to such practices. Democratic government and commitments to international human rights agreements also promised big improvements in prison culture. Unfortunately, however, old attitudes and structures are hard to change, especially when money becomes tight. Since the late 1990s, extreme financial pressures brought about by economic crisis and cutbacks on government spending in much of the region have combined with a ballooning crime problem to cause a rapid expansion of the prison population and deterioration in prison conditions. Reports from Zimbabwe in 2003, for example, refer to huge overcrowding and critical shortages of food. Inmates are lucky to get one meal a day, while prison guards struggle to get by on hopelessly inadequate salaries. It is a situation almost designed to encourage corruption and survival sex. Even in South Africa, with much greater resources and with strong protections of human rights in its constitution, journalists in 2002 reported from the Orange Free State how guards in the pay of powerful gang leaders corruptly provided them with young prisoners for sex.

Making matters worse in the Zimbabwe case has been the growing politicisation of the police and security services. Since the rise of a serious political opposition movement against President Robert Mugabe and his ruling party, reliable reports have emerged that tell of homosexual assault being used as a political weapon. In a recent case, Kindness Moto, aged nineteen, told how he was arrested during a protest against Mugabe at the World Cup cricket match in 2003. In addition to being starved, electrocuted and beaten, he was repeatedly raped by police officers. The *Sunday Times* newspaper also found this to be common amongst Zimbabwean refugees in South Africa. In fifty-two interviews, no less than thirty-eight of the men reported that they had been raped or forced to engage in anal sex with other victims by agents of the state. Even one of the opposition members of parliament was gang raped in an act of political terror. As the South African doctor who treated the men explained: 'In their culture rape is worse than death and all my patients are being treated for depression and mental trauma. In my thirty-five years as a doctor, I have never seen such brutality.'

When confronted with such allegations, the ministers responsible for prisons in both South Africa and Zimbabwe have, in several cases, simply denied the problem. A spokesperson for the Zimbabwean prison service, for example, sounded almost like a colonial-era bureaucrat when he was confronted with a sensational news story about widespread, sometimes violent lesbianism in the system. 'It was', he said, and intending no irony whatsoever, 'highly unlikely for acts, such as homosexuality, to occur in prison cells as guards were always present round the clock'.

⁓ ⌣

This history tells us several things that could help us to understand present-day issues around same-sex sexuality in southern Africa. In the first place, sex in prison is not something new; it can be traced back to the very beginning of the prison system in the region. Also, official denial, willful ignorance and corruption are old stories. There is a remarkable continuity between colonial, apartheid and post-colonial officialdom in this sense. It may even be that the denial and corruption are actually worse now than under colonialism, which tells us that reforms are urgently needed.

A second point is that same-sex sexuality in prison has often been violent and dehumanising, just like many other aspects of prison life. A *wyfie*, in most cases, was thus a good deal worse off than a wife on the mines. Whereas a *wyfie* was pretty well stuck in the role for the duration of his sentence, an *inkotshane* could move to another mine or eventually graduate to become a husband in his own right. We should therefore be careful not to think of mines and prisons, or any other same-sex institutions like boarding schools, as all being more or less the same thing.

That said, violence was not always present within the prison system. There clearly were cases where men and women, who were apparently heterosexual before going to prison, engaged in sex with their own gender out of choice or desire. Some took considerable risks by breaking gang rules in order to build more satisfying relationships. Some even continued with a homosexual relationship after leaving prison. This then reinforces the idea that human sexuality is not very stable. Those who defend compulsory heterosexuality with the argument that it is 'the will of God' or 'nature' are clearly on very shaky ground.

Zimbabwe's first gay rights activist: Sarmiento, 1788

The Marquis de Sade, or Donatien-Alphonse-François Sade, was a key influence on the development of gay literature and of modern homosexual identities. It is little known that Sade was also 'Zimbabwe's First Novelist'. This honour is based on a story that Sade wrote while in prison in France in 1788. A large part of the story is set in Butua, the name of the kingdom that dominated the western part of Zimbabwe from the 16th century.

Sade never visited Butua and his portrayal of Africans is often laughably inaccurate. He failed, for example, to understand the importance of children in African society. But historical accuracy was never Sade's goal. Rather, he aimed to make fun of bourgeois Christian morality back in Europe. He does this through a character named Sarmiento, who defends the Butua way of life against the Frenchman Sainville. In one scene, the two characters debate the idea of prejudice against homosexuality. Sarmiento easily wins.

Here, then, is a shortened version of Sarmiento's (and Sade's) argument in favour of sexual rights, written over two hundred years ago. Sarmiento was not a real African, of course, but his words provide an early example of support for African and global struggles against homophobia.

In this scene, Sainville, the Christian, has just expressed his disgust at the Butuan practice of same-sex sexual initiation.

'Listen, my friend,' Sarmiento replied. 'from whatever angle you look at it, homosexuality is dangerous on a sole score: the harm that it does to the birth rate. But is this a real danger? What in fact happens by tolerating it? Throughout the state, I suppose, a smaller number of children would be born than usual. But is this reduction then such a bad thing, and what government is dim-witted enough not to know it? Does the state need to have a greater number of citizens than it can feed? Beyond that quantity, shouldn't all men be free to decide whether to reproduce or not to reproduce? I therefore actually don't know anything quite so ridiculous as this ceaseless howling for population growth, your countrymen above all, your beloved French, who don't seem to notice that if their government treats them with such indifference, if their exodus from the country, their deaths touch the government so little, and if their lives are daily sacrificed by inhuman laws, that this can only be the result of the population being too big. If the population were less, people would become more valuable to a state that otherwise so obviously doesn't give a damn about them.

'But let us leave these imbeciles to squawk at their leisure; let them make their disgusting plans to increase the population, whose excess is already one of the great evils of their state. Let us just see if what they desire is a moral good. I dare say no. I dare say that everywhere where population and wealth are moderate, equality will be more complete and, as a result, the happiness and well-being of the individual more assured. It is the abundance of people and the growth of luxury that produce the inequality of conditions and all the travails that follow. All men are brothers in a moderate and frugal society, which they forget when luxury masks them from each other and when a large population demeans their value. As the one thing feeds off the other, the rights of the strongest grow imperceptibly, they enslave the weak, despotism emerges, and the people are degraded and soon find themselves crushed beneath the weight of the chains that their own abundance has forged. That which reduces the population thus serves rather than harms the state: Politically speaking, in other words, this vice, which is so abominable, belongs in the class of virtues rather than that of crimes in all of the philosophical nations.

'Shall we check what nature has to say about it? Ah! If the intention of nature had been that every grain of wheat should germinate, she would have given the earth a better constitution. This earth wouldn't find itself out of action, fertility-wise, for such long periods of time. Always fertile, only ever waiting for seeds, there would be nothing one couldn't throw at her that she wouldn't produce.

'Take a quick glance at the female body and let's see if that's how it really is.

'A woman who lives to seventy years, I suppose, first of all spends fourteen of them without yet being useful; then another twenty when she is no longer so. That leaves thirty-six, from which we must subtract three months per year where her natural infirmities prevent her from working towards nature's end. That leaves us with, at most, twenty-seven years out of seventy that nature permits her to serve.

'I wonder, is it reasonable to think that she would consent to lose so much if the tendency of nature were that nothing should be lost?'

(Hmmm, Sainville thinks, how much less time would there be for fertility if the woman actually fell pregnant every year? For nine months, whatever the amount of seed the field received, it would not produce more. A woman's fertility, it would seem, hardly exists for twenty-four months out of seventy years!)

' ... and if this loss is directed by her own laws, can we legitimately make our laws punish that which nature herself demands? The propagation of humans is clearly not a law of nature, but rather something that she only tolerates. Did she need us to reproduce the first species? Hardly. In fact, when there is not a single man left on earth, nothing will go on any the less than it now goes; we enjoy that which we find but nothing was created for us; miserable creatures that we are, subject to the same accidents as other animals and born the self-same way, we take it into our heads to have pride; we take it into our heads to believe that it's because of our precious species that the sun gives its light and that the plants grow. What rubbish! Let us rather imagine that nature can just as easily do without us as it could the class of ants or the class of flies: and that, accordingly, we have no obligation whatsoever to serve her through the propagation of a species whose total extinction would not alter a single one of her laws. One could then spill some seed without offending her in any manner; what am I saying? We actually serve her by not augmenting a type of creature whose complete ruin would actually benefit the environment.

'And if homosexual desire isn't natural, how is it that we have been receiving that impression since infancy? Wouldn't it give way before the efforts of those who would educate us? But when one examines the youth who would be so imprinted, we can see that the penchant clearly develops itself, despite all the barriers erected to oppose it; it strengthens itself with the years; it holds out against advice, solicitations, the terrors of a life to come, of punishments, of contempt, of the spiciest attractions of the opposite sex; is it then the work of depravity that a taste so announces itself? And that whatever one would like it to be, isn't it most certainly the inspiration of nature? If this is so, does it offend her? Would that which outraged her have inspired her? Would she have permitted that which hampered her laws? Would she have favoured with the same gifts both those who supposedly serve her and those who degrade her? Let's study her better, this indulgent nature, before we dare impose limitations upon her. Let us analyse her laws, scrutinise her intentions, and never venture to speak of her without understanding her.

'And let us dare not doubt one final thing, which is that it is not the intention of this wise mother that the taste ever extinguish itself. On the contrary, it enters into her plans that there be men who do not procreate at all, and more than forty years in the life of women when they cannot, in order to convince us fully that reproduction is not amongst her laws, that she scarcely values it at all, that it hardly serves her, and that we are free to make use of this particular ability however it best seems to us, without displeasing her in any manner whatsoever, and without weakening her power in the slightest.

'So don't imagine for a minute that abuse and sarcasm, that chains or tortures could convert these heathen faggots more surely. Take that route and some men will be turned into idiots and cowards, others into fanatics. They will be guilty of stupidity and cruelty and, at the end of it all, we will not have one single vice the less'.

(Here Sainville is brought to reflect on yet another great philosopher: 'As for the punishments inflicted on those who offend the simple and chaste will of nature, they depend on the good character of the nation. Without that good character, laws which protect traditional values will be more dangerous than the infraction itself.')

5 • early colonial Zimbabwe

The colony of Mashonaland was created in 1890 by a small group of mostly white, English-speaking settlers coming from the Cape Colony. There were also some 'Cape Coloureds', Xhosa and Basotho acting as servants and wagon drivers, plus Afrikaners who arrived in separate treks. Commanding African labour, they quickly laid the foundations for an export-orientated capitalist economy with modern towns and institutions. They also introduced Roman-Dutch law to apply to themselves and to those Africans who took up service in the areas of the colony that the settlers declared to be European. The majority indigenous population continued to be administered by the chiefs under customary law overseen by a Native Commissioner. This dual legal and land-tenure system was then extended to Matabeleland after its conquest in 1894.

The grand ambition at the time was that the combined colony of Southern Rhodesia would serve as a model for friendly British–Boer relations and that the settlers would peacefully lead the African population towards 'civilised' values and economic progress. The move from company rule to responsible self-government in 1924 seemed to offer a political step in that direction with a promise of gradual introduction of democratic institutions.

We now know that those ideals were frustrated or betrayed in large part by the greed and racism of the white settlers. The colony's relative poverty also frustrated some stated good intentions. The dream of striking it rich with a second Witwatersrand, for example, was never realised. The mining sector of the economy thus remained seriously undercapitalised, which is to say unable to afford the kind of housing, or to pay the kind of wages that could compete with the mines of South Africa. In the early years, for instance, very few mines ever built compounds on the South African model; rather, most companies left it for the African workers to build their own shacks and find their own food and water.

The stream of African men from the poverty-stricken 'native reserves' of Nyasaland (Malawi), Portuguese East Africa (Mozambique) and Barotseland (Zambia) therefore mostly saw Southern Rhodesia as little more than a stopping-off place on the way to greener pastures in the south. Local men, meanwhile, mostly still had access to land and could pay their taxes and sometimes even made a tidy living by selling their farm produce. They remained independent peasants for as long as they could manage, rather than doing dangerous and humiliating work for the whites.

Policies to solve these labour problems led Southern Rhodesia to recreate some of the worst aspects of native administration and urbanisation that were found in South Africa. This then resulted in many of the same political injustices against Africans and many of the same bewildering changes to sexuality and gender relations as were happening in the Union. Among these was the emergence of a population of 'loose women' in town who brewed beer and sold sex and who were continuously on the run from the police and public-hygiene officials. The government, the missionaries, the chiefs and the majority of respectable African women and men alike regarded this development as the most scandalous effect of modernisation. However, male–male sexual relationships in the prisons and labour camps were also an early trickle-down effect of Roman-Dutch law and the migrant labour system and came to be known in whispers amongst Africans as mine marriage or *inkotshane*. In fact, the very same year that Leary and Taberer conducted their investigation into *inkotshane* in the Johannesburg area, an Ndebele police constable more than a thousand kilometres to the north told a Southern Rhodesian magistrate that *ingotshana* was a 'common practice' amongst certain types of men on the mines of that colony.

No official inquiry or policies to address 'unnatural vice' amongst African men was ever launched in Southern Rhodesia. There is not even any evidence that officials there were aware that their equivalents in South Africa were struggling with the same issue. Meanwhile, Roman-Dutch law lacked the means to detect and punish lesbian-like behaviour, which may have taken place but which remained totally invisible to the state. But Southern Rhodesia did have a relatively efficient district court system and a centralised bureaucracy that carefully preserved the records of hundreds of cases of male–male sexual crimes. These cases offer us some fascinating insights into the type of men who engaged in sex with males and how social attitudes towards African sexuality changed over the years. They enrich our understanding of the wide range of relationships that happened in a rapidly changing social and economic situation, challenging us, once again, to be careful of the stereotypes and over-simplifications that people often reach for when trying to explain or condemn taboo behaviour.

~ ⌣

The first man in Southern Rhodesia who some people say had homosexual tendencies was none other than Cecil John Rhodes, its founder. Rhodes never married and from a modern perspective some of his personality traits seem to have been almost stereotypically gay – a high, squeaky voice when he got excited, for example, and a limp, girlish handshake that positively embarrassed some of his military colleagues. He preferred the company of young males, or 'lambs' as he called them, and developed intensely close emotional relationships with some. No one has ever seriously accused Rhodes of having had a physical relationship with another man, but several historians have speculated that his repressed homosexual desires fuelled his imperialist ambitions: that is, because he could not allow himself to express his homosexuality freely, he instead let that energy out by working to expand the British Empire. A similar accusation, by the way, and perhaps with more evidence to back it, has been made of both the great conquering hero of Sudan and South Africa, Lord Kitchener, and

France's 'greatest colonial soldier', Marshall Hubert Lyautey.

Among the actual pioneers in Mashonaland there was scarcely a hint of homosexual scandal, despite the fact that the colony was effectively closed to white women for the first few years. The first white woman actually had to sneak in disguised as a boy. This was 'Billie', who later married into a very respectable social position as the Countess de la Panouse. Even after a decade, white males outnumbered white females by nearly three to one. But this imbalance did not result in a rash of male–male sexual affairs, either amongst whites or across race and power divides. Perhaps the enormous amounts of whisky that the pioneers consumed distracted them from the shortage of pioneer women; or perhaps it was the ready availability – sometimes by virtual kidnapping – of African women.

Whatever the case, in that whole first male-dominated decade of 1890–1900, only a single case ever came to court of a white man accused of assaulting an African male. Even looking over the longer period, instances of whites exploiting or seducing African males for sex were relatively rare. Between 1892 and 1935, magistrates heard about 450 cases of male–male sexual crimes in 52 district courts around the colony. Of these, only 39 involved whites accused of sexually assaulting blacks. Less than ten per cent of the activity, including many obviously false accusations, is much less than one might expect, given that whites made up thirty per cent to fifty per cent of the urban population overseen by these courts during this period.

The criminal courts, of course, are not a very reliable source for understanding something as complex as sexuality, especially when the police and magistrates were so busy with the whole range of racially discriminatory laws upon which the colonial order depended. The courts would have been blind to the vast majority of same-sex relationships, either because the partners involved were consenting or because the victim in a real homosexual assault was too scared or too ashamed to report it.

Still, in light of the view sometimes heard in Africa that Europeans introduced homosexuality there, the numbers alone contain some surprises. The very first five cases of sodomy to be heard in Mashona-land in the 1890s involved men described as a Hottentot, a Matibili, a Zambizi (which may have meant a Valley Tonga), two Manyika (that is, eastern Shona-speakers) and five unspecified 'natives', presumably local Shona. Over the longer run up to World War II, nearly ninety per cent of all recorded cases of male–male sexual crime involved black Africans on black Africans. In other words, Africans were lodging complaints against each other or were caught in the act more frequently than one might predict judging from the relative size of their population in town, let alone from what their cultural beliefs said about the central importance of marriage and sex for reproduction.

Who exactly were these African men who had the misfortune to end up in the colonial court system? In the early years, the large majority were migrants from outside the colony – mostly Chikunda, Sena, Chewa, Ngoni, Tonga and Lozi from the north and east, plus a scattering of Shangaan, Zulu, Basotho and Xhosa coming from the south. These 'alien natives' (as they were called at the time) probably ended up in same-sex relationships for much the same reasons as the migrants did in South Africa. Indeed, some may well have introduced the practice, along with the word for it, on their way home from work in Johannesburg or Kimberley. Far from home, lonely, fearful of gangs of local men and fearful of town women with their expensive tastes and sexually transmitted diseases, they took to *ingotshana* to protect their health and dignity as men until they reached home safely once again.

Just as in South Africa, one particular group of migrants soon became notorious for practising male–male sex. These were Nyanja-speakers from Malawi, who were known amongst the local people in Southern Rhodesia as MaNyasa or MaBlantyres. They were particularly despised and shunned by local Africans, in part because of their poverty and the fact that they were willing to take on the kind of jobs that no self-respecting Shona or Ndebele would ever agree to do. They were the lowest of the low – for example, the public-latrine cleaners. The men who did that foul job lived in hostels on so-called 'sanitation farms' on the outskirts of the main cities.

Perhaps in a mood of dark humour about their situation, the sanitation workers coined the term *matanyera* to describe themselves. *Matanyera* was formed from a Nyanja word for an especially horrible kind of diarrhoea caused by worms. *Nyera* was also used as an extremely strong swear-word back home in Malawi. It entered the Shona language by the 1910s and could be translated either politely as 'scavengers', 'street sweepers' or 'latrine cleaners', or more crudely as a terrible insult. By 1921, at least, *matanyera* had also come to mean men who had sex with other men because they were too poor and despised to find proper wives.

The Malawians, of course, like other migrants, almost never regarded Southern Rhodesia as the final resting spot on their journey. They carried the word with them to Gauteng – the place of gold. South Africa stopped recruiting Malawians for work in the Johannesburg mines in the 1920s. By then, though, their little joke upon themselves had already passed into other African languages. To eat *matanyola*, for example, came to mean 'have sex between the thighs' in Sepedi. By the 1970s and 1980s it was also said to mean 'male prostitute' in Sesotho. People by then had forgotten where it originally came from. One book published in 2003 even described it as an 'old, proper Tswana' word for homosexuality.

One of the many other ironies is that the Malawians themselves often managed to escape from their ghetto of unmarriageable latrine cleaners. Passing through Shona villages on their journeys to seek work, it was hard not to notice them as kind-hearted, fun-loving men. They came from a matrilineal society that clearly gave women more respect than Shona and Ndebele cultures did. Because of this reputation, as well as their hard work and careful savings, the Malawians proved to be successful at eloping with young Shona women and taking them as wives. This situation upset Shona men a great deal and they pressed the government to introduce laws to prevent the Malawians from poaching their daughters and wives. The result was the Native Adultery Prevention Ordnance of 1916, which gave Southern Rhodesian police the power to deport 'alien natives' who interfered with local women. Fear of this law may have contributed to some migrant men's decision to keep to themselves in the hostels.

The 1910s and 1920s witnessed other rapid changes in African society in the colony, above all the growing number of local Shona and Ndebele men who could no longer support their families by peasant agriculture or herding. As they began to abandon the land to join the flow of migrant labour to town or to the commercial farms, the number of indigenous men appearing in court for male–male sexual crimes also increased. By 1921, for the first time, the majority of men accused of male–male sexual crimes in Southern Rhodesia were Shona and no longer 'alien natives'. In the period 1924 to 1931, Shona men accused of male–male sexual assaults outnumbered Malawians by more than two to one. The language used in the trials reflected this change. Terms like *ingotshana* and *hlobonga* largely disappear. Instead there are variations of local sex terms such as *kubata, kurinda* or *kusvira. Shamwari*, the Shona word for friend, appears to have been widely understood at the mines as synonymous with *inkotshane* or 'sweetheart', even to non-Shona speakers.

The court records show something else that may be surprising. Only about a third of the total cases happened in prisons and mine compounds. Some of the main mining centres in fact recorded only a handful or even no cases at all of male–male sex. Gwelo (present-day Gweru), for example, was home to the huge Globe and Phoenix mine and was one of the few Southern Rhodesian mines that had South African-style hostels. One might assume that it would have produced a similar effect to that revealed by Leary and Taberer in Johannesburg. But in over thirty years, only four cases of indecent assault or sodomy against males were ever recorded from there. Salisbury (present-day Harare) and Bulawayo on the other hand, which did not have major mines but were the two biggest cities, were by far the most frequent sites of male–male sexual crimes. The remainder of cases occurred in a wide variety of locations spread all over the whole country, from commercial farms and isolated woodlots to hotels, police camps, hospitals, the veld between working and drinking places, private homes and even established African townships. Simonas, who also went by the name of Bye-Bye, for example, was a self-employed mattress-maker with his own private accommodation in Harare when he was found guilty of multiple counts of sodomy in 1923. In 1928, Bikinosi was caught mounting another African man in broad daylight in the park known as the Kopje, near Salisbury's red-light district.

Cases like these challenge the main stereotype of situational homosexuality in Africa, namely that men have sex with males only when forced by the lack of females. In fact, few of the Southern Rhodesian mine companies could afford or felt that they needed fenced compounds for their workers. Unlike in South Africa, therefore, the mine sites often developed into small villages where the men built their own huts. They shared these huts either with fellow workers or with women who came to brew beer and provide other feminine comforts. At Jumbo mine, about forty kilometres north of Salisbury, one old man told us that the mine owners actually encouraged female prostitution as a form of cheap, local entertainment for the workers. Even so, this did not stop male–male erotic dancing and homosexual affairs or sexual assaults from taking place. Some of the accused in those cases were locally married men with children. In one unusual case from Dawn Mine in the Hartley (present-day Chegutu) district, twenty-five-year-old Magopo sneaked into the hut where the complainant, Sam, was sleeping together with his own wife, and mounted the man.

Women were also present and growing in numbers in town, despite constant police harassment to keep them out. By the 1930s, there were almost as many women and children as men in some of the major African locations. They were there watching and laughing at the men's erotic dances on the weekends, and they were there as informal wives known as *mapoto* wives. True, these women were generally more demanding than traditional, submissive wives in the rural areas; true, as well, many men could not afford even short-term *mapoto* marriages let alone proper *lobola*, especially as the economy took a turn for the worse in the 1930s. But the fact remains that some men clearly preferred sex with males rather than with the available females, and there are cases where they went far out of their way to get it. In 1903, twenty-five-year-old Kimbunzi walked thirty kilometres from Penhalonga to Mutare to catch up on some intimacy with his former room-mate and male lover, Marasha.

Several types of male–male sexual relationships amongst Africans were recorded in early colonial Zimbabwe. At one extreme was what we would now call child abuse. This could involve boys as young as eight years old and a level of violence in the sexual act that left the child bleeding and utterly humiliated. The men in these cases also often used violence to keep the victim quiet, as well as showing cruel contempt for the feelings of the boy. Few cases illustrate this callousness and selfishness more clearly than Bisamu when confronted in 1907 by his accuser, Lindunda. Bisamu did not deny the charge of sodomy made against him but calmly defended himself with the words: 'I have emitted semen on you and it does not matter because you are only a lad'.

Such cases of violent sexual assault are actually not very common in the court records – indeed, they are extremely rare when compared to male sexual assaults on female children. Just as Leary and Taberer found in South Africa, and as oral history also supports, the commonest type of male–male sexual relationship ran closely along the lines of customary male–female relations. The person taking the role of husband provided for the person taking the role of the wife. He showered 'her' with gifts and other treats. The wife in turn provided the usual feminine services. In a few cases the husband went as far as to negotiate *lobola* payments with the father-in-law, generally in the form of cash. In one instance from the coal-mining town of Wankie (present-day Hwange), however, a *lobola*-like payment was made in the traditional form of cattle.

These consenting marriages could be stable for several months or even years. They usually ended with an amicable repayment of the *lobola*-like debt. Those that ended up in court rarely did so because of conflict or violence around the sex act. They came to court because of disagreement between the two partners over proper compensation or repayment of debt.

Prostitution was another type of male–male sexual relationship. It involved satisfying another man's short term desires for a negotiated fee. In the 1910s, the fee for a single act of thigh sex ranged from three to ten shillings, about the same as a female prostitute would charge for her regular service. Fees for anal intercourse were much higher, as much as one to five pounds sterling, or more than an unskilled worker could earn in a month. Very ambitious young men and boys could get even more if they threatened to expose the act to the police. Cases of blackmail can be found from as early as 1900. A fairly common pattern was for a boy, or group of boys, to seduce their victim and then demand money to keep quiet. Sometimes the claim was for relatively large amounts (15 or 20 pounds) but others simply wanted the satisfaction of revenge against unpopular *induna*s ('boss boys') or white bosses.

There were, as well, male–male sexual relations for the purpose of *muti*, or medicine. The Malawians had an evil reputation for this, but as we saw in Chapter Two, the highly secretive custom was also present in Shona and Ndebele cultures before 1890. It probably became more common, and perhaps less fearsome, with the rise of popular figures like Dhuri in the 1930s and 1940s. Dhuri originally came from Nyasaland to become a champion boxer in Salisbury township. He lived an open homosexual life throughout his career. Many thought that this explained both his success in sport and his mocking attitude towards the colonial police, for both of which he was widely admired by Africans in the township. That he was never punished for his illegal sexual acts or disrespect of the police just showed how well his *muti* worked.

James Mabala was another public figure who appeared to prove that the medicine worked. A Shona man, he rose to become the leader of the *Zvibengu* gang in the 1920s by following the notorious customs of the Ninevites or 28s in South Africa. Mabala also controlled a thriving illegal trade of *mangoromera*, a powerful *muti* that young men used to strengthen themselves for gang battles and success in boxing.

These different types of relationship were not always one-sided, with the husbands, 'johns', or gangsters as the dominant partner and the boys or 'wives' as the helpless victims. Twenty-six-year-old Matshela, for example, defended himself in court in 1924 by saying that he never intended to have sex with thirteen-year-old Tsi, but only did so because: 'For three days complainant [Tsi] played with my penis.' The case of Mashumba and Njebe referred to in Chapter Two also demonstrates the possibility of love between African men on a more or less equal basis. Mashumba (40) and Njebe (16) admitted that they had helped each other to sexual enjoyment over a period of three years. Njebe explained, 'Every time [Mashumba] had connection with me he allowed me to do the same to him. We did it in the hut and also in the veld ... I never objected to [Mashumba] doing what he did before because it was not painful and I did it to him.' He concluded simply: 'We loved one another.' This was in 1923.

African men charged with sexual crimes upon males showed different reactions when asked to defend themselves against the charges. Some had nothing to say at all, while others claimed that they did not know that they were committing offences. They claimed that such acts were simply play and that such play was normal and acceptable in their culture. One Shona man actually described his sexual act on a youth using the word *kumanga*. Since this means only to tease a child, how could he be accused of a crime? Other men did accept their guilt but blamed Satan or alcohol or even the fact that others were doing the same.

Colonial officials and police took a dim view of such weak justifications for what they regarded as despicable and inhuman acts. They were especially harsh in their punishment of white men who assaulted black men or boys, handing down sentences of up to five years' imprisonment with hard labour and one hundred lashes. This was because the guilty man had not only committed a terrible crime in the eyes of the law, he had also disgraced the dignity of the white race in the eyes of public opinion. By comparison, white men who sexually assaulted African women were only rarely and mildly punished in the courts since this fairly commonplace event did not challenge the basic power relations of the colonial system.

The majority of cases, which involved blacks only, tended to be treated lightly in comparison. With a few exceptions that involved violent rape, black men found guilty of sexual assaults on males were typically let off with a humiliating lecture and a light sentence – sometimes as little as a few days in jail or a fine of one pound. That amount was hardly more than the man would have paid had he gone to a willing prostitute in the first place. It is especially interesting to compare this with the level of punishment given out to some heterosexual crimes committed by Africans, above all, black men having sex with white women. Such so-called Black Peril cases ended with the death penalty for an estimated twenty African men up to 1934, often based on very flimsy evidence. It seems that male–male sexuality amongst Africans was actually less worrisome to the government than the alternative that they really feared.

Sentencing is also revealing of changing attitudes towards male–male sexuality over the years. The clear tendency was towards lighter sentences, suggesting a less serious concern as time went on. Also, over time fewer and fewer cases even made it to court. The busiest year in the pre-World War II history of Southern Rhodesia was 1927, when twenty-five cases were heard throughout the whole colony. After that, the number dropped off rapidly. Only a single case of sodomy was heard in the four years between 1928 and 1931 and this was discharged as a false allegation. In the first three years of the 1940s, not even a single charge of the lesser offence of indecent assault was laid. By the 1950s and early 1960s, the total number of charges stabilised at around fifteen to twenty per year, from which, on average, eighty to one hundred per cent were dismissed for lack of evidence.

Should we believe that the sex suddenly stopped? We know for a fact that it did not and that it briefly became a political issue in the early 1950s (as will be discussed later). What seems to have happened is that the courts were becoming so busy with other crimes as the cities grew that they could no longer cope with the pressure. As early as 1934, the government actively began to investigate ways to reduce arrests of Africans for non-violent, non-property crimes. The problem only worsened with rapid urbanisation in the post-war period, when the total number of reported offences rose from 87,000 in 1945 to over 127,000 in 1949. The police simply could not spare the time to chase after certain kinds of love affair or business deal that did not directly threaten property or political stability.

The magistrates themselves were also keeping in line with a wider international trend towards leniency in cases of non-violent male–male sex crimes. As early as 1913, a judge dismissed a case where the complainant had shown his agreement to the sex act by accepting the accuser's money. In 1915, the Attorney General likewise refused to prosecute a case of two men caught having sex who had consented with each other beforehand. African men who heard of cases like this probably assumed that the whites now approved of (or at least did not care about) male–male sexual relations. If that were true, there was little to be gained, and much dignity and expenses to be lost, by taking their complaints of assault to the police.

Some historians have interpreted this tendency of the state to turn a blind eye to male–male sexuality amongst Africans as proof of a quiet conspiracy to allow, or even to encourage, African men to engage in homosexual activity. There may be a grain of truth in the idea, at least in the prisons and amongst the mining companies that faced chronic problems of labour shortage. But there were clearly other factors at work as well. One may be that Southern Rhodesian officials did not really want to know what was going on. They certainly did not want to publicise it. For example, police did not list sodomy in their annual report on crime in the colony until 1927, despite the fact that such cases had been coming before the courts every year since 1892. Even confidential discussions about prison conditions by colonial officials avoided mentioning homosexuality.

Newspaper editors throughout the colonial era also seemed to censor themselves on the topic, even when sensational homosexual scandals might have helped their sales. A glaring example is that of James Noble, superintendent of the Thabas Induna mission near Bulawayo. Noble had been charged in 1929 with nineteen counts of indecent assault against one of his African teachers and thirteen of his pupils. Even though he was found guilty, the shocking story was not published in the *Bulawayo Chronicle*. In fact, the very first daily newspaper report on homosexuality did not appear until 1969. The first official police comment on the subject came in 1972. This was to explain an embarrassing case of a European man who was tempted into committing sodomy with a young African male who then reported it to the police, hoping to make money. The report promised that the Rhodesian police would in future be more active in protecting the dignity of white men from such embarrassments.

Why was there such silence around male–male sexuality in Southern Rhodesia, especially when compared to the inquiries, scandals and moralistic campaigns against homosexuality that periodically took place in neighbouring South Africa? No doubt the white Rhodesians and missionaries were deeply embarrassed by the topic and were ashamed to talk or write about it. But there could also have been a more subtle force at work that needs to be explored in more detail. This was the Southern Rhodesian need to build a distinct 'national' identity, in part by cultivating a sense of moral superiority over South Africans. By refusing to talk about the issue, the Southern Rhodesians could pretend it did not exist in their jurisdiction. Hence, by comparison with the South Africans, they looked like better, more modern colonisers. They even made their more powerful critics in the west appear uncaring towards Africans. As we will show in the next two chapters, a surprising number of people fell for this simple trick.

Women loving women

Until recently, historians have tended to focus most of their attention on men, often ignoring women altogether or leaving all but a few in the background. In part, this is because the main sources we rely upon to write history were overwhelmingly written or told by men. Whether it was oral traditions or written documents, these accounts focused mainly on men's activities such as politics, crime, inventions and so on. Despite some differences of opinion, both the colonialists and African patriarchs basically shared the view that women should marry and have children, should serve their menfolk loyally and should otherwise keep quiet.

If women in general are largely invisible in African history, lesbians and other women who loved women are more so by far. Fear of men's violence or of becoming social outcasts from family and community tended to keep these women very discreet, sometimes so secret in their feelings that they could not admit them even to themselves. So it is that even this research project, which was to a large extent inspired by the courage of present-day African lesbians, had a hard time finding evidence of lesbians or lesbian-like behaviour in the past. Zimbabwe's first black lesbians, for example, only became visible within the GALZ community around 1992.

We do know that there was a whole range of female–female relationships in traditional culture that may have been sexual but were not seen or described that way. But can we put our finger on actual cases of sexual love between women during the colonial era? What were their feelings like, and how did they manage to express their love in a patriarchal society that refused to recognise their sexuality independent of men? How have day-to-day experiences of women loving women shaped the struggle for sexual rights in Africa?

There are probably as many different answers to these questions as there are individual women and girls who have struggled with them. Below we reproduce a few snippets of lesbian writing over the decades that shed light on the wide range of experiences across time, race and class divides. Some are real historical characters dating as far back as the 1930s; some are fictional; some are 'modern' and some are 'traditional'. Please meet Vera, Irene, Fatou and Sibongile ...

People can say what they like, but I don't believe that there is anything sick or unclean about our love. Is it so unnatural to want you and not a husband or babies?

Your loving wife

Moira (Eastern Cape, about 1930)
– Hungochani

We were bisexual. We never thought of ourselves as ... lesbians. What we thought was: our feeling about sex was unique ... We had no idea that there were people like us all over ... Looking back we realised that many of the girls and women we had known were lesbian or bisexual, but no one talked about these things. We thought we had invented it ...

Julie Mullard (Durban, about 1950)
in Caroline Zilboorg's The Masks of Mary Renault

Back in Wynberg I started having a romance with a married woman. We were happy together until Mrs M, who has a smokkelhuis [shebeen], told her that I was a woman. Then she moved out of the area. Anyway, I don't have to worry. I have got a nice friend now who lives in Sea Point. We have been together for over a year. She does not know that I am a woman. But I will lose her too when this story is read by thousands of people in Cape Town.

Gertie Williams (Cape Town, about 1955)
– Defiant Desire

Dear Dolly, I am a 17 year old girl and out of school after completing my O-levels last year. My problem is that although I have many girlfriends there is one I adore and there is nothing in the world that thrills me more than my lover's kiss. I have heard of the word 'homosexual' but I don't really know what it means. Please tell me what it means and its advantages and disadvantages. I do not like boys at all; all I care for is this girl.

C.L. (Kitale, Kenya around 1965)
in K. Mutongi's 'Dear Dolly's Advice'

I told her I was 'M'atsepo Nthunya. So she said, 'I always see you passing here. Today I want to talk to you. I want you to be my motsoalle.*' This is a name we have in Sesotho for a very special friend. She says, 'I love you.'*

It's like when a man chooses you for a wife, except when a man chooses, it's because he wants to share the blankets with you. The woman chooses you the same way, but she doesn't want to share the blankets. She wants love only. When a woman loves another woman, you see, she can love her with a whole heart.

I saw how she was looking at me, and I said, 'Ke hantle, *it's fine with me.' So she kissed me, and from that day she was my* motsoalle. *She told her husband about it and I told my husband, and these two husbands became friends too. It was a long distance from my house to her house and she was lonely ...*

'M'atsepo Nthunya (Lesotho, 1960s)
– Singing Away the Hunger

From an early age I knew I was different. I never had feelings for men, and I always had deep feelings for women. But I never had anyone in the village to talk to about these feelings – in my village gays were unheard of. I tried to suppress these feelings, but eventually they came out. As I grew older, I decided I didn't care what society said – I would be myself ... Finally I met a girl who became my friend. We loved each other, but I was terrified to go to bed with her. I felt I needed to have a penis to satisfy her. As far as I knew, sex meant penetration by a penis. On the last day of school, after we had finished our final Standard 10 exams, most of the students got blind drunk during the evening by sniffing benzene. I eventually plucked up the courage to sleep with my girlfriend, and I was so surprised that I was not rejected. She was the first woman who could accept me without a cock.

Vera Vimbela (South Africa, 1980s)
– Defiant Desire

Even though I am bisexual, the things I feel for men are completely different to what I feel for women. As a bisexual I have, I hope, a perspective on both sexes. Sure, men and women are different, but both have wonderful attributes emotionally and physically. It's hard to say what one gets from either sex without taking into account the individual person you are involved with. Obviously, that plays the most important role.

Zubeida (South Africa, 1990s)
– Defiant Desire

I have a lover now. She is also a **sangoma***. We are both proud and happy to be lesbians. To be a* **sangoma** *has made me strong. I don't feel afraid of anything. Even when these rough boys come to me in secret, they only want advice and won't harm me. They fear me because I am a* **sangoma** *and a lesbian ... I don't know if the two have anything to do with each other. All I know is that it feels right that this is the way my life must go. I look after myself. I do feel for gays* *and lesbians who are confused, because sometimes they come to me for advice. As I am a* sangoma *I try to help, but I always tell these confused people they must look inside themselves for answers.*

Sibongile (South Africa, 1990s)
– Defiant Desire

... the tension with my family has lessened. We see each other often and, if anything, our relationship is better than it was before. However, we never mention what happened and nothing is said about my lesbianism. They also never ask me about marriage or boyfriends. What is also strange is that our community, after initially rejecting me, now seems to have accepted me too. I even get a separate invitation to social functions which is unheard of for a single woman; usually she is invited with her family. I still don't understand why I am now accepted, but I'm happy for it.

Farah (Zimbabwe, 1990s)
– Sahwira

I couldn't go to the church for support. I can't ever go back to the church. Once you are in the church they start on you – they humiliate you and exclude you and finally you are driven out of the church. They tell me that being homosexual is un-African. If it is not African, where did this thing come from? I am a black African and I will stay African. Nothing will change that. And besides, where in the Bible is it written to rape and beat and kill women?

Sarah (Namibia, early 2000s)
– More Than a Name

Of course I am scared, because the law forbids it and my mother thinks it's immoral. I don't plan to tell them. I have to make it secret. I keep it secret because I feel insecure and since the law doesn't agree with it. I can't stand to lose my family.

I used to go to church, but currently I don't go because when I used to go to church those pastors, they used to criticise what I am and I felt so bad ...

I don't go [to church] because I know God is everywhere, so I can pray to Him whenever I want.

> *Tessa, Marci and Jackie (Kampala, Uganda, 2000s)*
> *– Tommy Boys*

Some time ago, I was lying in bed, flipping through a sex-toy catalogue. I had decided that I'd like to get a dildo. The selection was most impressive. I circled The One and asked my man, Richard, in England to go shopping for me. Richard is a Zimbabwean now living in England who generously sends many different papers, books, videos, etc. to the gay community in Zimbabwe in a personal commitment to easing our isolation. He set out to find 'Dave' in a sex shop in Cambridge. Outrageous that the dildos are pre-named, but what can a girl do from a distance? In a month or two, Dave was delivered disguised as a bookend and tightly wrapped, all very neat and tidy and far too inaccessible for a not-so-diligent Zimbabwean postal worker to investigate further.

Let me say now that, for the most part, I don't give a crap if the whole world knows that I have a dildo in the drawer. I mean, big deal. But, like I said, having lived a lot of my life in anticipation of a raid in the middle of the night, the thought of the conservative creeps from central police headquarters ferreting through my stuff just wasn't appealing. So my sex toy(s) – Dave got a friend, Roger – have never been very close at hand.

For a long time, Dave lived in a motorcycle helmet in the top cupboard in of the bedroom. Then he was moved to the right pocket of my girlfriend's furry white terry-cloth robe. Then he was stuffed at the bottom of our voluminous sock basket. After that, he was moved to a vase in our kitchen. And finally, he ended up under a bougainvillea in the garden – the purple one by our neighbour Malcolm's wall.

Luckily, my dog Frank never got hold of Dave. What then?

Finally, I thought: This is ridiculous; let me stop forgetting where I've left Dave (and Roger) and give them the boot. I decided to toss them into a storm drain. On the way to dinner at my girlfriend's parents' house, I got ready but couldn't find a drain in the dark. When we drove into her parents' driveway, I saw that their rubbish bag hadn't been emptied. It was innocently waiting there for more items to be added for the next day's removal. But, as you can imagine, this suggestion didn't go down too well with my girlfriend, especially because Zimbabwe is in the grip of a fuel shortage and waste removal is therefore an erratic affair. It was likely that my in-laws would be saddled with Dave and Roger longer than was decent. So Dave and Roger stayed in the car while we had dinner.

On the way home, I noticed how many rubbish bags were lining the roadside hopeful of a truck with fuel in the morning. In the end, perhaps it was the unsuspecting Mr and Mrs F living at No. 3 Ardmore Close that finally took ownership of Dave and Roger. Or perhaps their gardener smiled to himself when the rubbish wasn't taken the next day.

Who knows?

Bev Clark (Zimbabwe)
– Website, Entry 3, Wednesday, Aug. 6, 2003

Why don't we all take a shower and go down on each other? It wouldn't be copulating, it would be a lot of petting, smooching, and caring.

Abioye (Nigeria, 2000s) in Unoma Azuah's
The Emerging Lesbian Voice
in Nigerian Feminist Literature

She stretches me out on the bed, crouches down on my buttocks. I close my eyes when she massages me. First the nape of the neck, then the back, the thighs, the legs, the feet. My skin rolls between her expert fingers, and other carnal universes open up to me, more gigantic still. She pours these massages onto me, sighing quasi-orgasmically ... I don't

112

understand her, so I just savour the ecstasy of her tongue as it lavishes my —

Irene and Fatou (Cameroon, anytime)
in Calixthe Beyala's Femme nue, femme noir

6 • homophobia in settler society

Homophobia means an irrational reaction to the idea of homosexuality. This can be as simple as feeling slight nervousness or discomfort with the topic. Homophobia is also commonly expressed by the ostracism or shunning of people who are suspected to be homosexual, by jokes and stereotyping, or by misguided attempts to convert homosexuals to heterosexuality. Extreme forms include violent acts of gay-bashing, such as raping lesbians (supposedly to cure them), and even murder. It may also be directed against heterosexuals who are thought to be too sympathetic towards gay rights. Homophobia is also often internalised by LGBT people. Thus, young people who are unsure of their sexuality, or who are beginning to feel that they may be attracted to members of their own sex, learn from the wider homophobic society to despise themselves for their feelings. In that sense, even mildly homophobic jokes or looks can be deeply hurtful.

Many of the recent statements by African leaders condemning homosexuals are blatantly homophobic in that they inspire hatred, contempt and even violence against homosexuals and their sympathisers. Because those leaders generally claim to be speaking on behalf of African values, people in the west often assume that African culture as a whole must be homophobic. But, as we have already seen in earlier chapters, African cultures had sophisticated and humane ways of dealing with people who did not meet heterosexual ideals of marriage and fertility. The homophobia of people like Robert Mugabe is therefore embarrassing or even offensive to the guardians of tradition in Zimbabwe. After all, *munhu munhu, hazvienzani nembwa* is the old

114

Shona proverb saying that a person is a person and not to be likened to a dog. Zimbabwean member of parliament, Border Gezi, learned the truth of this Shona saying during the 1995 debate on 'homosexualism and lesbianism'. His rural constituents urged him not to talk in public about such matters. As far as they were concerned, if homosexuality went on in private then there was no reason to worry about it. This also seems to be a common theme emerging from personal accounts by LGBT people around Africa – as long as they do not publicly name themselves or their sexual preference, then they will be left alone.

This then begs the question, where did this untraditional intolerance of non-heterosexuals in modern-day Africa come from? In this and the following chapter we explore the argument that has been made by several scholars and activists – that homophobia, not homosexuality, is the real 'white man's disease' in the region. Let us start by taking a close look at attitudes towards homosexuality amongst the early European missionaries and settlers.

～ ✓

The word homophobia was coined in Europe in 1969 at the time of the emergence of the modern gay rights movement and the sharp political reactions against it in the United States. The attitudes and behaviours it describes, however, clearly existed long before this. Portugal, for example, produced crudely anti-homosexual literature in the 14th and 15th centuries. The Spanish Inquisition, from the 16th to 18th centuries, resulted in hundreds of executions for what was termed the nefarious sin. According to historian Mark Jordan, as many men were put to death for sodomy during the Inquisition as for the crime of heresy, usually by being burnt alive at the stake. This cruelty was justified by pointing to certain translations of select Christian texts. The judges also gave examples of God's violence against men who supposedly mocked His will. The Portuguese Law of Inquisition of the 16th century, for example, referred not only to the physical destruction of Sodom and Gomorrah described in the Bible: it also claimed that the political destruction of the Knights Templar in 1307 was a sign of

God's judgement against that crusading order for practising sodomy.

The Calvinist Dutch also performed executions for 'monstrous lust', including at Cape Town. Dutch settlers (Afrikaners or Boers) then carried the stigma against male–male sexuality with them when they expanded into the interior. No doubt they sincerely believed in homophobia on moral grounds, just as they believed in slavery, also considered moral according to a literal reading of parts of the Bible. Interestingly, however, the Bible does not condemn polygamy; in fact the Old Testament seems to honour the practice. For cultural reasons, the Dutch chose to overlook this aspect of ancient Jewish society, along with other traditions and rules that had come to seem barbaric.

This points to the danger of a selective reading of an ancient, much-translated and hotly disputed text. Indeed, it does not take long to find examples of Afrikaners selectively exploiting Biblical homophobia in order to achieve short-term political goals. As with the Portuguese and the Knights Templar, claims of anger and disgust against male–male sexuality could be a convenient way to score points against political enemies. In at least one famous case from the Orange Free State such claims almost provoked a war.

It was during a time of already existing tension, not long after the Boers had effectively won their independence from British imperialism. Some of the more radical Boer nationalists wanted to expel British settlers from their state altogether. At first, the radicals were held back by more moderate Afrikaner leaders like J. H. Brand. The behaviour of the first Anglican bishop soon after his arrival in Bloemfontein in 1863, however, gave them the ammunition they needed to provoke ill will against the British. The Reverend Edward Twells apparently engaged in unspecified sex acts with boys at his church. For several years this behaviour was covered up, as Brand attempted to maintain good relations with the British and as church leaders themselves struggled to avoid public controversy. In 1868, however, Britain openly sided against the Free State in another conflict by declaring a protectorate over the neighbouring Basotho. The hardliners seized their chance. Free State police issued a warrant for Twells's arrest and over the next few days, the Afrikaner press condemned the British in terms designed to enrage the population: 'God-defying', 'shameless and God-forsaken', 'satanic lust', 'animal-like behaviour' and 'pollute our children'. Twells narrowly escaped from the country and war between Britain and the Orange Free State was temporarily avoided.

A similar case of homophobia being used to denounce a whole group of people took place during the 1906 Chinese catamite scandal. Accusations of homosexuality against the Chinese were an attempt to mobilise the white working class and to embarrass the British government into deporting the Chinese from South Africa. The language used at the time reflects the deep disgust that the idea caused in British society. Even the courts expressed their horror. Hogoza, who was condemned to death in Natal in 1868, thus did not simply commit an act of violence: he 'did commit and perpetrate that detestable and abominable crime of buggery (not to be named amongst Christians)'.

Hatred and fear of homosexuality is thus a very old, well-established part of European culture that was transplanted into Africa in sometimes sincere, and sometimes opportunistic, ways. But the same religion that justified capital punishment or even war because of homosexuality also provided an alternative way of understanding the issue. That alternative understanding gradually led to lesser punishments or even acceptance in a minority of cases. The Christian ideals of forgiveness and of loving one's neighbour suggested tolerance rather than violence against homosexuals. The idea of submission to God's plan also undermined the consistency of anti-sodomy persecutions in the name of Christ. After all, perhaps it was God who had planted feelings of homosexual orientation in the first place.

Building from that idea, a 'cult of homosexuality' developed in the 19th century within the Anglican church. Like one strand of ancient Greek philosophy, this cult saw male–male sexual love as a way to achieve a purer knowledge of love and God than heterosexual marriage, in which love was burdened by child care and other household matters. The cult may partly explain how Twells reached such a high level within the church before anyone complained about his tendencies.

Another scholar has argued that repressed homosexuality was also idealised amongst the British military officer class during the age of colonial expansion. As long as they were not allowed to develop into actual sexual relations or to be openly named, very close homoerotic bonds between men were thought to build warrior discipline, loyalty and comradeship in battle. Ability to repress sexual desire was a sign of superior leadership quality.

Anti-Christian thinkers were making some of these same points, perhaps the most influential being the French author, the Marquis de Sade, an aristocrat who became an official of the state during the radical phase of the French revolution. He wrote extensively about the liberating effects of the free expression of sexual desire, including homosexuality, against the political and social tyranny of the Catholic church.

Adding to the confusion in the late 19th century was the emergence of new, scientific explanations of same-sex sexuality. The work of Sigmund Freud after 1890 was especially influential in spreading the view that sexual inversion or 'uranism' was not the outcome of free will or sin, hence it did not deserve punishment. In the view of Freudian psychology, all human beings were naturally bisexual from infancy. They failed to develop into 'normal' heterosexuals not through any fault of their own but as a result of bad or misguided parenting. Overprotective mothers, and those who kept boys at the breast for 'too long', were favourite culprits in that regard.

These new psychological theories were still stigmatising, but they tended to replace Christian fear and hatred with feelings of pity or concern with healing a mental illness. The fierce application of the law and religious opinion thus declined fairly steadily over the course of the 19th century. The French led the way in Africa when they extended their revolutionary laws to the four communes in modern-day Senegal, removing sodomy as a legal category as early as 1791. Among the powers that colonised southern Africa it was Catholic Portugal that took the lead when it dropped consenting homosexual acts from its new criminal code in 1852. In the British colonies, sodomy, or buggery as it was sometimes called, remained a criminal offence, but by the 1870s no more death penalties were carried out for it. By the 1910s and 1920s in colonial Zimbabwe, there was not only a clear tendency towards more lenient sentencing for male–male sexual crimes but also for the police to ignore all but the worst cases.

The decline of church influence and the growing lack of interest by the state in persecuting same-sex behaviour led to the emergence of the first openly gay subcultures in some African cities. In the 1930s, notably, a homosexual, cross-dressing 'moffie' scene had arisen out of what had formerly been the Coon Carnival or public parade by coloureds dating back to slavery times in Cape Town. By the 1940s and 1950s small gay scenes had begun to appear in other urban centres as well, including African townships like Mkhumbane, Durban and Dakar's *bidonvilles*. Officials meanwhile largely turned a blind eye to male–male sex in the prisons and mine compounds, including weddings and feasts to celebrate the occasion.

Not all men were pleased with these trends, to say the least. If the state was not going to enforce compulsory heterosexuality, some men were determined to take matters into their own hands. We have already mentioned one of the first of these cases – the Scotland gang, or 27s, which was formed in the early 1900s by black South African gangsters who wished to escape from the homosexual system of the Ninevites, or 28s. Similar evidence of privatised violence against male–male sexual assaults in Southern Rhodesia starts to appear in the courts a little later. Nyama, for example, came to court in 1927 with a broken collarbone. He had been beaten up by a man and his friends in revenge for an alleged sexual assault. In 1931, another victim of indecent assault by a man was Carl Beirousky. He explained that he had not reported the assault to the police but instead 'decided to get up a gang to give accused a hiding'.

Some of the Christian churches also took up a renewed struggle against sin whenever it appeared that the state was becoming too lenient or liberal. This time it was not by burning sodomites at the stake, but by education. The aim was to internalise fear and hatred towards same-sex sexuality (indeed, some would argue, any kind of sexuality)

119

and to toughen men up so that they could and would police themselves by guilty conscience and peer pressure. Some might call it colonisation of the mind. To achieve this, the churches engaged in constant propaganda against disapproved behaviour and towards the glorification of role models who demonstrated the ideals of proper masculinity and femininity. People were taught to live up to the example of these models and to be vigilant against any signs of deviance from them. For boys and men that meant repressing any feminine or passive characteristics in their own personality and sexuality. It also meant keeping a close eye on friends and peers and reminding them if and when they strayed from the path.

The sex-segregated public schools were a critical element in this transformation of sexually unruly white boys into refined gentlemen. Such gentlemen could, in turn, tame unruly women, Africans and the natural world itself. A whole branch of imperial literature celebrated this type of inner discipline, from *King Solomon's Mines* to *Jock of the Bushveld*. Periodic moral panics in the popular press also served to remind the white population to remain on guard against slip-ups in sexual conduct and fantasy life.

The colonial state may not have initiated this cultural movement but it was broadly supportive. Homophobic masculinity coincided quite well with the need to build up a class of whites who could manage the empire. It provided a politically useful argument: white men deserve to rule because they alone have the inner discipline to control the immoral tendencies in human nature. The same belief could be stated in public hygiene or scientific terms, notably that improper sexual behaviour led to disease and racial pollution and decline. It was then reinforced through everyday activities and socialisation. The sport of rugby, for example, was actively promoted amongst white youths in the late 19th century in Natal. With its controlled violence and homoerotic contact, rugby was thought to be an ideal means of building the moral character necessary for imperial expansion and management.

At the turn of the 19th century the main area of concern in this regard was not so much same-sex sexual acts but inter-racial sex and masturbation. Sex with Africans was especially feared as leading to the pollution and indignity of the supposed natural purity and strength of the master race. A host of laws were put in place to prevent it, backed by the threat of stigma, ostracism, or even deportation. Masturbation, meanwhile, was believed to cause both psychological and physical weakness. In boys it was said to cause hair to grow on the palm of the hand, or blindness; in girls it caused hysteria. So great was the anxiety that it actually became possible for medical doctors in the 1890s to earn a living from it, touring the country to provide advice to white parents, tutors and young people. The lessons they offered focused on how to cultivate racial pride by repressing their children's urge to fondle themselves.

As it turned out, white men in southern African proved their courage as warriors in World War I and worries about the ill effects of supposedly increasing masturbation were proven wrong. Attention then turned to rooting out homosexuality and effeminate behaviour. Men who were in the Natal public schools in the period after the war recalled how suspected 'real' homosexuals were mercilessly thrashed or mocked, often as much by fellow pupils as by school authorities. The situation grew worse in the 1930s when openly homophobic, fascist ideologies of masculinity and race were on the rise in Europe. These were promoted in the region by the fascist regime of Portugal and by right-wing Afrikaner parties. Fascism held a strong fascination for many South African whites, out of both admiration and fear. The most common fear was that their own comparatively lax attitudes towards male homosexuality might weaken South Africa for the expected war. It was this anxiety that seems to have sparked the region's first moral panic on the issue in February 1939.

The scandal began when the press revealed the existence of an organised white male prostitution ring in Johannesburg. The evil was said to have arisen in part from the system of youth prisons scattered around the city. But Dr Louis Freed argued that there was also a deeper cause. Freed was a Freudian psychiatrist who thought that white mothers were undermining their sons' virility by, for example, showing too much affection or taking too long to wean their boys from the breast (this is what supposedly caused African boys to grow up to be sexually irresponsible). Freed therefore recommended that the state take action to educate mothers on the critical importance of weaning boys as soon as possible. Fathers could help as well by keeping emotionally distant from their sons in early infancy.

No equivalent moral panics took place in the colony of Southern Rhodesia. However, the situation there was in many ways even more tense than in South Africa. Whites were much fewer in number relative to Africans. Hence they were both less secure in their dominance over Africans and more needy of an ideology of masculinity that reassured them of their moral fitness to rule. White men, meanwhile, hugely outnumbered white women for the first few decades of the colony's existence. 'Normal' family life was impossible for many to achieve. The need to keep up defences against 'abnormal' relations was therefore acute. Most of the public debate around appropriate sexuality for white men centred on how to control inter-racial sex, but the deathly silence around homosexuality also told a story. The topic was so taboo that even to admit the danger was a danger in itself. One of the only times it briefly raised its scandalous head in public discussion was when the government passed its Immigration Act of 1914. This included a clause that would block men convicted of sodomy or unnatural offences from settling in the colony. The wisdom of this exclusion was so obvious to everyone at the time that no debate was necessary.

Yet, despite all the homophobic propaganda, laws and threatening silences, small circles of men who enjoyed homosexual relations and did not regard them as sinful or criminal began to grow in the urban centres of the region. Ironically, the outbreak of war in September 1939 actually made matters worse for moralists as it gave rise to a gay scene around some of the military camps. It was not until 1948, when the National Party came to power in South Africa, that the government there determined to put an end to such things. In close alliance with the Dutch Reformed Church, the new regime often used old-fashioned religious language to justify itself, but it also linked the repression of male–male sexuality to international politics.

This was in keeping with new scientific arguments coming mainly from the United States. Freudian theories that blamed over-protective mothers for homosexualising American men had been used to explain the higher rate of post-traumatic stress syndrome, or battle fatigue, amongst American soldiers in World War II compared to previous wars. Combating poor mothering and homosexuality was therefore seen as crucial to preparing Americans for the next war, the worldwide struggle against Communism. Not only did homosexual men supposedly lack the moral fibre and fighting ability that would be needed for that struggle, their illegal desires also made them vulnerable to blackmail by Soviet spies.

These ideas filtered into official policy in the United States and many of its Cold War friends. Witch-hunts amongst state officials and suicides of accused homosexuals were amongst the results. Homophobic masculinity was also glorified in American popular culture, which flooded into South Africa in the form of Hollywood movies. A subculture amongst white, working-class youth arose in the 1950s that mimicked Hollywood images of masculine toughness. In this way, the apartheid state gained an unlikely ally in driving homosexuals deeper into the closet – white youth gangs. 'Moffie-bashing' or 'bunny-bashing' was one way for the gang members to show off their toughness to each other. Bunny-bashing expeditions by these gangs could be extremely brutal, including hunting down and torturing suspected gay men that they found at night.

This climate of hostility fuelled internalised homophobia amongst men and women who were not sure of their sexuality. The power of such internalised homophobia can be seen in the secret slang languages that gay-identified people used to find each other in this period, Moffietaal and Gayle. Gayle, in particular, is often openly homophobic in its terminology. It uses the word 'queen', for example, as a way to increase the stigma of adjectives, as if effeminacy magnified the wrongness. Hence Dora in Gayle means a drunk; but a *queen* Dora is a *fucking* drunk. Gayle also uses nouns that directly dehumanise homosexual lovers ('a piece', 'a number', 'a fuck' and, in Afrikaans, 'n pomp' or pump/hit). The effects of such dehumanisation can be seen in gay men's writing from South Africa in the post-World War II era. Men's repressed homosexual feelings or self-hatred come out in this writing through characters who publicly performed their homophobic rage, including the rape of women, in a misguided attempt to cure themselves of their own confused feelings, or the rape of men to show contempt. Suicide and other forms of self-destructive behaviour like alcohol abuse became attractive alternatives for many men and women trapped by such feelings. To the extent that sexual orientation became known to the public as a contributing factor in the suicides or alcoholism, it fed back into the public stereotype of homosexuals as a weak link in the chain of being.

The state itself first entered directly into the repression of homosexuals in the late 1950s, when police began to make raids on private parties and known male homosexual cruising areas in the big cities. As Cold War tensions mounted and the threat to colonialism and apartheid from African nationalist struggles grew, so did the determination of the state to eliminate any signs of moral weakness in white men. At least one high-profile case of an open homosexual who was also a communist seemed to prove the existence of the danger. Cecil Williams was imprisoned for anti-apartheid activity and then deported from South Africa in the mid-1960s. Also, beginning in 1960 – the year of Sharpeville, the year of Congo's independence, the year of Cuba's turn to Marxism-Leninism – the South African Defence Force launched a thirty-year crusade to identify and then 'cure' homosexuals in its midst. Soldiers suspected of homosexual tendencies were sent to a special psychiatric unit where they were given counselling on how to become heterosexual. In some cases they were also shown gay pornography followed by drugs or electric shocks to make them sick, a treatment known as aversion therapy.

The single most spectacular action to be taken against homosexuality, however, was the Forest Town raid of January 1966. Police had heard that a party for gay men was being planned in a quiet suburb of Johannesburg. Undercover agents posing as guests infiltrated the party where they were stunned to find more than 300 mostly white men dancing, kissing and cuddling each other. They called in a raid and made arrests. The scandal made headline news and sparked further undercover operations to find and round up suspected homosexual networks. There was panicky talk of conspiracies by decadent English and Jewish men corrupting the souls of innocent Afrikaner youth. The Minister of Justice, P. C. Pelser, went so far as to warn parliament that the survival of the nation was at stake. Referring to the ghosts of ancient Rome and Sparta, he thundered: 'Formerly glorious civilisations are lying in the dust and South Africa should beware of a similar fate. The canker of Sodom has to be sliced out before it ruins the moral fibre of the nation.' Not a single parliamentarian raised a voice in disagreement.

But the question remained: how was this necessary moral slicing to be achieved? In 1967, Pelser submitted a proposal to parliament that would give the police sweeping new powers to crack down on homosexuals. A Select Committee on the Immorality Amendment Bill was then formed to study the issue and make recommendations. For over four months, the Committee heard conflicting evidence from a whole range of experts about the nature and extent of the homosexual threat. It provided a very public forum for the expression of extreme homophobia and conspiracy theories. On the basis of these, it finally concluded that the state did indeed need greater ability to repress what it called 'immoral, indecent or unnatural acts'. This would include power to break into private social affairs in order to gather evidence, even a 'party' consisting of as few as two people. The new provisions also, for the first time, targeted lesbian sex by banning dildos. Men found guilty of immoral acts, so defined, or in possession of offending sex toys, could be imprisoned for up to three years.

As bad as this was, north of the Limpopo the situation was in many ways worse. Despite the official homophobia in South Africa, that country still had big cities with, by this time, well-established gay scenes and communities with international connections. The police largely left them in peace as long as they remained within their 'pink ghettos'. Southern Rhodesia, by comparison, was much smaller, with nowhere to hide. The same conservative Christian, Hollywood and Cold War influences were at work, but in addition LGBT in Southern Rhodesia faced constant intense propaganda to conform to an ideal of national identity. This was an old theme in the history of the colony but the pressures to conform grew more acute after World War II. A flood of new immigrants arrived in the colony, many from countries in southern and eastern Europe that did not share early Rhodesian attitudes towards sexuality. It became almost an obsession of the political and cultural elite to develop a sense of Rhodesian nationalism that would bring a diverse white population together.

This settler nationalism emphasised the rugged masculinity of the pioneer period and the more recent heroic role of Southern Rhodesians in the defence of Britain in World War II. It was a muscular masculinity that claimed a special ability for the colony's white men to fight and drink, but also to build, to protect the weak and to master nature. Idealised Southern Rhodesian masculinity also defined itself by what it was not: not socialistic, not effeminate and not wimpish. Complementing it was an ideal of settler femininity that emphasised domesticity and the management of children and households. In this view, the liberalism of the west (and even of South Africa) was a positive danger to civilised government and progress in Africa to the extent that it tolerated homosexuality and women's liberation from traditional domestic roles.

This hyper-masculine or macho-nationalism was endlessly reiterated through the popular media, including popular humour that idealised heterosexuality and mocked the gender-bending that was beginning to appear in the west. Just to be on the safe side, the Immigration Act of 1914 was revised in 1954. It prevented anyone thought to practise 'homosexualism' from even entering the colony as tourists (let alone settling in and effeminising the precious culture). In 1964, the Miscellaneous Offences Act made it a criminal offence even to wear gender-inappropriate clothing, empowering the police to arrest lesbians who wore trousers and men who wore lipstick or dresses.

There were not, by the way, very many of these people, and certainly almost none outside of tiny, private circles. The chilly climate for Southern Rhodesian gays and lesbians became even chillier, however, with the Unilateral Declaration of Independence in 1965 and the outbreak of the bush war soon after. The consequent militarisation of white society in the 1970s only made things worse for those who 'let the side down'. The political rhetoric of the regime emphasised the supposed Christian nature of Rhodesian identity and struggles. The common view was that the weakness of contemporary Britain to stand up to African demands arose from its abandonment of hardline Christian certainties around morality.

One can see the same themes dramatised over and over again in Rhodesian war novels from that period. These show the triumph of noble and virile Rhodesian manliness over communist, sadistic and/or homosexual enemies. John Gordon Davis, for example, in his novel *Hold My Hand I'm Dying*, has his Rhodesian hero rebuild his masculine and national pride by moving to the wild Zambezi Valley where he battles with terrorists. In *Seize the Reckless Wind* Davis rages furiously against 'lily-livered' (another way of saying cowardly or sissy) whites while seeming to admire the adulterous bed-hopping of Rhodesian society. The heroic policeman in Robert Early's 1977 *A Time of Madness* first rescues a South African man from moral decline in Johannesburg, then goes on to defeat a whole range of communists, terrorists, meddling whites from overseas and homosexuals. And so on.

The ultimate expression of this culture of homophobia occurred in 1972 when two white men, including a police constable, hunted down and beat to death a middle-aged gay white man because, as they said, he was a 'poof'. The climate of hostility against suspected gays became so bad that, the following year, the commissioner of police almost expressed sympathy towards them. He promised to make greater efforts to protect (implicitly white) homosexual men from juvenile (implicitly black) blackmailers. Little seems to have come of this, however, and as the war entered its final most brutal phase in the late 1970s, social space for tolerance disappeared almost entirely. As we will see in Chapter 9, there were still a couple of night clubs where men could wear drag, as well as a discreet cruising place for deeply closeted gays in Salisbury. However, LGBT persons who could, often preferred to join with the growing number of whites who left. In Rhodesian slang, they 'gapped it', or 'did the chicken run', for South Africa and overseas.

⁓

Settler societies in southern Africa were full of contradictory messages and trends. These included promising ideals of universal rights, on the one hand, yet, on the other, rationalising the widespread practice of racial discrimination and outright theft of land from Africans. Colonial regimes also commonly claimed to desire the emancipation of women while promoting their own deeply sexist culture. For at least a hundred years, but closer to two hundred in some cases, there have also been strong scientific, legal and moral arguments in favour of tolerance of sexual diversity both coming from the settlers' home societies and generated internally. Yet these arguments were offset by varying degrees of intolerance, mockery and active persecution of LGBT people, up to and including torture and murder. Well into the 1980s, the South African government continued to strengthen its ability to prosecute LGBT people and used accusations of homosexuality to smear its political opponents.

These contradictory messages unfolded over the course of colonial rule and apartheid before the watchful eyes of African populations. Africans were, by turns, resentful, admiring, hopeful, amused and angry towards settler culture. In the next chapter, we look closely at some of the specific ways that western and settler attitudes around homosexuality were heard and interpreted by those Africans, particularly those Africans who wished to climb the narrow social ladder of respectability that settler society offered.

April 1968. My Dearest John ...

The Select Committee on the Immorality Amendment Bill was set up in South Africa at the beginning
of February 1968 when nine committee members,
all senior white males, were appointed. Up until the
middle of June the Committee considered written
representations from more than 50 institutions also
overwhelmingly dominated by white men: religious
institutions, members of the legal profession, the police
force, the Justice Department and Defence Force, psy-
chologists and sociologists. There was one submission
from the National Council of Women. Seven un-named
white men and women also spoke about their own
experiences as gay men and lesbian women. The result,
amounting to 349 pages of text, helped guide the South
African Parliament to draft its repressive anti-homosexual legislation in 1969.

The following story is based on some of the statements made by witnesses to the Select Committee.
When reading the evidence, we kept imagining if one
of the committee members had been in the closet and
how he would have felt.

One out of nine is more than just a slight possibility ...

April 1968

My Dearest John,
    *We have another few days here, listening to more evidence
and submissions. We should be done by the end of April and
I'll be back home in your arms and all this will seem like a*

129

bad dream. I still have serious reservations about sitting on this committee and I still feel that I should have made some excuse and turned it down. But I also think that you were right when you said that it was an opportunity that couldn't be missed, given the recent hostilities against us. But I can't imagine the consequences if it should ever become known that a gay man helped to investigate what one witness described as the 'threat to the Republic' that men such as us constitute.

I have to say I'm finding it really hard going listening to what our informants have to say. And alarming even. I had quite a fright when a very senior police officer claimed to be able to accurately identify homosexuals without any trouble at all. It was easy, he said, looking me straight in the eye, for an experienced person such as himself to identify such deviants. I kept my cool and asked him how he managed it and he continued telling us, every word demonstrating his error, but with me unable to draw it to anyone's attention. Talk about frustrating! And for the most part, my fellow committee members accept such testimony as truth. Did you know that men like us 'caused the downfall of great empires, such as the Greek, Roman and Ottoman empires'? Had you ever realised what a powerful force we could be?

But it isn't all as scary as that. Some of the psychiatrists and medical doctors have said things that make sense, but not all of them. A Cape Town doctor told us the following story about a homosexual school principal. It was obvious that the man was a homosexual, our medical expert reported, because 'he always wore far too big a tie'. It was 'too big a tie, too large and too wide, and of too bright colours'. Worse still 'whenever he was talking he played with this tie, lifting and dropping it'. I didn't know whether to laugh or cry, but made sure my hands were firmly in my pockets and far away from my tie. I did notice that one of my colleagues on the committee changed his tie the next day though! I'm sure it was just coincidence!

It was the police officers who gave the scariest testimony, stating prejudice as fact time after time. 'It is universally recognised that homosexuals drink excessively.' Well that kind of logic suggests that a man who sleeps with other men, but who doesn't drink, isn't a proper homosexual at all. But I thought that instead of challenging him on this I should rather keep quiet. Another senior officer stated categorically that it was established as fact 'that every homosexual makes it his business to recruit as many homosexuals as possible'. I don't know what this means for those of us who have been in committed long-term relationships; presumably we also aren't proper homosexuals? The Deputy Secretary for Social Welfare and Pensions even stated that homosexual men routinely went about seducing boys as young as eight. I don't know of a single gay man who'd be remotely interested in having sex with children. I desperately wanted to say so, but didn't have the courage.

So we sit again tomorrow at nine o'clock. I have to say that, in hindsight, I don't think that my presence on this committee will have helped our cause very much. Although the committee members are decent people who want to do the right thing, they are being given so much rubbish in the way of evidence. I can't challenge it, or claim any expertise in contradicting such testimony without risking exposure, and it just keeps on piling up. When so many people repeat the same nonsense it develops a momentum of its own, and it is hard and probably futile to be the solitary voice contradicting it. I shall still try, but I don't want to precipitate a witch-hunt.

So I fear the worst, my love. I think that the committee, with the best intentions, will make some fairly severe recommendations, and that our lives will become even more difficult than they are now. As long as we can find some time together I can tolerate it.

All my love
Peter

7 • homophobia in the African nationalist movement

Colonial rule was a period of theft, violence and humiliation engin-
eered by Europeans against Africans. It is true that many Europeans
sincerely believed that they were doing a moral thing in building such
a system, and many Europeans did in fact bring material and other
benefits to Africa. But overall, the way they did it caused widespread
destruction and injustice. Apartheid in South Africa from 1948 to 1994
was in many ways, even worse, as it enforced racial inequality with
the full efficiency and ruthlessness of a modern, powerful, capitalist
state.

Africans responded to colonialism and apartheid in many ways,
including resistance through open rebellion, trade unionism and passive methods of non-co-operation such as downing tools or avoiding
taxation. Colonial authorities usually met this resistance with crushing military or police power and with divide-and-rule tactics that set
Africans against each other. The modern African nationalist movement grew out of African efforts to overcome these tactics and to
create unity where tribal and other divisions caused weakness. The
goal was never simply to achieve political independence: it was also to
restore the pride of Africans in their traditional values of community
and spirituality linked to their guardianship of the land – *ubuntu* and
hunhu are the Ndebele and Shona terms.

One of the great achievements of 20th century world history is
how African nationalist leaders built a mass movement that accom-
plished many of those goals. They forced the colonial rulers to hand
over political power to Africans much more quickly and thoroughly

than almost anyone imagined possible. African nationalist ideals also continued to play a crucial role after independence by providing a focus of resistance to neo-colonial pressures from western aid donors, international financial institutions and multinational corporations. African nationalism has achieved important successes in restoring the dignity of African cultures against the global tide of the western-dominated culture industry.

Unfortunately, however, in order to dismantle the master's house, the servants in this case borrowed many of the master's tools. That is, Africans adopted many ideas and skills from the colonialists in order to fight against colonial rule. On the positive side, these included ideas about universal human rights and democratic institutions, mass political mobilisation, and effective, modern military discipline and strategies. In other cases, however, European colonial values quietly corrupted the high ideals of African nationalism. The terrible ethnic conflicts that followed independence in many African countries, for example, can often be directly linked to the long history of European tribalism and the deliberate policy of encouraging Africans to distrust or hate each other. A similar argument has been made about gender relations. European efforts over a long period to impose their vision of proper behaviour for men and women resulted in boosting African men's powers over women and undercutting African women's traditional rights and dignities.

This chapter will focus on a less well-known trickle-down effect of colonial cultural imperialism, namely homophobia. Although it may not have seemed like a big issue at the time, in the long run, seeds of intolerance and hate planted in the colonial period have emerged as a corrupting influence within the African nationalist movement.

～ ～

African cultures, with all their pressures to conform to the ideals of marriage and family, could be quite oppressive around issues of gender and sexuality. For example, witnesses from several countries in the region told the 1907 Leary–Taberer inquiry that the death penalty was imposed for continued indulgence in male–male sex. Sokisi was purportedly sentenced to death by his king *in absentia* for his behaviour in taking male wives. Similar claims about African tradition have also been used in contemporary Zimbabwe to justify deportation, rape, castration, cutting off of the penis, and even execution of unrepentant lesbians and male homosexuals. Some African leaders today take pride in the boast that African cultures are fundamentally and historically intolerant on this issue.

Yet, truth be told, capital punishments were rarely carried out in ancient times. The terrible risk of avenging spirits in any case of unjust death made communities want to avoid extreme reactions to sexual misbehaviour. African cultures were also good at explaining or denying all but the most flagrant cases of same-sex sexuality on the principle that keeping families together was more important than naming and blaming individuals within them. This allowed considerable leeway for private sexual experimentation or play as long as public appearances were maintained. Among other things, many African cultures allowed pre-marital sex play such as *hlobonga*, which allowed young people to have sex without endangering the virginity of the girl. Christian missionaries and other Europeans were often shocked by this, denouncing it as immoral.

The missionaries were even more shocked when they realised that African men who travelled to the mines had a casual attitude towards *hlobonga* with males. The men who engaged in this practice in southern Africa expressed no strong shame or guilt about it. Since they were either already married or intended to marry and have children, they did not regard such short-term affairs as homosexual in the modern sense, or even sexual at all.

Far from being instinctively homophobic, African cultures generally had to be taught this new sexual dogma. Missionaries took the first steps with a campaign of direct propaganda against male–male sexual practices in the major mining centres of South Africa beginning in the early 1900s. Their message was not just that such conduct was bad but that it would be punished ruthlessly in the afterlife and for eternity.

No level of compensation to the victim would wash away the sin. No curtains, no level of darkness and no amount of threats against the victim to keep quiet could hide the act from the watchful eye of an all-powerful and all-knowing God.

Similar campaigns, it seems, also took place in other parts of Africa where male–male sexuality was a recognised part of traditional culture. Until they converted to Christianity in the early 20th century, elite warrior castes amongst the Azande and the Tutsi, for example, kept young boys as servants and lovers. In the case of the *kabaka* Mwanga of the Buganda kingdom, allegations that he sexually abused Christian converts fuelled the missionary propaganda machine against both him and the Muslim (Arab or Swahili) influence that was supposedly corrupting African morals. Mwanga's homo- or bisexuality, in that sense, actually helped to pave the way for the British conquest of Buganda in 1899/1900.

Many African men at first mocked the Christian vision of hell-fire and damnation. They kept to their ways for the most part, not worrying too much about the importance of private sexual affairs. However, evidence given to Leary and Taberer suggests that the missionaries were beginning to have an impact amongst African migrant labourers even as early as 1907. Bob Zandemela, a Chopi miner from Mozambique, explained his conversion to Christianity and to exclusive heterosexuality in these terms: 'I was *inkotshane* myself once; I gave it up when I heard it was an evil thing ... When I learned in the Book [the Bible] it was wrong I stopped it. I submitted to being an *inkotshane* because I did not know better.'

Christian propaganda was not just spread through sermons and select anti-homosexual quotations from the Bible. It was present in the application of the law as well. Those men unlucky enough to get caught by police were typically given a short but stern lesson in anti-homosexual theology. Their crimes were described as, amongst other things, 'detestable and abominable', 'unspeakable', 'revolting', 'despicable', 'unnatural' and 'un-Christian'. The first generation of Africans to be trained in the practical application of colonial law was also immersed in the social values behind it. We can see this in the Biblical-sounding language that black Zimbabwean magistrates have frequently used in their rulings on sodomy in the post-independence period. The words of one magistrate in 1991, for example, sound remarkably 19th-century in their Christian imagery and dogmatism: 'such unscrupulous acts', he said in his judgment against two consenting male partners, 'do in my view stink in the nostrils of justice, above all society does look at such offences with abhorrence'.

Christian homophobia was also taught to Africans by more subtle means, including the imposition of literal, crude translations of indigenous languages. The word *inkotshane*, to give the most obvious example, had originally included the meaning of servant without necessarily suggesting a sexual relationship. Yet, the missionary translations that made their way into popular understandings of the word stated the meaning, baldly, as 'sodomy'. Where African languages lacked an explicit word equivalent to the English ones, missionaries sometimes did them the service of inventing new terms derived from the Bible, such as *isono samadoda ase-Sodom* in McLaren's 1923 Xhosa dictionary, for example, or Hamel's 1965 *mosodoma* in Sesotho. Apartheid-era anthropologists and linguists did much the same by putting crude literal translations of European terms into the dictionaries of African languages that they wrote. Fischer's English–Xhosa dictionary in 1985 contains some of the most awkward of these, including *umntu obhinqileyo othandana nomnye okwabhinqileyo* (said to mean 'lesbian') and *ukwenziwa kwezinto ezingcolileyo phakathi kwendoda nenkwenkwe* (said to mean 'pederasty'). It is probably safe to say that no Xhosa-speaker would ever have used such expressions and few would have understood them.

Even more commonly, however, the missionaries showed their disapproval by simply ignoring indigenous words for same-sex behaviour as if, by writing the word out of existence, the practices themselves could be banished. Fr Michael Hannan did not include any word referring to homosexual in his impressive 1,014-page *Standard Shona Dictionary*, even though he did include many vulgar or dirty words.

Where words had a double meaning, he included only the 'approved' meaning: *matanyera*, for example, is noted as 'Latrine cleaner, scavenger', but not its other meaning of male–male sex. *Ngochani* is also omitted from the first edition of the first major Shona–Shona dictionary, *Duramazwi*, but it does appear in the second, larger edition without any reference to the stigma often attached to the word.

European fears about homosexual perversion were communicated through things as well as through language. For example, buildings like boarding schools, hostels and prisons were rebuilt over the course of colonial rule according to the European sense of what was sexually correct. Where it had been considered entirely normal, non-sexual and non-threatening for African men to sleep together under the same blanket in the nude in the early days of urban development (as had been the case in pre-colonial days), by the 1950s most institutions and public housing in Southern Rhodesia provided for separate sleeping quarters. Such arrangements were particularly admired by one South African 'expert' on African sexuality. Southern Rhodesia, he maintained, along with the Orange Free State, was a model for Johannesburg precisely because its superior urban planning supposedly protected African men from homosexual temptation.

Clothing was another way in which powerful colonialist messages about sexuality were communicated to Africans. Modesty in traditional terms could be achieved by covering the genitals and often little else. The missionaries, by contrast, regarded virtually the entire female body (and even words that made one think about it) as sexual. Modesty – and hence progress towards civilisation – in their eyes demanded a full cover-up for females. The unseen, the forbidden, in this way became erotic. As one elderly Shona man recalled to researcher Agnes Runganga: 'We grew up swimming with girls, without clothes. There was nothing sexual about the exposure. When I worked in Harare in the 1930s I realised for the first time that the female body was sexual.' The main danger in this development was that sexual thoughts were now introduced into the commonest daily interactions. This therefore required developing a new culture where constant self-repression could keep the thoughts, and the lust that followed, at bay.

A similar effect was also created around homosexual desire. A hint of this can be seen today in the transvestite or queen sub-cultures in Africa, where African men do not dress up and act as traditional African women. They wear the sexy fashions and make-up of a certain stereotyped western femininity.

New attitudes towards the body were also conveyed through lessons on hygiene, disease and body odour. These lessons were often given to Africans in deeply humiliating ways by whites, by African police, or by senior boys and girls in boarding schools. Women in Southern Rhodesian towns, for example, were sometimes rounded up by the police for compulsory vaginal examinations known as *chibeura*. If the doctor found evidence of a sexually transmitted disease, they would be deported from the city back to their rural home village. African men at work had their penises and anuses inspected and could be retrenched if the doctor suspected illness. All this was supposedly to protect Africans from disease. Endless propaganda about the smell of African bodies and the need to teach them the proper use of soap was also typically put in terms of health. But there was another cultural effect. Freshly scrubbed genitals came to mean a sign of modernity and progress. It was a short jump from there to associating cleanliness with marital and material success, an erotic association if ever there was one. Thus it is that many contemporary black gays remember the showers of boarding schools and hostels, rather than cramped sleeping quarters, as the scene of their first awakenings of homosexual attraction.

The Africans most heavily affected by this colonial obsession with controlling and changing African sexuality were those who hoped to advance into the middle class through western education and professional employment. The French term for such a person (*assimilé*) and the Portuguese (*assimilado*) refer directly to the need for these Africans to assimilate fully European values, or to transform themselves culturally into 'black Europeans'. They needed to win respectability and citizen rights in settler society by, first of all, distancing themselves from supposedly primitive aspects of African society, including polygamy and marriage using cattle as *lobola*. Initiation or circumcision schools and adolescent sexual experimentation like *hlobonga* were also taboo from the point of view of African middle-class respectability. In the 1930s these men and women were amongst the loudest opponents of the working-class sport of boxing, which was thought to inflame passions in a primitive way compared to more civilised sports. They were also supporters of strict controls on so-called loose women and on African access to hard liquor.

A small number of Africans did make progress up the colonial social ladder by demonstrating their 'civilised' qualities in these ways, and by becoming teachers, doctors, journalists and other professionals. But, by the early 1950s, it was becoming obvious that Africans had to do more than simply live in a modest, respectable manner in order to shake the settlers out of their racism. Indeed, it seems that almost no matter what they achieved in the white man's terms – including success at school, church, police, master-farming, monogamous marriage, hygiene, fashion, tea-drinking, and so on – Africans continued to be seen and treated as inferior or childish. African men remained forever 'boys' in the eyes of most settlers, blocked by law or an unspoken colour bar from the rights and respect given to white men.

Often this put-down was made in terms of comparative sexualities. The argument went that African men, unlike white men, could not control their sexual urges and therefore lacked the moral worth to exercise power or enjoy other rights and privileges that went to whites. Much of this was simply false and deeply hypocritical. Nonetheless, repeated over and over again, it had an impact on middle-class African culture and to a large degree shaped the development of resistance to the colonial system.

The influence of Christian teaching on efforts to assert African dignity is immediately obvious in struggles against both colonial and missionary racism and the traditional authorities who were promoted by many colonial regimes as their 'stooges' in the rural areas. Across Africa, various Moses figures emerged to lead the people out of the wilderness using language and concepts taken straight from the Bible.

This was aimed as much against colonial injustice as against tribal customs understood as superstitious, immoral or backward. Even the more radical Zimbabwean leadership that emerged in the late 1950s and 1960s was still the product of mission schools and, in many cases, of evangelist parents. Edgar Tekere's father was an Anglican priest and Robert Mugabe was educated at a Catholic school run by the Canadian Marist Brothers. Joshua Nkomo, president of the Rhodesian African National Congress after 1957 and a founder of the Zimbabwe African People's Union in 1961, described himself as a proudly monogamous, teetotaller, while Ndabaningi Sithole learned the manners of 'how to treat a lady' from Garfield Todd at Dadaya mission.

Public statements on gender made by these leaders during the liberation struggle generally reflected their conservative or even puritanical Christian upbringing. Indeed, despite their frequent appeals to African traditions, it was obvious that they had mixed feelings about African culture. Naomi Nhiwatiwa, a ZANU party official, for example, told a western audience in 1979 that ZANU had abolished *lobola* and polygamous marriage amongst its fighters, had banned divorce and adultery, and had condemned beer-drinking, when, in fact, these were all recognised in traditional culture. The Reverend Canaan Banana, a Methodist preacher who became independent Zimbabwe's first president, wrote several books that aimed to harness Christian theology to the goal of building a revolutionary society. In his book *The Woman of My Imagination,* for example, Banana refers to St Paul when he urges wives to obey their husbands. He also blames the sexually irresponsible behaviour of boys on 'the poor upbringing of the girls', meaning a lack of chastity.

What makes this advice so interesting to us now is that Banana's own sexual behaviour was less than the perfect model according to his own standards, as revealed in the multiple charges laid against him in 1997 of sodomy and indecent assault on males. Banana, who by that time taught Christian theology at the University of Zimbabwe, at first defended himself against the charges with a vicious counter-attack upon homosexuals and whites.

The class of educated Africans that produced most of the nationalist leadership did not only emphasise their Christian respectability, they also sought to prove their modern credentials and to win the whites' recognition as men by claiming a shared virility with white men. We can see this in the writings and speeches of the first and second generations of African nationalists from the 1940s to 1970s. Ndabaningi Sithole, for example, was one of the first blacks in Southern Rhodesia to earn a degree and was one of the founders of the modern nationalist movement. In his memoirs, he describes his relationship with white men in the light of their shared desire for sex with white women. The fact that white men refused to allow this desire to be consummated seemed to be his main, underlying grievance against colonial rule. Interestingly, in *Roots of a Revolution*, Sithole again harshly criticises the Rhodesians for 'castrating' African men and for making inter-racial love a crime. Yet, at the same time, he worries that punishments against male–male love are not tough enough under Rhodesian law.

The exact same point about inter-racial relations was also made by the pioneering African journalist Lawrence Vambe who described sex as the 'main root of the racial problem'. Didymus Mutasa was yet another early nationalist leader who pointed to the penis in the struggle for African dignity: 'The white man's civilisation will end', he predicted, 'when too many blacks want to urinate in the same place as the white man.' Robert Mugabe put it a bit more subtly, but one still gets the same message from the language he used to denounce international attempts to negotiate a compromise with the Rhodesians in 1979 – 'emasculated'.

The emphasis on shared virility between white and black men often translated into anger against black women who questioned that virility, or who seemed to take advantage of the colonial system to escape 'proper' controls by African men. Sithole hinted at this just after he had become a teacher in the early 1940s. He boasted of soundly thrashing a schoolgirl, an act of violence he saw as modern when compared to the traditional beliefs of the girl's father. During the first big industrial strike in Southern Rhodesia (Bulawayo, 1948) strikers also lashed out with violence against African women passers-by. Even worse was the mass rape of young women in Harare's female hostel in 1956, an atrocity that was justified by prominent African nationalist leaders. The women, they claimed, had not only refused to participate in a bus boycott but had mocked the jobless, unmarried young men who were enforcing the boycott. To Maurice Nyagumbo this was an intolerable provocation to the men and to the nationalist movement as a whole. 'Personally I had no reason to feel regret for the incident,' he later wrote. 'I actually believed the girls deserved their punishment.'

Reflecting this anger against women, prominent nationalist leaders began to attack western fashion, the mini-skirt above all, as symbolic of the humiliation of African men. They also commonly equated compromise or political moderation with femininity. Sithole's mentor, Obed Muteza, put his choice to go to prison this way: 'Clearly, the honourable choice is the life of hardship, even death, than to go down in the annals of a nation as a collaborator or indeed a woman. The choice before me is simple; am I a man or a woman?' To avoid being seen as a collaborator, men therefore had to show no tolerance for effeminate behaviour, homosexuality, or even close male–male friendship. As Muteza further explained: real African men repressed even the instinct to laugh or smile, abstained from sex before battle, and cultivated 'distance between man and man' to harden themselves.

There are hints that such attitudes were turning to focus directly on men who had sex with men from as early as the 1940s, when letters began to appear in the African press denouncing as disgraceful to Africans the 'coons' and the homoerotic dances associated with the migrant labour hostels. Charles Mzengeli, the leading African figure in Salisbury politics until the mid-1950s, actually once brought up the issue in a confrontation with city officials over the need for more married quarters and less harassment of African women in town. But intolerance of men who did not conform to the virile ideal became more and more entrenched as Rhodesian intransigence drove moderates like Mzengeli out of leadership positions in the nationalist struggle. An interesting sign of this came in the mid-1970s, when Zimbabwean workers were recruited in large numbers to replace Malawians in the mines in South Africa. The Zimbabweans emerged as the main critics of South Africans who engaged in or were tolerant of the practice of mine marriage. According to the sociologist, Dunbar Moodie, the better-educated and more homophobic Zimbabweans played an important role in bringing mine marriage as a system to an end.

Two other intellectual influences on that generation of Zimbabwean leadership were Marxism-Leninism and Freudian psychology. Both these traditions have socially conservative and homophobic tendencies that complemented the Christian vision. The effect could be seen when the Zimbabweans who went for training in communist China and the USSR returned to the region in the mid-1970s. Fay Chung, who went on to become Minister of Education in independent Zimbabwe, described them as 'puritanical, idealistic, Marxist *VaShandi* [workers]', who allied themselves with traditionalists to oppose what they regarded as a sexually loose atmosphere in the Zambian guerrilla camps. An internal ZANU document from July 1979 also denounced boy–girl affairs in the camps, arguing that their 'disastrous consequences' could include the girls' demand for birth control. Such a demand was seen to be weakening the struggle against white immigration to Rhodesia, colonial power and 'proper' female subservience to African men. Birth control also fitted with enemy policy to introduce secret, injection methods of contraception for black women as part of a strategy to slow the growth of the black population in relation to the white.

For a party that claimed to follow scientific socialism, and whose leaders came mostly from long-standing Christian backgrounds, ZANU's proposed remedies for boy–girl affairs and birth control were somewhat surprising: 'Intensify orientation on our [traditional] culture with emphasis on marriage and "internal discipline".' As well, according to Freedom Nyambura, a female freedom-fighter who was in the camps at that time: 'If you were caught with condoms you could be put in prison.'

The notion that internal discipline was needed to protect revolutionary Africans against homosexuality was never publicly raised by the Zimbabwean leadership. However, we know that it operated behind the scenes from the popularity of the French-trained psychologist, Frantz Fanon. Fanon used Freudian psychology to craft his most famous work, *The Wretched of the Earth*, 'the handbook for black revolution' as the publishers termed it. In *Black Skin, White Masks*, another influential book, he put forward the argument that homosexuality amongst blacks was basically a reflection of black men's sexual humiliation at the hands of white men. Black Martinicans in Europe were, he claimed as evidence, always passive to active white homosexuals, while racist whites hated blacks precisely because they caused whites to feel their repressed homosexual desire for black men. Such ideas were expressed in popular literature through characters who lusted after Africans: Arabs who raped African boys, alienated African-American gays, diseased coloured moffies, treacherous European lesbians and such. The African heroes in these novels triumphed over such non-African characters to regain symbolically the dignity that Africans had lost at the hands of foreigners over the centuries, whether by the slave trade, colonialism or neo-colonialism.

The influential Kenyan academic Ali Mazrui offered a similar type of pop-Freudian psychology in his analysis of the warrior tradition in African politics. In a 1975 article he associated the heterosexual virility of leaders like Idi Amin with their courage to stand up to imperialism. By contrast, he points to the downfall of the 19th century Zulu leader, Shaka. Shaka supposedly had a small penis, was a repressed homosexual and was therefore not a good African leader. Remarkably, Mazrui bases this judgement on speculation written by a European missionary and other colonial authors rather than African historians. While there may be some truth to rumours about Shaka's unusual sexual behaviours, without actual evidence how can we trust an old European man's fantasy that directly links penis size, sexual orientation and political behaviour? It seems that that fantasy suited a particular African man's political agenda in the 1970s rather than reflecting the truth about African history.

Finally, these ideas about the respectability and political value of homophobia to African nationalism were backed to some extent by the material experience of imprisonment during the liberation struggle. The Zimbabwean leadership has never said much on this topic, although Mugabe, Nkomo and many others spent long years in Rhodesian prisons. From South Africa, however, there are several accounts that may explain some of the deep anger against homosexuality. We have already mentioned the case of anti-apartheid activist, Moses Dlamini, who witnessed the white warders on Robben Island in the mid-1960s conspire with criminal gangs to rape the political prisoners as they arrived. At the very least, such experiences would have strengthened the stereotype of homosexuality as a symbol of the white man's oppression of blacks. Winnie Mandela herself infamously exploited this argument in her defence against charges of kidnapping and murder made against her by the apartheid state in 1991. Among other things, she claimed to have acted to protect an African boy from a white homosexual child molester, since homosexual practices had caused at least one of the boys under her charge to 'become mentally disturbed'.

We also know that nationalist talk of African male virility was often contradicted by the actual practices of the armed struggle. During the war of liberation in the 1960s and 1970s, young men on both sides had big guns and little respect for the old patriarchal order. They often heaped humiliation upon the majority peasant population, including public beatings of husbands who were accused of mistreating their wives, killing chiefs accused of being sell-outs or stooges, rape, seductions and calculated sexual torture or public shaming. Sithole, for example, describes the deep shame caused by the Rhodesian police when they dragged suspected African nationalists out of bed to expose their nakedness. Ex-Rhodesian soldier, Dan Wylie, also tells of stripping African men and mocking, or physically beating, their genitals as a military tactic. Young girls, meanwhile, took advantage of the presence of guerrillas and Rhodesian soldiers alike to escape from customary controls on their movement and their sexuality. In the guerrilla camps themselves, a high degree of sexual indiscipline took place. As Paulos

Matjaka Nare recalled about a camp high school: 'In the absence of their real parents and relatives, the children lacked proper guidance and counselling. Strange manners and habits were evolved.' In refugee camps, in concentrated villages or 'keeps', and in the urban townships, tensions around these strange manners and habits fed rising levels of sexual assaults.

All told, the war speeded up the process of destabilisation or breakdown of the old patriarchal order that had begun long before. The final year of the war was especially violent. According to traditional religion, such violence created innumerable 'avenging spirits' (ngozi), which in turn are one of the main causes of incurable sexual-identity problems. For many Zimbabweans today, failure to appease them with the proper rituals since the end of the war explains how not only out gays and lesbians but also 'uppity women' like feminists emerged with a high public profile in the 1990s.

Zimbabwean independence came in 1980. The new Prime Minister was a devout Catholic who espoused Marxism-Leninism yet advocated reconciliation with white commercial farmers and capitalist businessmen. As a leader, Robert Mugabe surprised many in the first few years by his encouragement of democratic institutions, freedom of speech, rural economic development, a huge expansion of the health care and education systems and the legal emancipation of women. Behind the scenes these policies were often contradicted in practice: for example, through the killings of civilians in Matabeleland and discriminatory action against female war veterans. On the whole, however, it was a time of great optimism in many ways, particularly when the risk of ethnic civil war was averted by the unification of the two main political parties. The Shona-dominated ruling party, ZANU(PF), absorbed its main Ndebele-dominated opposition PF-ZAPU with the stated goals of building national unity and focusing efforts on development rather than divisive politics.

The oppressive Rhodesian past began to be shed in cultural life as well. Despite the moral conservatism of much of the new leadership and its indebtedness to conservative rural patriarchs from the period of the bush war, the Zimbabwean government was, at first, self-confident enough to allow an unprecedented degree of sexual emancipation. The period beginning from the 1979 ceasefire and the arrival of Commonwealth peacekeepers was thus almost a golden age of gay life. New night clubs sprang up, exiles from South Africa and the west returned with experiences there of out gay life, the first-ever lesbian group was formed in 1982 and gay men could almost openly cruise in downtown Harare's Cecil Square. Even the state-controlled press advocated tolerance of homosexuals. 'Homosexuals break through barriers', the *Sunday Mail Magazine* reported as it broached the topic in a substantial article for the very first time in 1983. It advised readers not to be fearful of homosexuals since they were probably born that way and were therefore not contagious.

This relative golden age, however, was clearly fragile. To begin with, the old colonial laws against sodomy and indecent assault remained untouched. If anything, punishments tended to get harsher as relatively liberal white judges were replaced by more conservative blacks. The major media also fed into the stereotype of homosexuality as a white man's problem and encouraged blacks to laugh at it or to feel superior about their own culture. Identifying blacks as homosexuals remained taboo. Thus, all of the individuals described in the *Sunday Mail* article mentioned above were white or coloured gays and lesbians, while the emergence of black gay activists in South Africa simply passed without comment. The same paper also mocked the political rivals of the ruling party with a very Rhodesian sense of homophobic humour. A cartoon in 1983, for example, showed Joshua Nkomo in woman's clothing with his panties and large, womanly buttocks exposed to heighten his disgrace. Similar mockery was found in the way that gay rights activism and feminism in the west was covered in the *Sunday Mail* – in a regular column entitled 'It's a Weird Weird World'.

The shift to a more active and explicit backlash against sexual freedom was not long in coming once the first joy of achieving independence began to wear off. Independent women were the first to feel that backlash, in 1983. In Operation Clean-up, a huge, co-ordinated sweep of Harare's night-time streets, police arrested hundreds of alleged prostitutes and deported them to work camps in the rural areas. Gay men's activity in Cecil Square was roughly closed down soon after, although whether by freelance gay-bashers or by pro-government thugs is unclear. As gay rights activist Evan Tsouroullis recalls in his memoir from that time: 'It was sometimes dangerous. Once in a while gay-bashers would try and muscle in. Most of the activity stopped around 1986 when the Spanish ambassador was murdered. There was a lot of speculation amongst gay men at the time that the ambassador was murdered by a trick picked up at the Square. But that is one of Zimbabwe's untold stories.'

Feminists, alleged prostitutes and gay men were not the only groups to feel the increasingly repressive political climate: there were mass killings of so-called dissidents in Matabeleland during the mid-eighties as well. A sharp economic downturn then only made matters worse. In particular, the Economic Structural Adjustment Programme (ESAP) adopted in 1990 increased people's sense of disempowerment. Thousands of jobs were lost as industries closed down. At the same time, school and health-care fees were introduced and earnings were eroded by inflation. By 1991, workers in public administration took home only about half of what they had earned ten years earlier; for agricultural workers average wages were about a third lower. As the economy worsened, men faced the humiliation of no longer being able to support their wives and families, and mothers the pain of not being able to feed their children.

Under conditions of such terrible stress, people turned to behaviours that would have shocked the ancestors: alcoholism, suicide, baby-dumping, abortion and prostitution. The economic crisis also gave rise to a population of unwanted street kids for whom petty crime and selling sex were the only ways to survive. Most of that kind of prostitution was no doubt heterosexual. However, the possibility of earning some quick money drew increasing numbers of youths into homosexual relations regardless of their actual sexual orientation. They could earn the money either directly from a quick sex act or a more long-term 'sugar daddy', or from blackmail, that is, threatening to expose the homosexual affair to the police or to family members unless money was paid. As we have seen, this kind of opportunistic or 'survival sex' is an old story, dating back almost to earliest Southern Rhodesian times. But economic conditions today have not only made it more common and noticeable to the public, they have also, for the first time, brought a small number of African women into selling lesbian sex.

It would be a mistake to exaggerate this or to assume that it is mostly driven by the demands of international sex tourism rather than indigenous elites. Sex tourism in Africa, where it exists at all, is overwhelmingly heterosexual and is concentrated in a small number of resort centres such as Dakar, Banjul and Mombasa. Cape Town is almost certainly the only major exception to the heterosexual tendency as it markets itself as Africa's 'gay capital'. But one black woman, who was interviewed by a researcher at the University of Zimbabwe, explained how she preferred to have sex with white women because they paid more than either black lesbians or men of any colour. She also made it quite clear that she did not associate herself with the gay rights movement or identify as lesbian: 'I am not afraid of it [prostitution with women] at all because I am not a genuine lesbian,' she told Rudo Chigweshe.

HIV/AIDS appeared around this time as if to prove that the ancestors, or God, were punishing the people for polluting the land with their bad behaviour. Although many Africans originally regarded it as a gay white man's disease – indeed, this is the way it was often described even by scientists when it first appeared in the United States – by the early 1990s, HIV/AIDS was clearly taking a devastating toll amongst black heterosexuals. Fear of the disease caused people to behave in very different, and sometimes highly irrational, ways. Many Africans, for example, responded to the call to practise abstinence, to be faithful to one partner, and to wear a condom with partners whose sexual history was unknown. They were supported in this by the state, international donors, traditional leaders and a host of new, Pentecostal and fundamentalist Christian churches.

Others, however, reacted to the rising death toll in ways that made the situation worse, including women's and men's abuse of younger and younger children (supposedly to avoid HIV), the rape of virgins (said to cure the disease) and a fatalistic attitude towards sexual promiscuity (we are all going to die anyway, so why not indulge in the most conquests possible?). An air of moral panic began to creep into the popular media through letters and articles denouncing the new, dangerous sexuality and calling for a return to old, patriarchal values as a means to protect society. There were articles about women 'raping' men, for example, as well as whispered fears about *mupfuhwira* – a husband-taming herb that women were using to control men. Aside from the shame of being controlled by a woman, men feared that *mupfuhwira* could leave a man helpless: his penis could fall off or he could even be killed. The remedy, many believed, was for Africans to stand firm against moral corruption supposedly caused by non-traditional gender and sexual roles.

Perhaps surprisingly, a strong element in the international media said much the same thing: witness the extreme homophobia and misogyny in gangsta rap and some popular expressions of hip-hop youth culture that has flooded out of the United States since the late 1980s. The message to black youth seemed to be: ignore the politically correct propaganda of the liberal white establishment; have sex with women as much as you like and how you like it; blame gays for opening the door to further oppression by whites and uppity (feminist) women.

Justifying homophobia and misogyny on the grounds that it strengthened blacks in the fight against oppression by whites had a certain powerful logic that appealed well beyond youth culture. The fact was, while some of the whites who remained or came to Zimbabwe after independence adapted to the new situation in the full spirit of reconciliation, many others continued to live as before. They refused to accept that they had lost the war and continued to show blatantly racist attitudes towards Africans. Making matters worse, pressures on the government from the big international funding agencies like the World Bank and International Monetary Fund often seemed to reward whites and to frustrate the hopes and expectations of the black majority. Usually this was done in the name of economic productivity and efficiency. Sometimes, however, the funding agencies revealed that behind their best logic were racist or paternalistic ideas about Africans that were deeply offensive. Andrew Natsios, to give one of the most shameful examples, was the head of the powerful United States Agency for International Development when he opposed providing cheap anti-retroviral drugs to ease the suffering of the millions of Africans with HIV. Why? As he told the US Congress in June 2001, people in Africa would not be able to take the drugs properly because they 'do not know what watches and clocks are. They do not use Western means for telling time. They use the sun.'

This was a fertile field in which the political leadership could shift blame from its own errors in judgement to convenient scapegoats, primarily the white farmers and western neo-imperialism but also feminists and gays. In the early 1990s, discrimination against LGBT had not yet become state policy, but a growing number of mostly white and coloured gays and lesbians felt that things might be moving in that direction. The time had come to shift from partying and self-esteem-oriented activities towards a more organised political position. Only in that way could they actively defend against the threat of homophobia and prejudice. This then led to the creation of GALZ in 1990. By 1992 GALZ had a formal constitution and a vision to promote gay rights outside the relatively elite and urban centres where most out LGBT lived. It began to advertise its counselling services and to propagate anti-homophobic arguments in the national media.

In this effort, GALZ was at first blocked from access to the state-controlled press. But it soon found an eager ally in some of the increasingly outspoken independent press. Papers like the *Zimbabwe Independent* were hungry for stories that highlighted corruption and bigotry in ZANU(PF) and for issues that provoked the ruling party. They ran GALZ advertisements, praised the emergence of a democratic and gay-friendly South Africa, and published sympathetic stories on local gays and lesbians. In March of 1994 the *High Density Mirror* ran a story discussing the plight of local black gays in the townships, an implicit criticism of the ruling party. In 1994, Ngoni Chaidzo was formed, the first association for black gays and lesbians, in one of the historically black townships.

Such was the context for the appearance of the first openly homophobic statements and threats by ZANU(PF) officials in early 1994. The Minister of Home Affairs, Dumiso Dabengwa, reportedly described homosexuality as illegal and directed police to 'warn homos – net is closing in'. In January 1995, Dabengwa described homosexuality as 'abhorrent' and the state-controlled *Sunday Mail* ran an article denouncing foreigners who sought to pervert Zimbabwean culture.

President Mugabe himself first addressed the issue the following month with a speech in Bulawayo, where he said that prostitutes and homosexuals were basically the same thing. This occurred at the start of his long nationwide campaign for re-election as president. It inspired the editors of the Bulawayo daily newspaper to praise fellow Zimbabweans who 'loathe foreign ideas on morality' and to sneer at 'pseudo-campaigners for people's so-called rights'. Mugabe returned to this theme several more times over the next few months, most famously in his denunciation of homosexuals at the Zimbabwe International Book Fair in August of 1995. In September, Zimbabwe's parliament voted overwhelmingly to support the principle of increased persecution of homosexuals as a defence against western imperialism and 'reactionary forces'.

At the next Book Fair in August 1996, the courts declared that GALZ was within its rights to have a stand, but a vigilante group led by prominent ZANU(PF) members nevertheless threatened to close it down by force. On hearing that the group was approaching to carry out this threat, and having already distributed their literature, GALZ representatives made a hasty 'tactical withdrawal'. This was followed by a strategic decision to keep a lower profile at subsequent Book Fairs until tempers cooled.

Some of this surge of homophobia came out of the leadership's old Christian moralism and the puritanical ideals of the ruling party. Some of it, however, was clearly an attempt to score points against bigger political rivals. For example, many observers have noted how President Mugabe seemed to be disturbed by the emergence of a charming, charismatic and apparently gay-friendly leader in a free, democratic South Africa, namely Nelson Mandela. Denouncing gays and lesbians was a way for Mugabe's followers to raise their leader's profile on the continent as a 'real' African compared to 'pseudo-Africans' like Mandela and the other African leader most-widely admired in the west at that time, Desmond Tutu.

The homosexuality card was also a useful one to play against the political enemies of ZANU(PF) in the years that followed. After Banana's homosexual affairs were publicly revealed in 1997, for example, the *Herald* used the occasion to launch an attack on 'the establishment media across the Limpopo' (i.e. white South Africans). In a desperate and unsuccessful attempt to save himself from the charges of sodomy and indecent assault, Banana also made wild allegations of racist conspiracies. Mugabe at first stayed quiet. But he returned to the fray several times after 1999 in an attempt to smear international critics of his land-redistribution and other policies. At one point, he went as far as claiming that Britain had a 'gay government'. The state-controlled press also made clumsy homophobic accusations against internal critics, notably the outspoken Roman Catholic Archbishop Pius Ncube.

These tactics have not been particularly successful in political terms. They neither silenced Ncube and other critics of the regime, nor drove gays and lesbians underground. On the contrary, the attacks on homosexuality almost certainly did more to publicise the cause of gay rights and to win new black recruits to GALZ than anything else. GALZ continued to advertise its counselling and other services in the independent media, distributed its information at the Book Fair on the Human Rights stand along with other human rights organisations, secured its own stand at the Fair once again in 2003, and now operates its centre with the full knowledge of the local police.

While state-sponsored homophobia has been hurtful to LGBT persons and their families and has most certainly exposed some to increased harassment or blackmail attempts, an irony of the situation is that one of the first real victims of the government's anti-homosexual rhetoric was a prominent member of the ruling party itself. Alum Mpofu was Chief Executive of the Zimbabwe Broadcasting Corporation, the man who had allowed state television and radio channels to air blatantly homophobic opinions during the 2001 presidential campaign. He scored an own goal in April 2002 when he was arrested for allegedly fondling and kissing a young man in a quiet corner of a public pub.

African nationalism was not only necessary to rid Africa of colonialism and apartheid and to resist neo-colonial forms of western domination and exploitation in Africa, it was also, and remains still, an important force for the world as a whole. At its best, it offers a powerful criticism of racism, capitalism and amoral calculations of human and natural relationships. It offers a humane and sophisticated vision for building a better global society. It is a tragedy, however, that in the heat of the struggle some of the key elements of that vision – respect, tolerance, extended family, *ubuntu* – have been lost or forgotten.

The history of homophobia in Zimbabwe offers an important lesson, and one that probably applies to other African leaders who have claimed intolerance to be part of traditional values. It is true, of course, that indigenous culture had fairly strong taboos against publicly naming behaviours that did not fit with heterosexual ideals. But there were ways of dealing with those behaviours that did not require violence or shunning. To the extent that intolerance of homosexuality exists today, it clearly owes a debt to the ideologies, language, suspicions and abuse that were taught or demonstrated to Africans by European missionaries, settlers and pseudo-scientists. African leaders who today promote homophobia are promoting not traditional African values but a very modern mix of cultures – an invention that has clearly borrowed heavily from abroad.

Such an invention is open to manipulation for short-term political gain. Thus, the new homophobia creates danger from the national level right down to the family level, something that many traditional healers understand quite clearly. We end this chapter by reflecting on the wisdom of one old Zimbabwean *n'anga* by the name of Mbuya C. She was advising a GALZ researcher, Wallace Zimunya, to stick to the traditional ways of keeping a low profile with his sexuality: 'I don't want to talk of the government, probably there is something they find bad about these practices,' she offered, without understanding why. Zimunya then asked her if she thought society in modern Zimbabwe was capable of accepting homosexuality. Mbuya C replied: 'It all depends where one is. In the rural areas where culture is deep-rooted I think this should be understood. But the best way to deal with it is being quiet about it.'

Face-to-Face – *by Chris Dunton*

History

In October 1973 Tanzanian President Julius Nyerere was interviewed by the German writer Hubert Fichte. Their discussion was wide-ranging but at one point touched on the topic of homosexuality. Nyerere's contention that homosexual relationships are unnatural and should be outlawed is perhaps the first recorded instance of an African leader making a comment of this kind. When the interview was published, in the *Frankfurter Rundschau*, this part of the interview was omitted, for reasons that remain unclear.

A Story

The story that follows takes as its starting-point the historical fact of the Nyerere–Fichte interview. The interviewer in the story in no way represents Fichte. And although he is characterised as being basically sensitive and admirable, his views on homosexuality being a blind-spot, the President of the story in no way represents Nyerere.

When the young reporter from Africa Digest *enters, I shake his hand, motion him to sit down. Then I sit, too, with my back to the open windows and the veranda. Nowadays, this early in the morning, the light hurts my eyes.*

We exchange pleasantries, some personal questions from me to him, and he asks after my health. The knee's still a problem, I tell him, after my car accident.

'Is that the risk', he asks, 'of refusing to travel in a pompous motorcade?'

156

We laugh together. Godfrey serves us fresh mango juice.

The interview begins. I like the young man. He is well informed, candid and he seems well intentioned. He is no fool (good), no sycophant (better) and a man of good will (best of all).

After a little while, the questions grow tougher. But this is not a problem. I begin to enjoy the stimulus, the critical engagement.

'Mr President,' the young man says, 'despite your calls for Africa to free itself from the grip of exploitative western mining companies, these companies still have free rein in your country, extracting tin, potash, copper. Isn't there a contradiction here?'

'Certainly there's a contradiction,' I say.

Facing the President, I sit a little way from the table, so the tape-recorder rests on my knee, cupped in the palm of my hand in case it slides off. With the light behind him – amazingly bright even at this time in the morning – it's difficult for me to read the President's expression, but that helps me all the more to concentrate on his voice, his argument.

I like him. He is as personable, as frank as everyone says. Still, I am nervous of the questions I am keeping back for later.

'Certainly there's a contradiction,' he admits. 'We have the political freedom to air our principles. But in the economic sphere we remain shackled.'

'Do you have any answer, then, as to how to resolve that contradiction?'

The President takes a moment to consider. Behind him, through the open French windows, the veranda is spacious. A delicious, heady perfume comes from the guava trees beyond.

The veranda is partly shaded. At the back, though, there is a pool of brilliant light, shimmering white, cream, gold, where a young gardener is pruning bushes.

'We might hope to break that contradiction', the President replies, 'by a renewed effort at asserting our independence at the political level. But this could only come about as a result of a political initiative that is pan-African in scale. One country cannot go it alone.'

'And you fear that your fellow African leaders do not have the political will to achieve this?'

The President gives me a wry smile. Then shrugs.

I see the gardener has been joined by a second, equally young. I see they are chatting, though I can't hear their voices from here.

We move on to other topics, the parliamentary system, the justification – or lack of it – for the one-party state. Women's rights. Minority rights.

And at this point – nervous now, though I warm to the President – audibly nervous, now, I know – it must be done: I ask him the question I have been holding back.

'Mr President, what about the rights of homosexuals in this country? Would you agree that the rights of homosexuals deserve to be respected, as with those of any other minority?'

He answers swiftly. 'In your country homosexuals may constitute a minority.'

I wonder to myself, can he be suggesting that homosexuality is rampant over here?

'And in this country?' I ask.

'We have no homosexuals. Not even a minority.'

'But homosexual relationships are outlawed.'

'As they should be.'

'Why do you outlaw something you claim not to exist in your country?'

'As a precaution.'

Should I persist? I wonder.

The President gazes at me, head cocked to one side.

'Isn't that like saying that it doesn't exist, but just in case, don't do it anyway.'

The President grimaces. Then Godfrey comes in, apologises, bending over to whisper to the President, a paper

158

in his hand. Has this been pre-arranged?

Outside on the veranda I see the one gardener has placed his hand round the waist of the other. He is talking rapidly. The second gardener has turned his head, facing away from the first, gazing at the little grove of guava trees, but even from here I can see that he is smiling. He runs his fingers across the knuckles of the hand placed on his waist.

Godfrey leaves us. I think it is time to change the topic, but suddenly the President continues:

'The point is – and this is a point not appreciated in the West – the point is that homosexuality is utterly unnatural. In this country, our structure, our development, is weak enough already, after colonialism. You are sensitive enough and intelligent enough to appreciate that. We simply cannot afford to weaken ourselves further by engaging in activities that are unnatural.'

He sits back firmly in his seat, his hands now on the armrests. Inevitably – he has just signalled this should happen – we move to another topic.

Much of what he says now seems astute. Where appropriate, he is controversial. The firm, constructive engagement in issues that I had expected of him. That I had hoped for from him.

We talk, but even as we talk, I am mesmerised by the scene beyond the windows. That pool of light, cream and honey-gold, pulsing at the edges, hypnotically deep and bright. And the two gardeners.

I see the one now, still talking, extend his hand across the other's belly, across his navel, where sweat has gathered in the line of hair that must stretch down under the pants to the groin.

Suddenly he removes his hand, raises it to his lips, his hand now dripping with the other's sweat, and kisses it, then draws his finger across his lips.

The other laughs, gently, audible now from here.

A few more questions to the President from me. A few more answers. Then he rises to his feet and we move into closing pleasantries.

159

I apologise – I don't know why – hoping that my earlier question did not offend him.

He shrugs. And then, a little pompous, his hands indicating quotation marks, he tells me:

'But your good question received a better answer.'

I think, well, yes, how right you are.

8 • in the rurals ...

Up to now we have focused our attention on changes that were happening in the cities, in the industrial economy, and in institutions that had been introduced in the colonial period, such as prisons, the military, and mission schools. But what was happening all this time in the so-called traditional sector of the economy, in the Tribal Trust Lands (as they were called in Rhodesia), the Bantustans or homelands (as they were called in South Africa) and other African reserves and protectorates? Some African leaders who have complained about homosexuality in the cities and amongst westernised youth have argued that a return to traditional values, as they imagine them in these rural areas, would protect Africans from the further spread of supposed moral corruption. Could this be true?

In this chapter, we will explore both that African-values argument and the idea that homosexuality can be spread or caught. We can do this by taking a close look at one of the more famously traditional, rural societies in southern Africa. Lesotho, or Basutoland as it used to be called, was a protectorate under the British from 1868 to 1966. This meant that it had almost no white or Asian settlement. There were no mines, no hostels, very little tourism and very few boarding schools, prisons, or hospitals prior to the 1950s. Basutoland had precisely one kilometre of railroad. It also had precious few liberal-minded magistrates to interfere with or interpret the law. In fact, from the 1930s to the 1950s, the hereditary chiefs were actually gaining power in the government. They played a major role in the political party that led the country to independence (the Basotho Congress Party, BCP) and in promoting a strong national sense of identity and patriarchal culture. To this day, the Basotho cultural village in the former South African homeland of Qwa Qwa recruits its employees from Lesotho rather than within South Africa since, they say, only the 'real Basotho' still know the culture.

Of course, many Basotho travelled to South Africa and beyond, where they encountered the same conditions as other migrant workers. But even far from their wives and families they were said to take pride in keeping up their manly, heterosexual reputations. The Leary–Taberer inquiry in 1907 concluded that Basotho did not appear to participate in 'unnatural vice' in the mine compounds. The Basotho gangs known as *MaRashea*, to give another example, became notorious for the sexual conquest of women in the townships, often by abduction and rape. They also refused *hlobonga* with the women, which they regarded as a mere boyish thing for lesser tribes. One result of this attitude worried government officials, doctors and mine owners a great deal: by the 1930s Basotho migrants had by far the highest rate of syphilis of any of the African workers at the mines, more than ten times as high as the Shangaan who kept to their *tinconcana* (boy wives).

Some historians have claimed from this kind of evidence that the Basotho were able to resist the spread of homosexuality. Such claims invite closer investigation. Lesotho also offers a chance to consider what effects the migrant labour system was having on sexuality back on the other side of the equation, including what the 'women left behind', or 'gold widows', were up to. Could same-sex behaviours and relationships have taken place behind the scenes and without the trappings of the modern gay life? The evidence suggests so and strongly calls into question the stereotype that having sex with males will make a man less masculine, patriarchal, or less 'traditional'. It also shows that African women in the rural areas could be more sexually inventive than is usually acknowledged ...

⌒ ⌣

Basotho men's ability to control women's sexuality was a key element in Sesotho culture, governed by the concept of *hlonepha* (respect). The early missionaries, the first Basotho converts to Christianity and the first colonial government all agreed that this had to change. In the missionary view, once a Mosotho man 'bought' his wife with *bohali* (*lobola,* brideprice), he was free to use her as he desired, including loaning her out as hospitality to male friends and travellers. Her labour went to enrich his household and decrease his own responsibilities. The woman showed respect to her husband, to his and her families, and to the ancestors, by doing as she was told. In addition, Basotho men appeared to regard adultery as a sport to be boasted about, with no regard for the dignity or safety of the wives involved. As one Basotho Protestant described it in 1871: 'When a native talks of "Sesuto" [culture] he refers especially to marriage, the property in women, and the consequent rights and customs. Take them away and the whole fabric is broken in pieces – the native heathen customs become meaningless ... In our attempts therefore to introduce and propagate Christianity, our chief blows should be struck at this system.'

In fact, men's moral obligations and their economic dependency on women's labour limited men's ability to abuse their power over their wives, or to neglect them. Men had to protect their 'children' and respect the family into which they were married or else they would lose respect and standing in the community. Basotho women seemed to find this balance acceptable, at least judging by the very small numbers who converted to Christianity in the 19th century. Indeed, from the point of view of the missionaries and colonial government, Basotho women often appeared to be rather too willing to agree to men's demands upon them. By the 1920s, they had acquired a reputation for sexual looseness or prostitution that caused great concern to the governments in Basutoland, South Africa and even as far away as Southern Rhodesia. Other African women were also troubled by the Basotho. Especially worrisome were the effects of Basotho women's *labia majora,* which they manually stretched. As one Nguni woman in a Johannesburg township in the 1950s said: 'If your husband is in love with a Shoeshoe [Mosotho] woman he will certainly desert you. Don't you know they have 'traps' for men!'

As for homosexuality, Basotho chiefs in the 1870s claimed that it was so rare that they had no punishment for it. The magistrates' courts that were set up at that time seemed to agree. No cases of male–male sexual behaviour came to the courts until the 1890s and they remained extremely rare right up to independence. In 1956, there were only eight convictions for 'unnatural crimes' (including crimes against animals) out of a population of nearly a million people. Of course, most cases of same-sex behaviour escaped the attention of the state or even the village elders. After all, boys and young men could spend weeks tending their herds up in the isolated valleys of the Maluti Mountains, and who would relate the details of what went on between them? Basotho gays today maintain that thigh sex between herd-boys was common and point to the Sesotho word for male–male sex as proof – *maotoane,* which derives from words meaning 'little thighs'. Meanwhile, Basotho *ngaka*s, like many other traditional healers and spirit mediums in the region, were sometimes known to experience possession by an ancestral or other spirit of the opposite sex and to behave in unusual ways as a result. Also, as in other African cultures, Basotho women could formally marry young women or girls, although this was not regarded as a sexual relationship but one undertaken for economic and diplomatic reasons.

The first real evidence that Basotho men were in fact engaging in something suspicious comes from outside the country. A case involving Basotho men in Natal shows that they sometimes negotiated male–male sex even in the very early period of migrant labour. Moba was a railway labourer in 1878 on the newly constructed railway line heading west from Durban. He shared a tent with three other countrymen, one of whom accused Moba of assaulting him between the thighs. As Maseane explained to the court: 'When I said to prisoner [Moba] that I would report the matter to my master, he said don't do so as I will give you what money you want. *I said I would take a pound sterling. I would have taken a pound but he refused to give it me.*' The witness Umschweshwe agreed that the two had argued over money and that Maseane came to the police only after he had failed to get his due. In other words, these Basotho men were negotiating for sex in exactly the same way and for the same amount of money that other African men were later discovered to be doing.

Two cases from Southern Rhodesia also suggest that Basotho migrant labourers took part in the early development of the mine marriage sub-culture. They both involved 'John of Lesotho', also known as Shubela, a 30-something 'boss boy' or *induna* at Old Hartley mine near modern-day Chegutu. In 1908, he allegedly raped a Shona youth named Kadzwiti. This case was dismissed, but the very next year Shubela was charged again with indecent assault upon an even younger (nine- or ten-year-old) herd-boy. The assault this time took place in the veld near Inez Mine in Matabeleland. 'Come and work for me and we will sleep in the same bed', Shubela allegedly proposed before attempting to mount the unnamed boy. In his defence Shubela explained that he was very drunk, besides which he was 'only playing'.

Around the same time two Basotho testified to the Leary and Taberer inquiry in South Africa. Their comments also make us suspicious. Jerry, for example, claimed that he had no idea that the word *inkotshane* meant a sexual relationship. Yet he had lived for three years in a mine hostel where other witnesses described *inkotshane* as 'pretty general', 'very prevalent' and 'very common'. Was he really so blind or was he lying about what he knew?

Mlambo, the other Mosotho witness, did admit to Leary and Taberer that he knew about *inkotshane* as a sexual practice amongst the Shangaan. He did not express a negative opinion about it, describing it simply as the 'old custom' of 'playing with boys as with women'. He also freely acknowledged that he was curious about it and had been making his own enquiries. Japtha, a Zulu guard at the same mine, was very negative about the practice. But he, too, cast a shadow of doubt on Basotho purity on this question. 'The Zulus and Xoxas do not do it; I am not sure about Basutos. I see them sleeping together and the men buying food and things for the boys.'

Could it be that the example of helpful, caring, fun, rebellious and safe sexual relationships amongst the Shangaan and other African males at the mines were attractive to Basotho migrants? Allegations began to surface soon after the Leary–Taberer report that the Basotho were not, after all, as immune to *inkotshane* as had originally been thought. The Swiss missionary Henri Junod made the first accusation in his 1911 novel, *Zidji*. In it, an experienced Mosotho character forewarns a young Shangaan of the fate that awaits him at the mines. In a scene that is central to the novel's plot and Christian message, the character Zidji is introduced to the idea of 'unnatural vice' using a Sesotho spelling of the word, *boukoutchana*.

The Basotho were also singled out by a South African historian the following year. 'I fear that Natives from Basutoland have, to a certain extent, been demoralised by the example of their northern room-mates,' wrote William Scully, referring to the 'addicted' Shangaan. The Inspector of Mines at Germiston confirmed this in 1916 and took note of a new Sesotho word. Upon arrival at the mine, each new recruit had to *Komba-E-Kehle*, that is, 'choose a husband who will look after him and his interests'. A confidential report to the Director of Native Labour in that same year went even further, accusing the Basotho of inventing a new practice altogether. To make the sex act feel more like entering a woman's vagina, they placed warm, freshly butchered sheep innards between the thighs of the male wife. The Director first learned of this through informants amongst African Christians. The rising price of sheep organs on the market confirmed that there was a new and unusually high demand for them amongst the men.

South African officials and mine companies did not know what to do about this information. Any attempt to repress the practices risked disrupting production or even sparking an uprising amongst the African workers. The Basotho were regarded as an especially touchy, if not rebellious, tribe compared to other Africans and the mines simply could not afford to lose their labour. That possibility came frighteningly close to happening in a 1919 incident at Brakpan Mines. Albert Maama, an *induna* there, had forced a young Mosotho named Mokete to endure thigh sex every night for a month. When the boy escaped, Maama sent a troop of his men to give Mokete a thrashing and to kidnap him back. The mine manager eventually fired Maama for this abuse. To his surprise, though, the Basotho workers under Maama threatened to go on strike, while no less than forty-four deserted the mine in solidarity with him. The deserters were arrested before they reached the border. Far from being punished, however, they were all given their jobs back – even Maama, provided he agreed to pay a fine of three pounds.

A similar incident occurred at East Geduld in 1941. A group of twelve Basotho *induna*s were accused of organising erotic dances, which included greasing up the crotches of the wives in preparation for sex. They were all dismissed. Trouble immediately arose when an estimated 400–500 Basotho men violently demanded the return of their leaders. The words of Police Inspector of Boksburg show that this was a continuation of direct rebellion against mine authority: 'The Basutos are in the habit of holding dances in the Compound during the night and ... at these dances the young natives are dressed as women and squeezing and kissing are resorted to. Such dances are foreign to native custom and the Compound Manager warned the Basutos that these dances must stop. Later it was found that the dances are being continued and on the 20th October 1941, twelve of the ringleaders and organisers of these dances were dismissed and sent to Johannesburg. They all admitted that they continued the dances and disobeyed the instructions.'

Other references in novels and in oral history show that mine marriages amongst the Basotho continued to be common, at least until the 1970s, and that short-term, prostitution-like relationships have continued to the present. These did not result in the collapse of the patriarchal institutions and culture upon which the migrant-labour system and colonial rule depended. It did not even result in the triumph of communism, as Cold War propaganda in those days seemed to predict could happen if there were too many homosexuals. On the contrary, during the years when the mine marriage system became most developed, Basotho men flowed into South Africa in steadily increasing numbers. Far from un-manning them, the experience became part of a new form of initiation or test of manhood in idealised customary terms: to submit was proof of bravery and discipline; to take a male wife was also proof of an honourable masculine moral obligation to one's children and female wife back home.

Some of these male wives undoubtedly did experience violence and humiliation in *inkotshane* relationships, as in the case of the young Mokete noted above. It is important to remember, however, that this was also true for female wives in regular marriages. It may well be that regular heterosexual marriages were, in fact, more stressful than homosexual mine marriages under the circumstances of rapid social change where women were abandoning the old concept of *hlonepha*. On the whole, it appears that African men and youths maintained their dignity as men in the male–male relationship by following the pattern of traditional marriage and manners. This included the exchange of presents between partners and providing for both *hlonepha* and modesty. Modesty was achieved through screens around beds, by separate rooms for male–male sex, and by a collective agreement neither to talk about it nor to import the behaviours back into Lesotho.

Complicating matters were the new, modern ideas about sexuality and romantic love being pushed by the missionaries and through western popular culture. These ideas were said to be marks of progress and civilisation, without which no African man could be trusted to put his hands on the levers of the modern economy or emerging government structures. But how could young men practise the new ideas safely with young women? How to kiss the modern way? How to keep a romantic partner loyal and happy? How to treat her in public and so on? Heterosexual dating, where these ideas could be practised, was expensive and full of the risk of humiliation. That risk came from both the parents and from the 'modern' girls themselves, who might reject proposals or shift their loyalties in exchange for favours. Male–male relations, by contrast, provided a way to experiment with the new ideas and practices and to prepare oneself in a relatively safe way for a future modern-style marriage with a woman. Not only was there no risk of pregnancy, but when the wife decided to move on 'she' would normally reimburse the presents that 'she' had received from the 'husband'. A. S. Mopeli-

Paulus's novel, *Blanket Boy's Moon*, portrays such a relationship in a Johannesburg township in the post-World War II period while suggesting that similar love between men took place in the rural areas.

Despite its benefits, the system of mine marriage began to break down in the 1970s. The years 1973 to 1975 were a turning point. For political reasons, large numbers of Malawian and Mozambican labourers in South Africa were withdrawn from the mines. The men who replaced them tended to be more educated, more Christianised and more politically aware. Black Zimbabweans recruited from Rhodesia, in particular, harshly condemned the mine marriage system on both moral and political grounds. They saw, for example, that mine marriage served the interests of the white mine owners by distracting men from the efforts of the African trade unions to organise workers to achieve better wages and working conditions. Added pressure also came from anti-apartheid church leaders in these years. Desmond Tutu, for example, who later became one of the most outspoken supporters of gay rights, denounced homosexuality in 1973 as one of the most dehumanising effects of the migrant labour system. At that time he described it as equivalent to crime, prostitution and illegitimacy. A novel by Mpapa Mokhoane about Basotho migrants also refers to the wild denunciations of male–male affairs by a Mosotho Christian preacher, a message the men themselves regarded as 'mad'.

The mining companies responded to these criticisms with some fairly radical changes. For instance, they abolished the *induna* or boss-boy system that had allowed senior African men to abuse their powers over incoming recruits. Electric lighting, better-spaced beds and even closed-circuit television to keep watch at all hours also made it increasingly difficult to conduct sexual affairs in the hostels themselves. Meanwhile, political repression and increasing poverty in Lesotho and the South African homelands pushed women out of the rural areas in greater numbers than ever. As more women moved to town, it became easier for men to strike up relatively stable urban families or to negotiate cheap sex with female prostitutes. Many gave up the idea of ever returning to a rural home. The conversion, since 1944, of many of the male-only hostels into family accommodation also meant that more women were available to the men in town, further reducing their 'need' for mine marriage.

Interestingly, while the growing presence of women in town contributed to the demise of the mine marriage system, the construction of married quarters and the expansion of townships also presented new possibilities for same-sex relationships compared to the male-only hostels. They made it possible for some men to move out of the compounds and settle down in modern, openly gay relationships. As Pule Hlohoangwane, a gay South African Mosotho, explained: 'It is very difficult for gay people to stay in the hostel because you have to bath with men, forty-two men around you naked ... it was very irritating ... So he [the husband] realised that I had a problem and he said to me it's better for me to hire a flat in town because you are a *real* homosexual person.' This they did, settling down together. Hlohoangwane adopted the dress and manners of a respectable modern, middle-class housewife and adopted children to complete the marriage.

Other changes in the South African economy since the early 1990s have affected male sexuality back in Lesotho. Above all, the opportunities to find employment on the mines have been hugely reduced. Tens of thousands of Basotho men were retrenched in 1991 and fewer now migrate to South Africa than ever did in the last century. One effect of this has been that men who prefer sex with men, whether they consider themselves gay or not, now more often remain in Lesotho than previously. A discreet, gay-friendly saloon opened on the outskirts of the capital city to cater to them. New highways have also made a change in that it is now possible to make a weekend trip from the heart of the Maluti Mountains to the capital, Maseru, or even to Johannesburg. One can be a farmer during the week, married and with children, and still commute to the city to enjoy the gay-ish life there or earn some quick dollars through prostitution. With the agricultural economy stagnant or declining, and with jobs in the new export-processing factories going mostly to women, prostitution is now, in fact, one of the few relatively well-paid options available to young Basotho men.

For some it may even be a necessity: without a source of income, how could they afford *bohali* to marry?

⌢ ⌣

Hlohoangwane's remarkable story touches upon another issue: what did the real (female) wives think about their husbands having sex with men? Did the men keep them in the dark for nearly one hundred years? Did the women know? Were they homophobic in the sense of being opposed in principle to same-sex behaviours as some people now claim, or did they not really care? As Hlohoangwane told it, in his case at least, the answers to these questions might be surprising to many people. It appears that women not only knew about the secret but they, in fact, had good reason to approve of it:

> My husband is a bisexual. He's married in Lesotho, he's got a wife with two children and I'm accepted as the second wife of the family. The first time when she realised that I was maybe going out with her husband it was a little bit confusing because she used to visit the hostel where the husband was staying but only to find that the man is no longer staying in the hostel but in town. 'With whom, who is that lady who has taken my husband?' Then he brought her to my house. 'Here is the person I am staying with, meet her'. She said, 'Oh, is it you? I'm very lucky that my husband is going out with a gay. I thought maybe he is going out with a woman whereby maybe he can make other children and all that stuff.'

The possibility that male–male sex could enrich the emotional quality of heterosexual relationships is also raised by one of Dunbar Moodie's informants. He put it this way when asked if taking male lovers at the mines made it harder to find female wives back home: 'No, it actually helps because you understand the woman's point of view. You learn to be more gentle.' This seems to have been the view of Hlohoangwane's co-wife as well. According to Hlohoangwane, she was grateful that his love and patience were teaching their shared husband to be more caring and more responsible with money: 'And since you came into my husband's life,' she told him, 'there is some [positive] changes that I see. Thank you very much. Please, if you've got any problems with my husband let's come together as a family and sort it out, completely!'

But what about the women themselves back in Lesotho? How were they affected by the long absences of their husbands and the changing ideals around romantic love and sexuality? The common assumption is that they either remained faithful and abstained from sex while their husbands were away, or committed adultery and prostitution with other men migrating to and from the mines. Basotho men and colonial officials certainly worried a great deal about the latter. But is it possible that Basotho women and girls turned to each other in their loneliness and need for physical intimacy? After all, at the height of the migrant-labour system, villages in Lesotho commonly had three or four women to every man.

We do know that Basotho women and girls shared similar ideas with men and boys about the importance of regular sex for their health. But they were also well aware of the dangers of heterosexual play or dating. For a daughter to get pregnant before marriage was to stain the reputation of her parents. It also put the future marriages of her brothers at risk owing to the reduced *bohali* the parents would receive for a 'spoiled' daughter. Meanwhile, for a wife to get pregnant by an adulterous relationship was to risk a severe thrashing and other retaliations from the husband, now shamed in the eyes of his family and friends. The threat of ostracism or excommunication from the church was also an important issue to many women, especially after the 1930s when Christian pious associations known as *likopano* or *manyano*s spread in popularity throughout the country. One of the main functions of the *likopano* was to guard over the virginity of daughters and to watch out for signs of adultery amongst churchgoers. 'Gold widows' thus probably often felt that neglect and poverty justified their turning to prostitution or committing adultery. But they were mostly kept from carrying it out by this combination of customary and Christian controls over their sexuality.

Sesotho culture partly solved this problem of sexual tension by allowing a limited amount of female–female physical intimacy, provided it was discreet. Sesotho recognises, for example, that new brides coming into a polygamous household from a far-away village would naturally form a close bond with a co-wife, especially if the husband was away.

Co-wives were allowed or even expected to express close physical affection including kissing and snuggling. Sesotho culture also recognised several types of female–female marriage. Most commonly, a widow who had the resources could pay *bohali* and take a young woman in marriage. The wife in this type of marriage was supposed to get pregnant by a discreet arrangement with a male lover, who would have no claims upon the offspring. However, the female *ntate* (father, Sir, or Mister) was entitled to show affection for her wife as well. No one in the extended family or wider community would ever dream of asking about what exactly took place in the hut at night.

The Sesotho word for female–female affection of this nature was the very same as that used for neglected wives who had extra-marital sex with men – *setsoalle*. Obviously the physical acts were different in the two situations, and the word *setsoalle* could be further broken down into different types: 'fat' and 'yellow'. Fat *setsoalle* meant that it was beneficial to the husband in a material sense, such as in a case of adultery that added children or compensation to his household. Female–female *setsoalle* was yellow by comparison, that is, it had no material benefits or costs. Its emotional benefits, however, were widely accepted and admired, including by the husbands themselves who appreciated that a strong *setsoalle* friendship not only made a wife more loving in general but could also help keep a wife from looking to men for company. One Mosotho woman who recalled the late 1950s was strongly nostalgic about this dying custom. In the words of Mpho 'M'atsepo Nthunya: 'The woman chooses you the same way [as a male lover would], but she doesn't want to share the blankets. She wants love only. When a woman loves another woman, you see, she can love her with a whole heart.'

Girls meanwhile could manually assist each other to lengthen their *labia majora*. The reason usually given for this was to increase the future husband's pleasure and so keep him faithful to the marriage. It seems likely that the practice was also a means for women to learn to achieve orgasm so that they could enjoy the sex as much as men.

These cultural norms eventually allowed for the development of

a lesbian-like relationship amongst Basotho girls and young women
known as 'mummy–baby'. Anthropologist Judith Gay found it to be
widespread when she did her research in the 1970s and speculated that
it became popular following the expansion of girls' boarding schools
after the 1950s. In fact, girls-only boarding schools date much farther
back in time, and the mummy–baby relationship may have its origins
amongst the small middleclass from as early as the late 19th century.
As with the lengthening of *labia majora*, and in fact much like *boukoutshana* amongst the men at the mines, the mummy–baby relationship
was modelled on heterosexual norms of courtship and marriage, not on
any notion of a mutual homosexual affair. Gay's informants described
it as a way of preparing themselves for marriage by allowing them to
practise their kissing, petting and flirting skills while avoiding the
risks of practising these things with boys. They also exchanged gifts
in a way that reinforced a code of moral obligations between unequal
partners. The mummy played the role of the husband, while the baby
was the wife.

This type of practice, or play marriage, gained in importance as the traditional means of courtship and sex education faded under the influence of
the Christian missions. New ideas about romantic love and companionate
marriage challenged old ideas of female *hlonepha*, or female subservience to men. Increased gender tensions between males and females that
grew out of the migrant-labour system and deepening poverty also contributed. Indeed, forced abductions and rape were becoming more and
more common in the 1930s. The mummy–baby relationship thus helped
African girls learn to be heterosexually attractive in a situation where
heterosexual courtship had become more dangerous and individualised
than had traditionally been the case. In other words, despite the non-
traditional partner and the modern way of talking about romantic love,
these relationships were basically conservative and non-threatening to
the concept of a male-dominated heterosexual marriage. Gay even found
cases of love triangles, where the mummy would both have her baby
and be a baby herself to a boyfriend. In some cases the relationship
extended beyond school years and even after marriage to a man.

Evidence from Lesotho of the spread of same-sex sexual relations enriches our understanding of similar developments elsewhere in the region. Above all, it casts serious doubt upon both the 'they-were-forced-to-do-it' argument and the view that same-sex sexual relations are necessarily immoral. Evidence from peasant and working-class Basotho women and men also seriously undermines the claim by some African leaders and intellectuals that intolerance of same-sex sexuality and intimacy are fundamental to African culture. The evidence shows that Basotho men, and later girls and young women, did not passively catch a homosexual infection owing to conditions or abusive bosses that left them no choice. Of course, there were times where force or extreme cultural pressure was applied. For the most part, however, the individuals involved actively chose to maintain sexual relations with members of their own sex because they appreciated the numerous advantages. Those advantages were not limited to sexual release or safer sex in a context of huge gender imbalance and rising tensions created by colonialism, Christianity and racial capitalism. They also included developing emotions, social skills and a sense of moral obligation or anchor that was otherwise under profound threat in the dominant culture. In that sense, both the *boukoutshana* and mummy–baby relationships could actually be *more* moral than the exploitative and abusive heterosexual relationships that were becoming increasingly common as early as the 1910s and 1920s at both ends of the migrant shuttle.

These relationships were not static. Research in the 1990s found Basotho women continuing to negotiate new forms of relationship with men and with each other in response to rapidly changing circumstances. A small but growing number of women, for example, had independent access to income. Those who desired to avoid the complications of heterosexual marriage and the danger of heterosexually transmitted HIV or other diseases could now afford to do so either by remaining celibate or by engaging in lesbian-like affairs. Hence, the

American researcher K. Kendall found that the old custom of *setsoalle* had gained new life, including some remarkably modern-sounding lesbian sex acts. *Hlonepha* was maintained by keeping such behaviour firmly behind closed doors.

The possibility that these kinds of same-sex relationship will be extinguished by the same factors that gave rise to political homophobia in Zimbabwe and elsewhere in Africa is certainly there: African nationalist reaction against liberal 'excesses' in South Africa and the west; men's 'emasculation' by poverty and women's relative empowerment by formal employment and legal reforms; the spread of fundamentalist Christian churches and homophobic ideas and images imported from the west; and so on. For now, however, that does not seem to be happening. Back in 1991, poor, underdeveloped, 'traditional' Lesotho was one of the first African countries to agree to the idea of expanding human rights to include the protection of sexual minorities. A gay-friendly saloon operated openly in a sprawling village at the edge of the capital city. A gay Mosotho man, when asked if there were any lesbians in Lesotho, responded with a touch of pride: 'Plenty!'

It seems that the Bible was definitely right in this respect: Seek, and ye shall find.

Finding love on the gold mines

This is a fictionalised account of one man's story of his life on the mines, told, let us say, in a rural location in the hills near Lusikisiki in Pondoland around 1985.

I have tried to keep as close as possible to the stories told to Vivienne Ndatshe and me, but this narrative combines the accounts of a number of the men we talked to. The story goes as follows:

I went to work on the mines as a young man. My friends came too. In those days the Mpondo liked to work on the mines. We had heard from our fathers that it was hard work and that men were beaten underground there, but we went anyway. I remember one time as a child, my father brought back his gumboots from the mine and, when I worked herding the cattle, I wore those boots. They were too big for me, but I felt like a man. The old men would laugh at us when we spoke of going to the mines. They would say to us: 'You will think of your mothers when the white man is kicking you underground.' But we wanted to feel the pain for ourselves. Besides, we needed the money for lobola, so as to marry our girlfriends and set up households of our own.

I ended up at City Deep. My friends were scattered all over. On weekends we travelled across the Rand on the trains, from Roodepoort to Boksburg, Benoni, even Springs, to spend time together, practising our dances, drinking and sharing news from home. We would sit in a semicircle and talk about home events and our girlfriends as all the young men always talked about such things when at home. That's how we enjoyed ourselves on the mines.

It was a tough life: very hard work. We were afraid of the white miners, the boss-boys hit us, the boots we wore were heavy and the heat was terrible. It was dangerous. You had to listen to the rocks talking underground. Sometimes they fell and people were injured. I have seen many stretchers coming up with men lying hurt on them. Every day you were grateful to come out of the mine. But I survived. Eventually I came back home to where my parents still lived and I bought some cattle.

Next time, I joined at Crown Mines. I worked there for nine months as a driver of the ingolovane, *the underground train. Then, without going home, I went to Simmer and Jack where I worked as a boss-boy. As a boss-boy, it was very difficult to control the miners. They were cheeky and some preferred to be ordered by a white man than by me. One had to be very strong and had to talk to them, sometimes with cruelty, but politely to those who paid one respect. In the end they obeyed because the boss-boy had authority. We were encouraged to hit them. Boss-boys who were not obeyed lost their jobs and went back to shovelling again.*

I worked on many mines as a boss-boy: Robinson Deep, State Mines, Modder B, Marievale, Luipaardsvlei. I bought more cattle, married my wife and she looked after my homestead, working in the fields, brewing beer and being helped by neighbours and other clan people. I trusted my wife to show strength of character like a man when I was away, to see to it that all was well. Now we stay together with our children and I no longer go to the mines. I receive cattle from young men now on the mines who are betrothed to my daughters. I sit at the court of the district chief and help decide cases. People treat me with respect. I am generous with my oxen and plough, which I lend to others who are away. In exchange, they brew beer for me and my friends. Life is good.

In the countryside when women brew beer, they invite friends and neighbours and clansmen to join together to drink and converse. We men sit around the fire and share stories of our days on the mines. We remember friends who have absconded, left their wives and children and settled down near the mines with women from town. Sometimes, later, they come home, very poor, and cast themselves onto the charity of their wives and sons. If they are lucky, the wives are kind to them but their sons often despise them because they have seen the mothers suffer. The sons now preside over the homestead. Such men seldom join the beer-drinks. They are ashamed.

One had to be strong to resist the temptation of town women. They made themselves very beautiful. They used soap and water successfully, and all sorts of cosmetics (perhaps even love-potions) to make themselves attractive, choosing clothes to make them look really smart. I remember at Modder B I had a Basotho friend. One night he took me to the township and introduced me to his town woman. She had a friend there who entertained us with strong liquor. I had some money, but not too much, and when I proposed love to her she came to me. I can tell you, she really knew how to love, how to do her job in bed. I went to her sometimes after that, but not too often because I had to keep my eyes on the promise of country life.

We were at the mines to make money for cattle, and town women were a dangerous distraction from our mission. At the mines, when we gathered in the compound and drank and ate meat, we constantly reminded one another of this. We would watch over friends who were tempted, even trying to keep them from leaving the mine to go to their town women, but some could not resist. They evaded us and moved to other mines without telling us where they were going. Now many of them are home again, abandoned by the town women, living in poverty in their sons' homesteads, pathetic creatures without full manhood, skulking like dogs at the edges of country life. We, we who remained true to our calling, now live respectable lives, happily presiding over our own homes.

Sometimes at beer-drinks in the countryside, when we reminisce about life on the mines, someone will mention mteto ka sokisi, *the practice by which men take other men to be their wives in the compounds. Everyone will laugh because they know that even amongst us, sitting here around the fire, drinking good country beer made by our women, are some who also did this. In fact, I also did it. When I first got to City Deep, I was approached by my boss-boy, a nice man from Qumbu who didn't hit people too much, only occasionally to teach us how to work well, as we do also with young men in the country. He proposed love to me, saying that seeing me in the shower was driving him crazy and promising to double my wages if I would sleep with him. I agreed because I was on business at the mine, working for cattle. I moved into his room and cared for him, washing and ironing his clothes and fetching coal for him. He arranged for me to do softer jobs underground so that I still had the energy to care for him. At night we slept together. He would rub his manhood and 'breathe out' between my thighs, even as we used to do with the girls at parties in the countryside. Amongst my people, that practice is called* ukumetsha. *We would not make love when the others were conversing in the room, though. We would wait until everyone was asleep.*

I can't say it brought me much pleasure, that sex, but my boss-boy was a nice man and quite gentle with me so I didn't mind too much. My underground work was lessened and I doubled my wages. Payment was enforced by the black authorities on the mine. In the case of disputes men could be fired for not paying their boy-wives; or the induna *would fine the culprit for breach of contract. Even the* indunas *had their own boys. In most cases, in fact, the* indunas *were the first to choose from the newcomers. When I came home after that first join, my father saw all the money that I had made and he smiled at me. 'I know what you have been doing, my boy,' he said, but he didn't mind because I could buy more cattle.*

Later, when I became a boss-boy myself, I found a boy from Basutoland who looked like a women with shapely thighs, fat and pretty. I proposed love to him in the compound;

called on him in our spare time. I promised him some of my pay but not all of it as some men did. Then he agreed. I loved that boy very much. I think he loved me too but he had to control his feelings because he was my girlfriend. I found much pleasure in the warmth of his body and the softness of his skin. I was not really close to him: I had other friends from my own age group with whom I shared my innermost thoughts more easily. Our boys would wait on us when we socialised together. But later in the evening it was time for 'legs' and I found comfort and happiness in him. We parted when we left for our homes. After that we didn't write to one another. It was only friendship on the mines.

When I was at Robinson Deep, again, I was a boss-boy. There, I had an induna as my best friend and he took me to the township. Again, at Robinson Deep, I had a boy, and my friend the induna had one also. But in the township we both had girlfriends. When we went to the township we left our boys in the compound. But we never stayed overnight in the township; we just took a few hours with our girlfriends and then went back to our boys. We loved them better. Indeed, some men grew so fond of boys, they were lost to the mines and never came home at all.

As for myself, from my mine work I bought cattle and maize for the family. I have a household and children, and my wife was in charge when I was away. I trusted my wife and nothing went wrong in my absence. Now we stay together and I no longer go to the mines. I own my own place and plough my lands with oxen bought while I was on the mine. I am happy now to be independent. But sometimes at beer drinks when the men laugh and joke with one another about that business of mine marriages, I feel sadness and a tug of longing for 'legs' and the boys we loved on the mines.

9 . gay rights to sexual rights

The emergence of an organised gay rights movement in Africa is a very recent development, although, to be fair, it is not very old anywhere else either. This relative newness contributes to the ability of its enemies to portray African LGBT groups as foreign or foreign-influenced. In addition, LGBT groups remain so scattered and small in number that their achievements have tended to be overlooked, even by scholars and activists who, in theory, share their basic concerns about human rights and sexual health. The objective in this chapter is to demonstrate the mistake in that thinking and to draw attention to the important roles that LGBT associations in southern Africa have played in the general development of civil society over the past three decades or so. We will argue that minority sexualities are not some little sideshow to the great dramas of underdevelopment and racial conflict in southern Africa. Rather, their work on behalf of the vulnerable *majority* population on these issues not only deserves recognition but also may offer important lessons for other civil society groups.

〜〜

Small networks of LGBT people and organised gay events appeared in South Africa from at least the 1920s, most famously with the Coon Carnival and so-called moffie sub-culture of Cape Town. Not until World War II, however, did a true homosexual scene begin to emerge. The war brought together hundreds of thousands of women and men from around the country into tightly knit camps where, for example, white women were able to discover each other as lesbians in significant numbers for the first time. By the end of the war, there were gay and lesbian bars and cruising areas concentrated in the Joubert Park area of downtown Johannesburg. After the victory of the National Party in 1948, activity tended to go underground, to be more secretive or closeted, and to stay within small 'gay ghettos' in the major urban centres.

Still, from evidence provided to the South African parliament in the late 1960s and in the recollections of LGBT immigrants from England, like Mary Renault, the gay scene clearly remained an active, relatively open and relaxed one even compared to England at that time. South Africa actually made a contribution to the growing self-assurance of gay rights advocates in the west by nurturing Renault as an author. Renault had settled in Durban in 1948 with her lifelong partner, Julie Mullard. Although she had hinted at lesbian sexuality in earlier writing, her 1953 novel, *The Charioteer,* was one of the first in the English language to deal frankly and non-judgementally with a male homosexual love affair. Her treatment of male–male sexuality as normal in subsequent historical fiction about ancient Greece and Persia made her a central figure in the emerging gay liberation movement in the west.

The apartheid state's attempts to repress homosexuality amongst the white population gathered strength in the mid- to late 1960s. The gay rights movement in Africa dates from this time. Leading South African universities first picked up on research from the west that reduced the moral stigma of homosexuality, notably through the work of another lesbian, the psychologist Renée Liddicoat.

The world of Johannesburg theatre, meanwhile, produced one of the leading figures of the early anti-apartheid movement, Cecil Williams. Williams never made gay rights an explicit part of his politics in the late 1950s and early 1960s. However, his passionate anti-racism, communist ideals and completely open homosexuality combined to shake the thinking of African National Congress (ANC) leaders such as Oliver Tambo and Nelson Mandela. Williams challenged the ANC's respectable, Christian-influenced homophobia and opened the leaders' minds to the possibility that sexual orientation might be considered a human right worth defending. Other African nationalist leaders in prison during this time were also challenged by African men who had experiences of loving homosexual marriages at the mines. According to Moses Dlamini's account, the Pan-African Congress began consideration of the issue of gay rights as early as 1963, despite the dominant homophobic thinking in the movement.

Also, however weakened by the effects of apartheid, South African courts remained fairly independent from government interference in the 1960s and relatively capable of protecting individuals who were threatened by homophobic violence or blackmail attempts. Most whites also probably assumed that a democratic parliament and free press still functioned. This assumption may have contributed to an over-confidence in the rich, white gay community that in January 1966 led to the big party and the police raid in Forest Town. The scandal and state crackdown that followed from that event were no doubt terrible shocks to the hundreds of men involved. In the long run, however, they were advantageous to the cause. Some consider the Forest Town raid to be South Africa's Stonewall, named for the 1969 riots against the police in New York City that launched the gay liberation movement in North America. The raid led to the formation of the Homosexual Law Reform Fund (or Reform Movement), a well-spoken lobby group seeking to end state harassment of homosexuals.

The Reform Movement was made up of mainly white, middle-class liberals who drew upon civil rights arguments and the latest medical and psychological theories then emerging in the west. They hoped to block a proposed new law that would have made it a crime to be homosexual, not just to be caught in a homosexual act. Not all members of the police supported this proposal: they were probably worried about having to watch over citizens' private thoughts and urges. And, because of their moral disapproval of homosexuality, not all liberals supported the reformers. The Black Sash, for example, did not support one of its members, Renault, in her appeal to parliament to protect LGBT rights. And so, despite its strong scientific and legal arguments, the Reform Movement failed in its main goals. The new Immorality Act, passed by parliament in March 1969, gave police sweeping new anti-homosexual powers, including the power to arrest suspected lesbians.

On the other hand, the fact that an articulate and respectable-looking opposition could come together on this issue under such a morally conservative government seems to have influenced the police. Over the following years, they did not in fact take much advantage of their expanded powers. As long as LGBT people kept a low profile in their private homes and health clubs, the police basically left them alone. This allowed for new confidence to grow amongst gay rights activists, especially as the international scene seemed to be turning in their favour in the early 1970s. Not only did Stonewall make gay rights a much more visible civil rights issue than before, but soon after, in 1973, the influential American Psychiatric Association took homosexuality off its list of psychological disorders. This meant that LGBT people had to be considered mentally normal and blameless for their sexual feelings, a very powerful political statement given the recent history of homophobia in the United States.

In South Africa, meanwhile, these were years of economic boom and the migration of huge numbers of young people from the rural areas and small towns into the big cities. The numbers and the openness of the gay scene grew rapidly under such conditions, most especially in the Hillbrow district of Johannesburg. It was not long before some of them took up Stonewall-inspired political radicalism. In 1972, the first group to call openly for gay revolution was the South African Gay Liberation Movement based at the University of Natal-Durban. It disappeared very quickly. Then, in 1978, the first commercial gay magazine was established. *Equus* was not explicitly revolutionary but the mere fact of its existence to some extent normalised homosexuality in the country. Discreet nightclubs and social clubs catering to gays and lesbians began to spring up in the smaller cities of the country.

These clubs and networks were linked into the national Gay Association of South Africa (GASA) in 1982. In 1984, GASA brought together the first Christian homosexual study group and worship meeting. This eventually became the Gay Christian Community with its own gay-friendly magazine, *Perspective*.

Conscription for the wars against African nationalism in these years also played an unintended role in spreading a modern gay identity. As had been the case in World War II, compulsory military service brought tens of thousands of young white South African men and women into an institution that actively promoted homophobia and sometimes cruelly punished suspected homosexuals. Yet, military service also allowed for the emergence of small pockets of tolerance for limited homosexual activity, including fashion shows of men in women's clothing (drag shows) and quickie sex. Ironically, one unit in the South African Defence Force earned a particular reputation for being gay-friendly. This was the mental hospital where homosexuals were sent to be treated by aversion therapy.

North of the border, the hotting up of the bush war in the 1970s similarly brought together large numbers of young white and coloured Rhodesian men for military training. Numerous American and other Western mercenaries joined in the fighting on the government side. In that way, the state unintentionally helped the expansion of off-duty gay networks. Drag contests began in the late 1970s and there was at least one gay nightclub and a lively underground scene. One GALZ member, Leonard, even recalled sneaking affairs with fellow soldiers while on patrol in the bush.

When the Rhodesian regime collapsed in 1980, the scene grew even livelier. Exiles returned to the country from abroad. Gay-friendly nightclubs suddenly blossomed in the capital city, notably one called The Chicken Run. These were disproportionately attended by whites, coloureds and non-Zimbabweans, not least of all by white South Africans hoping to escape conscription into their country's army. They nonetheless represented the beginnings of a public expression of an African gay identity. Those black men who were no longer content to hide homosexual behaviours behind customary closeted roles began to come out in this party scene.

Lesbians also began to organise in the early post-colonial period as white society loosened up from the oppressive atmosphere of Rhodesian nationalism. The first regular group, consisting of ten white lesbians, began their meetings in 1982 in what they called the Women's Cultural Club, later the Monday Club. A similar process of opening up occurred in Namibia through its liberation struggle in the 1980s and following its independence in 1990.

Early attempts at organising public gay rights associations were often torn by deep disagreements amongst members. The economic, language and cultural divides between whites, blacks and other racial minorities or ethnic groups sometimes caused bitter feelings, just as they did in the non-gay community. Whites in Cape Town, for example, made no secret of their snobbery against, and exploitation of, so-called Persians, that is, people of mixed race. There were also problems of extremely conservative gender politics amongst drag queens and butch lesbians who often seemed to imitate the most oppressive aspects of heterosexual society such as wife-beating and polygamy. Bev Ditsie, one of South Africa's first out black lesbians, actually organised a black lesbian beauty contest to draw attention to the hurtful and divisive behaviour amongst some members of the community. As she put it to journalist Mark Gevisser: 'Our biggest problem amongst lesbians is that our butches feel they need to behave like real men, and in our African culture this means beating up their girlfriends and of course – just like any 'real' African man – practising polygamy and having as many 'wives' as they choose.' It also proved difficult to negotiate lesbian and gay identities when so many gays and lesbians also took opposite-sex lovers. In Zimbabwe, part of the tiny lesbian community split from the Monday Club to form a Tuesday Club of women who saw themselves as 'purer' than the Monday bisexuals.

Ultimately, even more divisive was the growing unhappiness amongst those activists who wanted the gay rights movement to pay more attention to broader injustices in South African society. GASA at first claimed that it wanted to avoid political confrontation over the big social divides, race in particular. It simply wanted to encourage LGBT people to come out of the closet and to feel good about themselves. The majority of its members were white and often unaware or uninterested in the nature of apartheid. For them, simply coming out, having fun as individuals and trying to heal from the experience of growing up in a sexually repressive society was politically radical enough. But the growing violence of the state to suppress opposition in the 1980s sparked increasingly heated debates about how to move gay rights forward. Those debates often focused on how racism, misogyny, homophobia and capitalism all seemed to feed upon and support each other. For those who just wanted to party, these were boring topics. For others, however, the moral dilemmas of allowing some members to enjoy freedom and wealth while basically exploiting others stimulated internal debate and new forms of activism.

GASA was the first big casualty of this difference of opinion about strategy and political priorities. In 1986, the association broke up after its leaders hesitated to condemn the harsh state crackdown in the black townships that had begun the year before. Blacks who split from GASA formed the Rand Gay Organisation, while those whites who felt frustrated by the partying and self-esteem politics of GASA formed Lesbians and Gays Against Oppression, later called the Organisation of Lesbian and Gay Activists, or OLGA. Remnants of GASA fought back in that year by launching the first gay pride festival in Durban. However, in large part because they remained so overwhelmingly white and male in their membership, these clubs fuelled the perception that they supported, or at least enjoyed, the exclusions created by apartheid. The GASA clubs eventually died out to be replaced by organisations that better represented the social diversity of the nation.

Steps to heal the racial split succeeded in 1988 when the various groups joined to form the Gay and Lesbian Organisation of the Witwatersrand or GLOW. Where GASA had tended to shy away from politics in the partisan sense, GLOW openly embraced the social democratic ideals of the anti-apartheid United Democratic Front (UDF) and the ANC. Simon Nkoli, an openly gay black man and UDF member who had been imprisoned for treason in 1986, quickly emerged as a leader who symbolised the complex struggles for freedom of gays and lesbians.

UDF and ANC leaders also took note of Nkoli's courage, leading to the recognition of gay rights as a legitimate part of the freedom struggle. In his short memoir, Nkoli describes the uproar in the UDF-affiliated Congress of South African Students after he first came out about his homosexuality in 1981. All the usual homophobic accusations were made against him but, ultimately, comrades voted four-to-one in favour of Nkoli continuing as a movement leader: his public strength of character mattered more than his private sexual orientation. Similarly, despite initial homophobic reactions by his co-accused during the Delmas treason trial in 1986, Nkoli's fellow prisoners publicly stood by him.

Around the same time, Ivan Toms, one of the founders of OLGA, also emerged as a leader in the anti-apartheid End Conscription Campaign. As well as raising awareness within the white community that tended to support the main legal opposition to the National Party, he consulted with ANC leaders in exile. When pressed in 1987 to clarify his party's position on the question of homosexuality and the anti-apartheid struggle, future President Thabo Mbeki was thus able to make a clear statement: 'The ANC is very firmly committed to removing all forms of discrimination and oppression in a liberated South Africa. That commitment must surely extend to the protection of gay rights.'

Mbeki's commitment received a setback in 1991 when Winnie Mandela used homophobic arguments in her defence against assault and kidnapping charges. But this was followed soon after by a warm letter of support from the ANC for GLOW's annual Lesbian and Gay Pride march. Winnie Mandela's subsequent divorce from Nelson Mandela symbolically distanced the mainstream of the party from her brand of African nationalism and opened the way for the ANC to move decisively to embrace the demands of gay activists. Most importantly, the party decided, in May 1992, to include in its manifesto a commitment to entrench sexual orientation as a category of human rights that would be protected against discrimination in South Africa's post-apartheid constitution. The proposed clause basically said that sexual orientation would be considered as equivalent to race, colour, creed and gender amongst types of discrimination. It implied a political will to both radically re-write South African law in order to get rid of its homophobic elements and actively challenge popular prejudices against homosexuality.

The other major parties, meanwhile, all quickly accepted the sexual orientation clause without serious dispute. Even the National Party, which introduced the notorious Immorality Act, which instituted aversion therapy in the armed forces and which as recently as 1988 extended homophobic laws to enable police to arrest lesbians for 'indecent assault', now saw political advantage in accepting the principle of gay rights. The supposedly Zulu-traditionalist Inkatha Freedom Party likewise put up no serious obstacles to negotiating what is arguably the most gay-friendly constitution in the world.

Many theories have been put forward to explain this dramatic development, including pressure from the international community, a desire by the ANC to win praise in the west as the most progressive liberation movement in Africa, and hopes of tapping into the international gay tourist market. No doubt there is an element of truth in all of these. Most politicians, however, probably had short-term, narrow, local interests at heart. Most also still probably assumed that LGBT people were a relatively small minority and of little concern to the majority of their constituents. To agree to LGBT rights was, therefore, a small price to pay to win agreement on the principle of protecting rights for other, bigger minorities in the battle, such as whites and Zulus. The fact that the ANC later fought against the legal challenges to discriminatory laws does suggest that it was never really committed to the cause of gay rights, using it only to achieve other ends.

One party did stand up to protest political opportunism around this issue. The African Christian Democratic Party (ACDP) was formed by Africans to fight against the sexual orientation clause and against other liberal attitudes, such as favouring women's rights to abortion. On the grounds of defending 'African family values', it threatened to whip up homophobic feelings in the other parties and in the wider population.

Gay activists responded to the threat in several ways. First came the establishment, in February 1994, of the Hope and Unity Metropolitan Community Church (HUMCC). The HUMCC grew out of Johannesburg's only gay bar with a predominantly black clientele. Its leader was the Revd Tsietsi Thandekiso, a theologian whose homosexuality had led to his disgrace and removal from the Student Christian Movement. Thandesiko aimed to provide a safe place where black homosexuals could express their Christian spirituality openly. He included offers to bless homosexual marriages and to allow the kind of dignified mourning for deceased members that the mainstream Christian churches often denied to LGBT people. He also opened a direct dialogue with the ACDP and with other Christian leaders who used the Bible to justify discrimination against gays and lesbians. According to Graeme Reid, the HUMCC succeeded in convincing the ACDP to remove some of the most offensive expressions of homophobia from its political platform. It has also been successful in encouraging Christian parents to mend their relationships with ostracised gay and lesbian children.

The major front of gay activism in democratic South Africa, however, was fought by the National Coalition for Gay and Lesbian Equality (NCGLE), established in December 1994. NCGLE co-ordinated the many local LGBT associations, including the HUMCC, to counter ACDP propaganda and to lobby the other parties not to crumble before popular prejudices on the issue. It also sought to recruit new members, to politicise those members who still thought that coming out and partying were sufficient activism, and to expand its international contacts so as to keep up the pressure on the ANC. Through these combined strategies it achieved what can only be described as spectacular success. In December 1996, South Africa's first democratically elected president formally enacted the new constitution with the sexual orientation clause intact, the first national jurisdiction in the world with such a clause.

Following this victory, NCGLE focused its energies on using the theoretical principles of the new constitution to press for change in actual legal practice, policing and government policies. This meant overturning discriminatory laws case by case, often with the ANC opposing the change. One of its first and biggest triumphs came in 1997, when it convinced the Constitutional Court to declare unanimously that the old Roman-Dutch sodomy law discriminated against gay men. Because the law ruled against male–male anal sex but not against male–female anal sex, it was judged to be unconstitutional and dropped from the books.

Other legal victories followed. NCGLE won an important case in 1998 representing Jolande Lagemaat, a police officer who sought spousal benefits for her lesbian partner. In the following year, it succeeded in convincing the High Court to criticise the Ministry of Home Affairs for discriminating against non-South African gay and lesbian partners of South African citizens. In 2002, the Constitutional Court confirmed that same-sex couples could legally adopt children. In another recent victory, it upheld a High Court ruling that same-sex couples should receive the same benefits as married heterosexual couples. In November 2004, Marie Fourie and Cecelia Bonthuys won their case against the government's attempt to defend the traditional definition of marriage. The Supreme Court of Appeal ruled that same-sex couples could not be denied the right to marry and it instructed parliament to proceed quickly with making the necessary changes to the law. This came into effect in December 2006.

NCGLE also actively worked to re-educate the police away from old homophobic habits, especially the attitude of turning a blind eye to acts of gay-bashing or blackmail. Problems remain, of course, particularly within the prison system. Yet here, too, there have been successes that are remarkable even in comparison with much older democracies. The gay press in South Africa is now full of stories of police heroism in protecting the gay community and praise for the transformation. The police have even developed a website that gives hints on safer cruising for gay men. And following the gruesome massacre of eight gay men at a club in Sea Point, Cape Town, in January 2003, not only did the police assign their top investigator to find the killers, there was also an outpouring of sympathy for the victims from politicians across the political spectrum. A telling sign of the changing times was that Winnie Madikizela-Mandela joined in by offering to give financial assistance to the victims' families.

Gays and lesbians in Zimbabwe followed a similar path to political engagement, although with less dramatic success. The gay scene that first flowered in post-liberation Harare was dominated by whites and coloured queens, the latter playing an especially important part in the drag pageants. The scene was also, at first, dominated by the party and self-esteem vision of gay rights. This began to change in the late 1980s. The worsening economic and political situation and the example of GLOW in South Africa inspired the formation of Zimbabwe's first formal gay rights association in September 1990. Gays and Lesbians of Zimbabwe aimed mainly to bring the many small, informal social groups and individuals together to support each other in the face of homophobic laws and blackmail attempts. GALZ also hoped to raise public awareness about LGBT issues as a step towards winning social acceptance.

Membership at first still tended to be white and urban, but non-whites were welcome and present in the association from the beginning. Specific efforts to encourage black lesbian and gay people to join as active members were given a boost in 1992–93 when Tina Machida and Poliyana Mangwiro (Tsitsi Tiripano) joined up as Zimbabwe's first publicly self-identified black lesbians. Mike Boaz, in conjunction with Machida, further raised the visibility of black gays and lesbians by forming Ngoni Chaidzo, or Sisters of Mercy, in the township of Epworth. In this it received aid and encouragement from GALZ, although deep philosophical disagreements over strategy sometimes strained the relationship. Where GALZ was increasingly drawn to the type of gay rights activism that was winning so many battles in South Africa and internationally, Boaz favoured a more gradualist approach to win social acceptance in African communities. This emphasised the politeness, harmlessness and blamelessness of LGBT people. From a gay liberation point of view this sounded like internalised homophobia; from the gradualist point of view, just getting food on the table and maintaining family ties were more important than winning legal battles or theoretical debates.

The anti-homosexual campaign by the government from 1994 did not solve this difference of opinion, and, indeed, many members left GALZ out of fear that it was attracting too much attention and making too much noise. Ironically, the anti-homosexual campaign had a positive effect on the broadening of the black membership simply by publicising so widely the idea of a homosexual identity and the existence of an organisation devoted to gay rights. Since the 1995 Book Fair controversy in particular, GALZ has transformed itself from a mostly white to an overwhelmingly black membership. It has also built up a network of international supporters, professionalised and indigenised its executive, and assisted in the opening of regional offshoots, known as affinity groups, in smaller cities and black townships around the country. GLOM, for instance, was formed as a branch office in Bulawayo to represent the Gays and Lesbians of Matabeleland, while Rainbow was formed in Chitungwiza, the main African suburb of the capital city. GALZ took ownership of a house in Harare that now serves as a secure, permanent counselling and social centre and provides support for LGBT members who have broken with their families.

GALZ has also taken a lead in forging co-operative links with similar organisations as they have emerged elsewhere in the region. Among those are The Rainbow Project and Sister Namibia in Namibia and LeGaBiBo in Botswana. Another very promising link was made in West Africa in 2002 when Fanny Ann Eddy arrived in Zimbabwe seeking political asylum from her war-torn homeland of Sierra Leone. She received guidance in the setting up of an LGBT group before she returned to Freetown, where she established the country's first sexual-rights association. Together with the Johannesburg-based website, *Behind the Mask*, GALZ has also been closely involved in efforts to organise a pan-African network of LGBT groups from as far afield as Sierra Leone, Nigeria, Rwanda and Tanzania. Known as the All Africa Rights Initiative, the network first announced its aims in 2004: 'To respond to human rights crises in Africa with a unified voice, and to share experiences that could lead to greater self-confidence and reduced dependence upon Western gay rights associations and other foreign donors.'

As in South Africa, these successes have been accompanied by set-backs, splits and sometimes bitter disappointments or tragedy – the murder of Fanny Eddy in 2004, for example. Also worrisome has been the growth of homophobic 'moral rearmament movements' and religious fundamentalisms that have resulted in increased persecution against new LGBT groups in Uganda in particular. Nonetheless, an underlying success has been the extent to which LGBT associations have managed to forge alliances with other civil society groups and to transform activism that was narrowly focused on winning rights for LGBT people into broader struggles for sexual rights and democracy for all citizens regardless of how they identify their sexuality. The 1995 decision by the Zimbabwe government to ban the participation of GALZ from the annual international book fair, for example, was based on the claim that it had the right to censor publications without even seeing them – a huge threat to the freedom of speech and expression of all citizens. GALZ won its case against the government in the High Court in an emergency ruling that gave them the right to display their educational materials at the Book Fair.

To give another example, in November 1996 the Zimbabwe High Court ruled that the police had unlawfully detained a GALZ member. Not only was the victim awarded monetary compensation but the police were also required to apologise. This was a huge, although admittedly temporary, victory for all citizens. Other legal victories in the region spearheaded by the NCGLE and The Rainbow Project have included forcing governments to overturn laws that discriminate against gay immigrants and to promise to take a stand against xenophobia.

NCGLE disbanded itself in 1999 in favour of another association that focused on fighting legal battles, namely the Lesbian and Gay Equality Project, or simply the Equality Project. Many NCGLE activists at that time also moved into other associations that linked gay rights to broader struggles for human rights in the region, groups like the

AIDS Law Project in South Africa. Founding members of GALZ, Bev Clark and Brenda Burrell, took a similar step in Zimbabwe by establishing a website to monitor human rights abuses in general in order to co-ordinate the responses of non-government organisations against government abuses of power. Called the NGO Network Alliance, it has criticised western-backed structural adjustment policies, Zimbabwe's crippling war in the DRC, abuses in the land-reform process and suppression of freedom of speech. It has repeatedly called for an independent judiciary and free and fair elections.

In combating discrimination in Zimbabwe, GALZ itself has also sought to position itself in alignment with other feminist and human rights organisations. As a member of the National Constitutional Assembly, for example, GALZ played a role in sinking the proposed new constitution in February 2000. During the gathering of public submissions, the abusive way that pro-government commissioners treated GALZ members alerted observers to the undemocratic, closed-minded nature of the exercise. The proposed constitution ultimately contained no real human rights protections against expansive presidential power. As 'a sop to the international community' and 'a gigantic fraud' (in GALZ's words), the proposed constitution was subsequently defeated in a national referendum in February 2000.

Such interventions make GALZ a frequent critic of Robert Mugabe's regime. Yet by no means is GALZ dogmatically hostile to the president or an uncritical parrot of western or partisan political propaganda. On the contrary, consciousness of the hypocrisy of the west is high amongst GALZ members. Evershina, for example, as quoted in an article by Margrete Aarmo, was saddened and angered by Mugabe's attacks upon gays and lesbians: 'But I still admire the President for his courage to tell the West to go to hell.' Similarly, while the defeat of the proposed constitution in 2000 hugely strengthened the main political opposition, the Movement for Democratic Change (MDC), GALZ has cautioned the MDC against statements that could contribute to political violence or which equivocate on issues of human rights.

Another promising area of activism has been on the health front, above all in the struggles against HIV/AIDS. HIV first appeared in the region in much the same way as it did in the west, amongst white gay males. While the main body of GASA initially played down the danger, the Cape Town branch in 1982 established the region's first AIDS Action Group. When the disease began to strike at the black, mostly hetero-sexual population, Simon Nkoli founded the AIDS Township Project. NCGLE president, Zackie Achmat, and other homosexual leaders also led the way in the establishment of the National Association of People with AIDS, the Positive African Men's Project, the AIDS Law Project and, in 1998, the Treatment Action Campaign, TAC. TAC, inspired by the charismatic Achmat, has since scored several enormous legal and moral victories on behalf of the most vulnerable populations, popu-lations that are not primarily LGBT people but poor, black, married, heterosexual women and their children. It spearheaded the campaign to force multinational pharmaceutical companies to lower the prices of life-saving anti-retroviral drugs and to make exceptions to strict patent-protection laws that restrict the availability of drugs. This, in turn, allowed cheap generic brands to be produced or imported in order to start supplying the huge needs in the region.

TAC later successfully sued its own government for refusing to take advantage of these concessions. It conducts research and provides com-munity outreach services to improve local knowledge of treatment amongst the poor. It also relentlessly questions, and criticises if neces-sary, official efforts (or lack of them) to tackle the crisis. In February 2003, for example, it exposed dangers in US President Bush's promise of $15 billion to HIV/AIDS activism in Africa and Haiti. In a letter to the President and US Congress, TAC expressed its 'concern, regret and anger that your government has failed in its commitments to the Global Fund Against HIV/AIDS, Tuberculosis and Malaria'. At the same time, it organised the 'largest march in the history of the AIDS epidemic, not only in South Africa but in any developing country'. Beginning in March 2003, TAC began a national civil disobedience campaign to maximise the pressure on the South African government and remind the ruling party of its social democratic roots.

Almost all mission statements from gay rights associations else-where in the region now place HIV/AIDS education amongst the central, defining services that they offer. Their frank approach to sexu-ality issues typically stands in stark contrast to mainstream media, which still tend to tiptoe around taboo topics or to moralise about 'proper' sexual behaviour. GALZ's counselling services thus avoid the simplistic and demonstrably ineffective emphasis on abstinence and sexual faithfulness within life-long monogamous relationships that are favoured by some governments and international donors. Instead, it emphasises equipping people with explicit knowledge of, and self-confidence in negotiating, safer sex. This includes increasing aware-ness of the health dangers, particularly for women, which occur within heterosexual marriages and apparently stable relationships.

Some of this education is presented in the secular language favoured by western AIDS service organisations. However, most African LGBT groups also encourage spirituality in their approach to fighting the dis-ease, to such an extent that they have made converts amongst leaders of some of the mainstream Christian churches. The Revd Njongonkulu Ndungane of South Africa is notable in that regard for having spoken out against the harsh homophobia of his fellow African Anglican arch-bishops in their reactions against the ordination of gay ministers in the west in 2004. The Revd Allan Boesak went even further that year by publicly supporting the principle of gay marriage in South Africa.

Gay marriage is not, in fact, a high priority for most African LGBT people: indeed, many fear that pushing for it, at least at this stage in time, would simply invite a backlash against them from the major-ity population. A preferred strategy is to devote energy to fighting the stigma against people living with HIV/AIDS. Such stigma has resulted in the abandonment, shunning and unnecessarily lonely, humiliating deaths of people with AIDS. It has even resulted in the murder of indi-viduals who have come out about their HIV infection, including the stoning to death of HIV/AIDS activist, Gugu Dhlamini, in a Durban township in 1999. Stigma, or AIDS-phobia as it is sometimes called, directly interferes with efforts to contain the spread of the disease.

AIDS-phobia also interferes with efforts to provide dignified lives (and deaths) to the millions of *hetero*sexual people, including children, who are living with HIV/AIDS.

A press release from GALZ made the link between stigma and denial brilliantly clear, as well as their further inter-connectedness to bad governance in general. The occasion was a speech in which President Mugabe honoured Chenjerai Hunzvi, the outspoken racist and leader of the invasions of white farms by so-called war veterans. Mugabe used the occasion to deny that AIDS had caused Hunzvi's untimely death. To suggest as much, Mugabe argued, was basically anti-Zimbabwean, perhaps even in league with the colonialists. GALZ immediately spoke up to denounce the president's dangerous rhetoric. Alone of the human rights associations in the country, it drew attention both to political corruption in the land-reform process and to Hunzvi's thuggery in particular. But it focused on the irresponsibility of leaders in the region who failed to recognise the social aspect of the AIDS pandemic: 'It is deeply unfair and irresponsible to stigmatise and blame people living with HIV or AIDS ... It is the duty of our national leaders to set a good example and support those within our nation living with the HI virus and to concentrate their efforts not on apportioning blame but providing access to affordable treatment for all people living with HIV and AIDS regardless of their social background, their gender or their sexual orientation.'

⁓ ⌣

Ironically, the gay rights movement in Africa today owes something of a debt to the continent's most outspoken homophobes. One of GALZ's first black African members, Herbert Mondhlani, expressed it this way: 'Mugabe is our inspiration. His sacrifice during the war of liberation is what is inspiring us to fight for our cause.' Others point favourably to Mugabe as their most effective publicist. His speeches have drawn international attention and money to support GALZ and other gay rights organisations region-wide. He has introduced homosexuality into day-to-day Zimbabwean discourse in a far more powerful way than GALZ could ever have achieved on its own. However negative and abusive in intent, this discourse has broken the taboo that existed against the frank discussion of sexuality in traditional and colonial cultures. He has, like Winnie Madikizela-Mandela, Sam Nujoma, Yoweri Museveni and others, helped to mobilise activists from a narrow party and individual self-esteem type of politics into broader struggles for sexual and human rights. In a similar way, the confusing and often stigmatising rhetoric by Thabo Mbeki and some of his ministers around HIV/AIDS has drawn gay rights activists into leadership positions and key alliances with other civil society organisations.

Hostile or denialist politicians have thus unintentionally helped gay rights activists to win a higher, more widely respected profile in southern African society than otherwise might have been the case.

None of this should be taken to be a claim for a special leadership role for gay rights associations in the struggles against anti-democratic political regimes and unhealthy patriarchal cultures. There are many civil society groups who contribute equally or more in those struggles. Moreover, African LGBT people will be amongst the first to admit that elements of anti-democratic and patriarchal culture still remain within the gay rights movement as they do within wider society. Incidents of blackmail, petty corruption, fraud, homophobia, selfish consumerism and political opportunism within the community have thus sometimes derailed the broader idealism. Yet, on the whole, it seems fair to conclude that the 'abomination' of gay rights (as Mr Mugabe put it) remains one of the brighter lights on the developmental scene in southern Africa today, and potentially throughout the entire continent. There is every reason to suppose that the gay rights movement, linked to a wider struggle for sexual rights for everyone, will continue to spread, despite – or even because of – the efforts to discredit and suppress it.

A special sort of sisterhood

To be gay or lesbian is not just about sex. There are as well rich, shared sub-cultures of language, style and references. In the big cities of Africa, gay sub-cultures often seem, at first glance, to be very western in their ironic or 'campy' references to western fashions, literature, film and personalities. But the fact is that many Africans are attracted to this way of expressing difference, both for the way it values a sophisticated, cosmopolitan outlook and for the sense of brotherhood or sisterhood that it offers. Although the dominant gay sub-culture in the west has a history of racism, African LGBT are now a part of that culture and are shaping the way it develops on the international scene.

The following story gives us a tiny peek into this subculture. While set in 'Harare North', it speaks to a style that increasingly knows no borders and to a kind of emotional bond that is often missing for straight men and women in modern urban society.

In Harare, I thought, there would be purple jacaranda blooms, blue sky and dazzling bright sunshine. Here, in London, rainwater seeped through my shoes and my umbrella flapped in the wind as I trudged through the autumn leaves. I needed a break from the solitude of writing my thesis and was looking forward to lively dialogue with Jonathan.

In a wet pocket, my phone began to buzz. It was him.

'Sister!'

'Sisi … I'm still coming but I'm running late,' he said

anxiously, 'and I'm a bit drunk.'

Dammit! When would we ever manage a sober meeting?

'You need your bottom smacked girl!'

'Sisi, I've had a row with my husband. He's trying to control me ... '

It wasn't the first time they'd argued. 'I'm sorry to hear that,' I said. 'But can you just whisk your slender self down to SOAS asap? Zimbabwean Literature, remember? We need to chat. We agreed.'

'Oh, Sisi, my head's spinning from wine ... and a joint or two. I'm not lucid at all.'

We lost the signal so I wandered into the SOAS bar on my own, found a table and settled down with a glass of red wine. There were leaflets everywhere announcing a mass demonstration against the imminent war in Iraq.

I thought back to the last time I'd seen Jonathan, about six months ago. Politics was also the background. Peter Tatchell had been invited to speak on 'Why I tried to arrest Mugabe'. True to form, the controversial activist had created quite a stir.

In the SOAS bar afterwards, we'd drunk a few pints to unwind from the heated discussion. Then we'd strutted into Soho in search of a 'husband', an African husband if possible – to take two 'wives' – both Zimbabwean, one white, one black. Why not? Central London was a magnet for such men, Jonathan had said. Actually, I thought he – with his long slender figure – was the magnet: in Harare, he could easily have been Jacaranda Queen!

As soon as we set off, a cab driver, blowing kisses from across the road, u-turned and offered us a ride – for free. Cheeky bastard. A 'ride' indeed! What kind of 'girls' did he think we were?

'No thanks, darling,' Jonathan had said. He wasn't our type. Next, he'd skipped into Charing Cross Road, causing a riot of horn-blowing and wolf-whistling. What a night!

Staring into my wine glass, I twitched my nose to inhale the distinct smell of burning weed. Yes, a trademark of SOAS! The bar was filling up, the haze of smoke was thickening, and there was a humdrum of student chatter. I emptied a pile of books from my rucksack, and began to sort through some candid 'queer' episodes I'd found in Marechera, which I wanted Jonathan to comment on.

By the time I looked up, heads were turning towards a figure, carrying a glass of white wine and a wriggling chihuahua, descending the stairs like a late actress. Around his neck was a purple woollen scarf, with long silver tassels.

'Mhoro *Sisi* … Yebo *darling* … Kungani *sweetie* … *Hello handsome.'* He was greeting some Zimbabwean girls – fellow students at *SOAS* – and a stranger, a bemused young man on his way to the toilet.

My mood shifted suddenly to elation. Enjoying in the spectacle, I waited my turn, then waved my arms like a windmill to get his attention:

'Sisi! I'm here, Sisi.'

The dog barked and took a flying leap towards me.

'Andrew!'

'Darling!' *As we kissed he transferred dollops of sparkling lip-gloss onto my already rosy cheeks. 'It's been forever.'*

'Sorry I'm late. How are you?'

The dog began licking my face.

'Tired. You know, the thesis. But otherwise okay.' *His eyes were bloodshot, and I wondered if he was also burning the candle at both ends. 'Fabulous scarf, by the way! You look great! How are you? What have you been up to?'*

'Ooo-la-la,' he said, 'So much to tell. I've been a naughty girl. Remember Mark, lovely Mark who we met last time?'

'The NGO guy who went to Malawi?'

'Yes. I've had an affair, Sisi. Ooo-la-la!'

'Oh … Nice?'

'No. Gorgeous, Sisi.' *The dog squirmed.*

'Have you met Chipo, darling?'

By now we were already acquainted but he held the chihuahua to my face for another long doggy smooch.

'See, she likes you. She thinks you're her Daddy. Why don't you hold her, Sisi?'

Chipo wriggled uncomfortably on my lap.

'Sorry to hear about the row with your husband. Is everything alright?'

'Ahh – men, darling ... you know ... '

'And how's your work coming?'

'I haven't written anything for months ... but I've been reading a lot. Theory actually: Bakhtin, Fanon, Gilroy, Appiah, Foucault, Cixous ... '

I leaned over, intently, eager to interrupt and engage, but just then a strapping barman caught our attention. Canadian James – I'd heard about him. He stretched across the table to wipe it, then downwards to stroke Chipo on my lap, before Jonathan introduced us. I tried to pick up where we'd left off when James returned to the bar, but Jonathan's mind was now elsewhere.

'Sisi,' he said, 'what do you think of James?'

'Nice guy.'

'Husband material?'

'Maybe.'

'Share him?'

'That's thoughtful, but no thanks, dear. I've decided to give monogamy more of a chance. One of these days, Sisi, I'd love to have a sober discussion with you over a pot of strong coffee.'

'Ooo-la-la, la-la ... ' His attention had drifted elsewhere.

A big dark man, with a broad grin, was moving our way, flirting quite obviously with Jonathan. 'Sisi, can you look after Chipo? I think I've found my new husband.'

This time it was Samson, from Nigeria, whom we discovered already had a girlfriend, Sophia. She didn't look at all pleased, on her way back from the Ladies, to find Samson chatting and chuckling, with an amorous arm around Sisi. There was an awkward moment before Samson sheepishly said his goodbyes and they left.

By now I was feeling very tipsy and warming with admiration. 'I'm amazed at the range of men you attract, dear: single, married, straight, gay, bisexual, African, European ... '

'Actually, you know my first sexual experience, when I was very young, was with a white guy.' He's married now, with children. But I remember it was just ... very innocent and intimate.' I loved the way Jonathan's voice rose and fell in pitch and tone, especially when he became serious. He paused, struggling to express something, which we both knew was important. 'What am I saying? ... Andrew, when it comes to desire, sex, a relationship – whatever the intimate connection – there are no rules as far as I'm concerned.'

I felt so close to Jonathan at that moment because I knew we totally agreed on something. We looked directly at each other as if we shared a secret – something quite obvious to us both, yet obscure to most. This was our point of connection.

'You know, Sisi, I'm not always such a terrible flirt,' he continued.

'What's terrible?' I said. 'I think it's great.'

'But I often yearn for a simple life, a traditional husband from the countryside. Tsholtsho or Chimanimani maybe'.

'Mmm ... I can see the appeal, but don't you think the idyllic existence is a bit of a fantasy, dear?'

'Maybe. At any rate, it's not an option. Not here in Harare North. Sisi, do you think I should go back to my ex?'

'I don't know dear. Let's get another drink and talk about it.'

At closing time the exit was as dramatic as the entrance. Jonathan released Chipo on an elasticated leash as he strolled onto the pavement, still sipping a full glass of white wine. The dog yapped and raced across the road, then ran round and round my ankles till I nearly tripped. I swore and laughed and told Jonathan I'd always remember the image. We hugged, kissed, and promised to keep in touch by email. Then he hailed a cab to his ex's in Notting Hill and I got the last tube from Russell Square Station – energised.

A lesbian affair on nigerian video (a film review)

Nigeria is Africa's most populous country, with hundreds of distinct cultures. Anthropologists have written about same-sex rituals and relationships in some of these cultures, including the *'yan daudu* in the city of Kano (often translated as 'transvestite' or 'homosexual'). In recent years, however, Nigeria has become better known for a harsh stance against gay rights, even to the extent of the federal government attempting to criminalise gay rights activism (homosexual acts are already illegal). Small LGBT groups have, nonetheless, made known their identities and political beliefs within this hostile climate. Nigeria's booming movie production industry, or 'Nollywood' as it is known, has also begun turn out video films showing same-sex relationships and practices. No fewer than ten have appeared and have been marketed throughout Africa in the last five years.

Emotional Crack is one amongst those films that ventures into the formerly taboo topic of lesbian sex. In this, our final vignette, we review the movie and wonder if it helps to make the idea of sexual rights less threatening to the majority population than they so often seem at present.

Crystal Ezeani (played by Stephanie Okereke) is a young female graduate accountant and a loving, doting but unhappy wife. Her husband is an irrepressible Casanova named Chudi Ezeani. Played by Ramsey Noah (a familiar male figure in Nigerian romantic films), Chudi opens the film by flaunting his Casanova credentials in a steamy romantic scene with an equally sexually irrepressible girl named Camilla (Dakore Egbuson). Camilla, though, as it turns out in a surprising twist as the film progresses, enjoys sex with both men and women. It is she who would introduce Chudi's wife, Crystal, to a whole new range of sexual possibilities.

What eventually drives Crystal into Camilla's arms is not so much sexual dissatisfaction. Nor is it so much about her husband Chudi's philandering. This is, after all, a patriarchal society where male sexual privilege or double standard is regarded as the norm. The real problem is that Chudi has a short temper and a quick, battering hand. Camilla makes her move after Chudi had beaten Crystal up again, this time at a party.

Neither of the women knew the other before this, though they were aware of each other's existence. For Camilla, Crystal is only the legitimate wife of Chudi who deprives her of fuller benefits of her illicit sexual relationship with Chudi. For Crystal, Camilla is only one of those shadowy figures her husband philanders with on occasions. They did not meet until the night of the party. Camilla had gone to catch a glimpse of, and probably make some trouble with, Chudi, who had begun to make himself scarce. In a pre-arranged move, Camilla emerges singing down the staircase into the party room. With her stylish earrings and short dreadlocks, she looks irresistibly sexy. She quickly engages another man in a romantic dance. Chudi, enraged by jealousy, disengages from Crystal and goes to accost Camilla at the other end of the room, thus creating the opportunity for another male waiting in the wings to dance with Crystal. This is what earns Crystal her public beating from Chudi and sends her tearfully to the toilet rooms.

Camilla comes upon Crystal crying in the toilet and consoles her with an embrace. It is not clear if this is a spontaneous ('force of nature') or pre-planned move, but the two maintain contact and the heat builds. Soon, Camilla declares her love for Crystal.

Crystal's initial reaction at this declaration is shock followed by an attempt to distance herself from Camilla. Next, she goes through a period of self-doubt and emotional turmoil. Her encounter with Camilla keeps haunting her, the lingering embraces recreated in flashbacks against the background of love music. Soon she finds herself seeking out Camilla. A whirlwind, emotionally laden relationship follows complete with two love-making scenes between the women in Camilla's bedroom.

Absolutely nothing has prepared the audience for this twist. The unfulfilled expectation is that Crystal might end up in the arms of another man should her husband continue to abuse her, but surely not in the arms of a woman! That this woman is also her husband's secret lover intensifies the drama, the intrigue and the sense of scandal.

Is the lesbianism situational or does the experience activate a deep, hidden sexual orientation or desire? The director leaves room for uncertainty. Yes, the affair is presented as an emotional prop for both women against the background of a painful heterosexual experience and humiliation by a man. But could there be more? Crystal herself confesses to Camilla: 'I don't know what is happening to me,' and to her unsympathetic twin sister: 'I just can't help myself.' It is also not clear if Camilla goes into the affair only to spite Chudi for deserting her, or if her orientation is naturally bisexual. Her violent and ultimately fatal insistence on taking Crystal away from her home only deepens the puzzle. When Crystal suggests that Camilla is raving mad, she admits that she is indeed mad, 'if loving you is madness'.

The plot moves quickly to its tragic conclusion. In a desperate move, Camilla arranges for Chudi to catch her and Crystal in bed, 'to see how good we look together and that you belong to me and not to him'. The move is meant to force Chudi to abandon Crystal to her, and simultaneously force Crystal into a helpless situation with no option but to remain in an open lesbian relationship with her. Camilla's scheme, however, backfires. As is to be expected, pressures from parents, siblings and friends move in to prevent the *affair from developing any further. When Crystal eventually jilts her, Camilla turns violent, threatens Crystal with a knife, and, with a final twist to the movie, turns the knife on herself.*

Emotional Crack *is no champion of gay rights. Even the camera tends to be more generous towards heterosexual romantic scenes, while dropping the veil rather quickly on same-sex acts. Nonetheless, the depiction of Camilla and Crystal's affair tends to imply the possibility and potential of same-sex love, even when society disapproves so strongly. The sound track, for example, is generally neutral between the different types of love affair in the film. The song accompanying Camilla and Crystal's romance is as much about love as the one accompanying heterosexual romance. The former song actually insists that 'love conquers everything.' One gets the impression that the love between Camilla and Crystal may well have blossomed but for pressure from society.*

conclusion: homophobia hurts everybody

Homophobia is not just hurtful or dangerous to LGBT people and the families and friends who love them: it damages everyone, particularly, we believe, in the way that it contributes to the spread of HIV. The crisis of HIV/AIDS in turn frustrates or has even rolled back many of the economic and social gains made since independence in much of Africa. It should motivate us all to face up to the homophobia problem with as much boldness as we can muster.

We therefore want to conclude our history of African homosexualities with a brief discussion of how specifically the struggle against homophobia (and related prejudices and blind spots like heterosexism) can be beneficial to the wider non-gay population in relation to HIV/AIDS education. This means moving beyond vague statements about gender equity and the empowerment of women that many African governments have made. Important as these statements and the commitments to gender equity are, in some ways they actually distract attention from issues arising from same-sex sexuality. What is needed is to get down to specific details and strategies whereby we can learn to see, and then to fight against, forms of discrimination that are often taken for granted as normal or natural. Such discrimination, in fact, plays a major supporting role in the persistence of the kinds of inequalities and injustices that fuel the spread of HIV/AIDS and other sexually transmitted diseases.

~ ⌣

HIV/AIDS did not originate amongst gay men. One of the very first suspicious deaths to be noticed in 1977 was of a Danish woman. Blood samples taken from presumably heterosexual African villagers have meanwhile revealed the presence of the virus as far back as 1959. This suggests that it may have mutated from a pre-existing animal virus even earlier, perhaps as early as the 1930s.

It is true, however, that the virus first became known in the early 1980s from the gay subculture of North American urban centres like Los Angeles and New York City. This subculture had arisen in large part as a reaction against the oppressive homophobia of North American society in the decades before. Among other things it celebrated sexual freedom and an abundance of sexual experience with many, often anonymous, partners. So closely did the first big wave of AIDS-related deaths match the men who took part in this scene that scientists at first, mistakenly, labeled the disease GRID, or Gay-related Immune Deficiency. This honest mistake fuelled public anger against LGBT people. Bisexuals were especially blamed on account of fears that they were transmitting the disease from the homosexual population into the heterosexual population. A typical sentiment was to blame gays for having brought the disease upon themselves, or that AIDS was God's punishment for their supposedly immoral behaviour.

Such beliefs then made it difficult for mainstream politicians to justify spending taxpayers' money on research and prevention. One indication of this is that, by the time US president Ronald Reagan made his first public reference to AIDS (31 May 1987), over 20,000 Americans were dead. This slow reaction has been directly compared to the rapid response to another new disease that appeared around the same time. Legionnaire's disease caused only a tiny fraction of deaths but it affected older, white, respectable, heterosexual men and therefore attracted almost immediate generous funding for research.

The numbers of dead from AIDS-related illnesses are now in the tens of millions worldwide, the clear and growing majority of whom are young heterosexual women. Yet there are still leaders around the world who cannot seem to pronounce the word 'AIDS' owing in part to their discomfort with the idea of homosexuality and 'the gay lifestyle'. In fact, there is no such thing as a single gay lifestyle.

Homophobic misconceptions such as these are sometimes so strong that they blind leaders to important truths, above all, the fact that HIV in the world today is predominantly spread by *hetero*sexual intercourse and intravenous drug use. Homophobic fears in the general public make it politically risky for leaders to express gay-friendly opinions or to propose policies that would help the LGBT minority to protect itself.

A further tragedy of homophobia is that it often goes hand in hand with racist or xenophobic discrimination. Because the stigma of homosexuality is so high in some cultures, people typically want to blame it on foreigners and to deny that it occurs within their own society. This blame game has had a particularly terrible impact in southern Africa. Encouraged to believe that AIDS was a rich, perverted white man's disease, most Africans at first assumed it was not a threat to them. When it became obvious that this was not the case, blame was cast upon Malawians or other African migrants. They became scapegoats. This in turn meant slow government responses and, in many cases, flat denial or suppression of evidence about the spread of HIV in the indigenous population. The years wasted by such denial allowed HIV to explode past the point of containment.

Sadly, as we have seen throughout this book, many politicians and religious leaders have not only shied away from the political risks of educating the public and challenging old stereotypes. They have actually made matters worse by inflaming xenophobic or racist stereotypes about homosexuality. African leaders are by no means alone in this, although they have tended to attract a great deal of international attention owing to the sheer extremeness of some of their claims. Leaders like Peter Akinola, Yoweri Museveni and Sam Nujoma have all urged patriotic citizens to drive homosexuals and their sympathisers out of their countries and church communities in the disastrously mistaken belief that this will defend Africans against both disease and western imperialism.

Such homophobia builds upon old colonial laws that criminalise consenting same-sex acts. It serves to drive LGBT people deeper into the closet, that is, into a secretive life that places them at great risk. The stigma of talking and providing honest education about gay sex means that young people who are attracted or curious about it may enter into sexual relations whilst lacking the most basic knowledge of how to protect themselves against unsafe practices. A further risk is the constant danger of blackmail attempts against male homosexuals in particular. HIV makes this even more serious since people can claim that they have been given HIV by someone. The maximum prison sentence in Zimbabwe for wilful transmission is twenty years, practically equivalent to life. A person entrapped into, or even falsely accused of, an unprotected homosexual encounter stands to lose so much that paying hush money makes sense. In the long run, however, it only fuels the culture of secrecy and stigma that created the problem in the first place.

Internalised homophobia also puts young LGBT people at risk by, for example, undercutting their sense of self-worth at a critical period in their emotional development. Shame, guilt and fear of confused sexuality then often lead young people to alcohol and other substance abuse. This, in turn, increases vulnerability to sexual assault or exploitation, to arrest and imprisonment, and to intravenous drug use, all of which are amongst the highest risk situations for contracting HIV. Much of this could be avoided if the whole range of human sexuality were presented to young people in non-blaming, fact-based language.

Internalised homophobia can also lead to nasty political behaviour. Powerful men who suspect and fear their own sexuality may loudly encourage those suspicions and fears in the wider society as a way to deny or hide from themselves. For example, we now know that the three men most closely associated with the anti-Communist and anti-homosexual witch-hunts in the McCarthy period in the USA all secretly participated in the underground MSM scene, namely, Joseph McCarthy, J. Edgar Hoover and Roy Cohn. Self-hatred, in other words, inflamed by ambition and ideology, fuelled a notorious political movement.

The paranoid Cold War mentality did not merely poison social life in the USA and result in suicides or ostracism of men accused of homosexuality. By demanding interventions against suspected Third World and African 'communists', it had a long-term destructive effect on African politics and development.

Perhaps even more worrisome than individual homophobic leaders is the emergence of broad alliances between fundamentalist Christian groups in the west and like-minded groups in the developing world, including Islamist movements that otherwise share very little in common with the Christians. Many Africans are leaving the old churches and traditional forms of worship for these new movements. This is not a bad thing in itself. In fact, spirituality is without question an important resource for giving people hope and for building communities that can resist the spread of HIV and offset some of the worst impacts of AIDS. But fundamentalist groups have tended to add fuel to the fire of homophobic blame. They have blocked their own governments, the United Nations and multilateral donor agencies from providing education and prevention that is aimed at (or even honestly discusses) homosexuals and homosexuality. Their language of Satan, slavery and bestiality and the like further distracts attention from the real issues fuelling HIV, above all, the disempowerment of women in general. Indeed, direct attacks on homosexuality often serve as veiled or indirect attacks on feminism or women's rights. Women's disempowerment in the law, in culture and in economic security all increases female vulnerability to violence and sexually transmitted diseases.

Homophobia also directly increases risks to youths who consider themselves heterosexual. In the first place, it increases peer pressure on them to prove their 'normal' credentials. For male youths and men this often means publicly demonstrating their machismo and virility by getting their girlfriends pregnant. For girls and young women, it may mean giving in to a boyfriend's pressure for sexual intercourse or even seeking to get pregnant as a show of 'normal' female sexuality. This not only exposes them to sexually transmitted infections like gonorrhoea and chlamydia, which enormously enhance the ability of HIV to enter the blood stream. It also engages young girls in sexual activity for which their bodies are not yet mature enough. Indeed, young girls are at high risk of vaginal tearing from intercourse, creating small internal wounds through which HIV can enter.

Meanwhile, many people who consider themselves heterosexual and may even be happily married and have children, also sometimes engage in secretive sex with members of their own sex. Guilt, fear of exposure, self-denial and ignorance expose them to unsafe sexual practices. Guilt may be further inflamed by biphobia, that is, stereotypes that present bisexuals as undecided or treacherous people who transmit disease and immorality across supposedly natural lines. One effect of internalised biphobia is that men who sometimes have sex with men are afraid to admit, even to themselves, that they have potential problems this way, including fear of their own sexuality, and the fear and prejudice of others. Not wanting to admit or understand their feelings, they do not take precautions or learn about the risks.

Another important term for understanding how attitudes towards same-sex sexuality have affected the spread of HIV/AIDS is heterosexism. This means a blindness to or ignorance about homosexuality, bisexuality and transgender issues. It describes a culture where people simply assume that 100% heterosexuality is normal, natural and good. People who are heterosexist may not be actively prejudiced in the way that a homophobe would be. However, they passively accept the existence of discrimination and insults against LGBT people that are built into our language, culture and laws: laws, for example, that criminalise male–male oral sex but not female–male oral sex, or laws that ban same-sex educational literature as obscene but not heterosexual pornography. Heterosexism also results in sex education and HIV awareness in schools being totally dominated by heterosexual images and lessons, with nothing to inform LGBT. Counselling training, to give another example, will typically promote skills and awareness of heterosexual family relationships but not LGBT families. Although LGBT families are not yet recognised in law in most of Africa, they exist in fact: for example, same-sex couples looking after the children of an uncle and aunt who have died from AIDS. Even the advertising of condoms assumes that the users are heterosexual and hence it shows images of loving heterosexual couples and wedding dresses that do not speak to LGBT needs or interests.

People who are heterosexist do not stand up to support calls to end such discrimination or invisibility; rather, they typically assume that these are the concerns only of a privileged and self-indulgent minority. From a heterosexist perspective, gay rights actually represent a luxury compared to other urgent development needs. They ignore the argument and all the evidence that protecting the rights of LGBT people is to protect the sexual and other human rights of all citizens.

Heterosexism also leads people to make incorrect assumptions about 'proper' sex that then negatively affect HIV-prevention strategies for the majority population. For example, sex-education programmes directed at presumably heterosexual youths typically assume that straight people do vaginal intercourse, while anal sex is what gay men do. In fact, heterosexual couples also engage in anal sex – sometimes for pleasure, sometimes for birth control and sometimes out of the grossly mistaken belief that it protects them against sexually transmitted diseases, including HIV. Men may not even be aware that their female partners might guide them 'the wrong way' during intercourse. In other words, heterosexuals are also put at risk when knowledge about anal sex is withheld from them owing to misguided assumptions about what is normal and natural.

Finally, heterosexist popular culture creates the impression that opposition or disgust towards homosexuality has more or less been the norm around the world throughout history. Gay-tolerant or gay-friendly attitudes coming from the west today are seen to be an exception to the rule of history and probably a sign of western moral decline. In reality, attitudes towards people whose sexuality, manner, or style of dress differ from heterosexual ideals have varied a great deal over time and across cultures. In ancient Greece, the homosexual relationship between a man and a youth was valued highly or even idealised as spiritually superior to the husband–wife relationship. Among many First Nations (indigenous) peoples in North America, the social category of *berdache* provided respect to so-called two-spirited people. In southern Africa, as we have seen, hundreds of thousands of men over the past century took male wives while they were absent from home for long periods of work on the mines. These so-called *ngochani* or *matanyera* relationships were an open secret that did not call the men's roles of patriarch and provider into question. Societies in which leaders today proclaim that homosexuality is un-Islamic meanwhile erase a long and rich history of diverse same-sex relationships in Islamic literature, poetry and music.

And so this aspect of heterosexism feeds into the stereotype that the west today is, in general, a sexually decadent and corrupt place. That stereotype makes it easy to forget that, in reality, the west is only just emerging from a period of extremely strong homophobia. And indeed, homophobia and misogyny still remain very strong and politically appealing in much of the west outside the big cities. Once you get away from this false image of generalised western moral decline, you can see that human rights activists in Africa actually share a great deal in common with civil society groups in the west, including gay rights and feminist activists. The cultural divides between west and non-west suddenly seem less difficult to overcome.

How then can non-gay AIDS service organisations (ASOs) and other development agencies begin to address all these issues and to learn from the lessons of gay rights struggles? The first step is surely to reach out and establish contact with local LGBT associations or informal networks. They would probably be all too happy to receive a polite invitation to explain the subculture and politics of their struggles and ambitions in the local context. The GALZ experience in Zimbabwe has certainly shown that even police in a state with a well-earned reputation for homophobia can respond well to education on this issue. The experience in South Africa is, in some ways, even more remarkable. The once notoriously gay-bashing apartheid police have become highly respected allies of LBGT associations in that country, even to the point of educating LGBT about the risks of certain behaviours.

Beyond these local contacts, education is required to enable people to tackle head-on the heterosexism or blindspots in the dominant approaches to sex education and HIV prevention. This would include coming to understand that same-sex behaviour is a universal phenomenon that takes place regardless of how conservative a culture may appear or its leaders may claim it to be. Appearances not only can be, but very often are, deceiving on this issue; a growing body of research shows how same-sex sexualities have been secretly expressed and explained in different cultures, worldwide.

Once ASOs have become familiar with this research, they can then take a leadership role in normalising the idea that sexual and other human rights include those of LGBT people. This could be achieved, for example, by publicly supporting local LGBT associations in speaking out against homophobic speech and in explaining the links between homophobia and other discriminations in society. It can also be achieved by including frank discussion of same-sex sexuality in education aimed at presumably straight audiences. It is crucial that such a discussion not 'otherise' same-sex sexual practices, for example, by presenting them as foreign to the culture or recently imported from the west. Many of these practices are, in fact, not necessarily very different from what some heterosexual couples sometimes do. Moreover, indigenous terms for most practices can be found with fairly minimal effort. It may be necessary to cleanse these terms of the insulting, homophobic meanings that they carry in the dominant culture, but sometimes just pronouncing them removes their power to shock. Breaking taboos on saying the words opens the way to discussions without blame and without introducing irrelevant and misleading side issues.

Of course, there is a risk that local authorities will be embarrassed and that attempts to destigmatise homosexuality will bring about homophobic and possibly xenophobic reactions from politicians and religious leaders. The risk that homophobic gangs will take matters into their own hands is also a real one. ASOs and Africanist academics, who are otherwise open-minded or sympathetic to gay rights, have probably kept relatively quiet on this issue for so long in part because of this fear. On the other hand, LGBT people themselves have taken bold steps in speaking out in the last few years and have shown that the worst of those fears are often overblown. Moreover, the risks of not speaking out are now clearer than ever. To remain silent in the name of cultural sensitivity or politeness is basically to accept attitudes and practices that we know condemn so many Africans to lonely and painful deaths. The slogan of early AIDS activists in North America is thus at least as valid in Africa today: 'Silence equals death.'

Yet despite the homophobia, sexism and racism of many of the most vocal opponents of sexual rights and women's empowerment, and despite widespread heterosexism even amongst our friends, there are strong reasons to be cautiously optimistic about the future. LGBT communities are becoming organised and are winning acceptance in civil society around the world, including Africa. ASOs, in particu-lar, have emerged as key close allies. Institutions like the military, police and prisons, formerly amongst the worst offenders in promoting homopho-bic values, are beginning to learn how homophobia makes their own work more difficult, and, in some cases, they have been reformed to such an extent that they too are now important allies in the struggles for sexual rights. The simple fact that this book could be researched and published in Zimbabwe also suggests that homophobia may some-times be loud but it is not necessarily very deep. The potential to build from here a new culture of sexual honesty, sexual rights and sexual health is actually greater than the discouraging or sensational head-lines often suggest.

Of course, no one claimed it would be easy, but we hope that this book makes a small contribution to the efforts in that direction.

further reading and watching ...

Homosexuality was once an obscure if not taboo topic in African studies. By now, however, there is a fair amount of material available for those who want to learn more about the history and the present-day struggles of African gays, lesbians, bisexuals, transgender and intersex persons (or 'same-gender-loving people' or 'tommy boys' and other people who do not conform to heterosexual norms, however they call themselves). This chapter briefly recommends and describes the best books, websites, and videos on the subject. They may not always be easy to find in Africa outside the major urban centres and universities; nonetheless, most of them can be found, borrowed or bought through the Internet and from the many friends around the wide world with whom the Web puts us in touch. For that, it is best to start this chapter with a nod in the direction of the website *Behind the Mask* (www. mask.org.za). This was the first and remains the best Internet source for information on LGBT activities throughout Africa. It contains links to numerous international human rights and sexual health organisations. It highlights news, debates, and announcements from around the continent, interviews with activists and artists, book and film reviews, job opportunities, and discussion forums for people simply to meet and share ideas with like-minded people.

For serious researchers, you can link from *Behind the Mask* directly to the Gay and Lesbian Archives of South Africa located on the campus of Witwatersrand University (www.gala.wits.ac.za). The archives are a small but growing treasure of artefacts, photographs, diaries, and other written material by or about LGBT people in southern Africa.

The shoppers and tourists among you can also link directly to a website for gays and lesbians called *Q*, run by South Africa's *Mail and Guardian* newspaper. Current events, culture, and debates relating to LGBT struggles and concerns from South Africa and around the world are covered best on a site called *Gmax* (www.gmax.co.za). A struggle-oriented website out of Zimbabwe that seamlessly weaves together debates about gay rights, feminism and human rights in general terms is *The NGO Network Alliance Project* (www.kubatana.net).

Scholarship on Same-sex Sexuality

The book you are reading at the moment derives from research that has been published elsewhere mostly in an academic or scholarly form. For those who are curious about the sources of the various claims and the characters that we present here, please consult *Hungochani: The History of a Dissident Sexuality in Southern Africa*, by Marc Epprecht (Montreal: McGill-Queen's University Press, 2004). Other invaluable academic references include two books edited by Stephen O. Murray and Will Roscoe. These are *Islamic Homosexualities: Culture, History and Literature* (New York: New York University Press, 1997) and *Boy Wives and Female Husbands: Studies in African Homosexualities* (New York: St. Martin's Press, 1998). The first focuses mainly on the Asia but also contains fascinating material from the Swahili coast, Egypt, Sudan and Muslim Nigeria, in some cases dating back hundreds of years. The second (*Boy Wives*) is a wide-ranging collection of contemporary scholarly articles and descriptions of same-sex sexuality and gender inversion among Africans going back as far as the early 1700s. This book alone makes it well nigh impossible to argue that Europeans introduced same-sex sexual practices into Africa.

The issue of mine marriages in South Africa was first closely analysed by the sociologist T. Dunbar Moodie, who together with Vivienne Ndatshe conducted interviews with retired Mpondo miners. They published a book called *Going for Gold: Men's Lives on the Mines* (Berkeley: University of California Press, 1994) that includes chapters on work, drinking, faction fighting and sex. The historian Patrick Harries also published a book in same year that focuses specifically on Tsonga or Shangaan migrants called *Work, Culture And Identity: Migrant Laborers in Mozambique and South Africa, c.1860-1910* (Portsmouth NH: Heinemann, 1994). It uses primarily the Swiss missionary Henri Junod's observations (and denunciations) of mine marriage, plus interviews with retired miners, to gain an understanding of why the Shangaan in particular became notorious for the practice.

Studies of female–female sexuality in Africa have been few and far between until very recently, with a chapter here or an obscure article there, not easy to be found. *Tommy Boys, Lesbian Men and Ancestral Wives*, edited by anthropologists Ruth Morgan and Saskia Wieringa (Johannesburg: Jacana Press, 2005) is the key exception. It contains an overview of how patriarchy, homophobia and secrecy affect African women who love women differently from the way in which those issues affect men who have sex with men. This is followed by ten chapters from all around eastern and southern Africa, including Uganda, Swaziland, Kenya, Tanzania, Namibia, and South Africa. For the most part, they involve African women giving personal reflections on their experiences as women who love women, from some who live in cities as out lesbian activists to some who live in the closet or in relationships that follow the form of customary woman–woman marriages.

Opponents of homosexuality still often use the Bible to justify their position, quoting select references to Corinthians and the like. Yet there are many Christians who deny that the Bible really says what the homophobes claim it does. There are three wonderful books that shed light on these disputes. First, John Boswell's *Christianity, Social Tolerance and Homosexuality* (Chicago: University of Chicago Press, 1980) looks at the different ways in which gay people were treated in Western Europe from the beginning of the Christian era to the 14th century. It concludes that the teachings of the church changed enormously over time. There were periods of oppression and stigma, yes, but there were also times when open homosexuals were actually welcomed within the church, even to the extent of allowing men to marry men in a church ceremony.

Paul Germond and Steve de Gruchy's *Aliens in the Household of God* (Cape Town: David Philip, 1997) and M. B. Alexander and James Preston's *We Were Baptized Too: Claiming God's Grace for Lesbians and Gays* (Louisville KY: Westminster John Knox Press, 1996) include chapters that discuss the theology to show how this was possible. They include insights into the specific original Greek and Hebrew texts relating to homosexuality that are usually quoted in their English (mis)translations. There are also personal testimonies by gay and lesbian Christians in South Africa who tell of the pain and confusion that Christian homophobia causes them and their families. The Foreword in the Alexander and Preston volume is especially powerful. There, Anglican Archbishop and Nobel Peace Prize-winner, Desmond Tutu, goes so far as to say that Christians who encourage hatred or intolerance of homosexuality are blasphemous, meaning that have they misunderstood the message of the Bible on this topic so badly that they have broken from the spirit of Christian teaching. Gay-friendly interpretations of Islamic spirituality are meanwhile explored on the website *Queer Jihad* (www.well.com/user/queerjhd/reading. htm#SPIRITUALITY).

African gays and lesbians have written their own memoirs, fiction and poetry to add personal insights to the discussion. The first collection of these was gathered together by Matthew Krouse and Kim Berman in *The Invisible Ghetto: Lesbian and Gay Writing from South Africa* (Johannesburg: COSAW, 1993). Soon after, GALZ put together *Sahwira: Being Gay and Lesbian in Zimbabwe* (Harare: GALZ, 1995). A second edition, published in 2002, was updated to include reflections on the changes that happened after the Book Fair controversy. In both these works, African LGBT of all colours and creeds express their deepest feelings about growing up, learning to love, and learning to be confident in themselves and amongst their families in a homophobic or heterosexist environment. An insider's detailed perspective on the coming out of Zimbabwe's gay rights movement can be found in

Keith Goddard's 'A fair representation: The history of GALZ and the gay movement in Zimbabwe', published in the *Journal of Gay & Lesbian Social Services*, Vol. 16(1), 2004, pp. 75–98.

Another essential collection of articles by gays and lesbians is *Defiant Desire: Gay and Lesbian Lives in South Africa*, edited by South African journalist, Mark Gevisser, and High Court judge, Edwin Cameron (Johannesburg: Ravan, 1994). This book includes scholarly analysis by a wide range of researchers, with especially helpful chapters on the law, on early efforts to organise a gay rights movement, on gay language and culture, and on HIV/AIDS activism. There are also interviews with and memoirs by homosexuals, notably the activists Simon Nkoli, Ivan Toms, and Zackie Achmat. *Defiant Desire* can be particularly appreciated for its huge achievement of including many lesbian and black African authors.

Bart Luirink, who first set up and still manages *Behind the Mask*, wrote one of the first books to cover areas outside the well known gay centres of South Africa. He travelled around the region in search of LGBT people in largely rural places like Swaziland and Lesotho. He met with mixed success but what he found, or did not find, is described in an easy-to-read, journalistic-style book called *Moffies: Gay Life in Southern Africa* (Cape Town: Ink Inc, 2000). In a more serious vein, Scott Long of the United States-based Human Rights Watch also travelled around southern Africa, in this case looking for evidence of the hurtful impact of homophobia. He found plenty. Although it tends to be over-negative, *More Than a Name: State-sponsored Homophobia and Its Consequences in Southern Africa* (New York: HRW and IGLHRC, 2003) is one of the few sources of information available on LGBT life in Zambia, as well as giving good accounts of Namibia and Zimbabwe. Another tour of sorts can be found in a book of photographs by Michael Meyersfeld with text by Daniel Somerville of *Behind the Mask*. Called *Gaze: Just One Look* (Johannesburg: Bell-Roberts Publishing, 2003), it offers a story in pictures of the diverse LGBT communities in South Africa.

Two more specialised studies from South Africa are *Gayle: The Lan-*

guage of Kinks and Queens by Ken Cage (Johannesburg: Jacana Press, 2003), and *'Daai ding': Sex, Sexual Violence, and Coercion in Men's Prisons*, by Sasha Gear and Kindiza Ngubeni (Johannesburg: CSVR, 2002). Cage studies the way that LGBT people in South Africa developed a secret way of identifying and communicating with each other so as not to attract the attention of homophobes in wider society. It also includes a strong analysis of how internalised homophobia is reflected in gay vocabularies like Gayle or an earlier form known as Moffietaal. Gear and Ngubeni, meanwhile, give a sometimes chilling and often very explicit account of life for men behind bars. What is especially impressive about this study is how it relies on the words of the men themselves to describe homosexual relationships in prison. Language and identity are also the focus of attention in much of *African Feminisms Vol. 2: Homosexuality*, a special issue of the journal *Agenda* (number 67, 2006).

Three other historical memoirs that touch on this topic of prison sex are by the South African gangster/musician, Godfrey Moloi (*My Life. Vol. 1*; Johannesburg: Ravan Press, 1987), Pan-African Congress activist, Moses Dlamini, (*Hell Hole, Robben Island: Reminiscences of a Political Prisoner in South Africa*, Trenton NJ: Africa World Press, 1984) and *A Snake with Ice Water: Prison Writings by South African Women*, edited by Barbara Schreiner (Johannesburg: COSAW, 1992). Zimbabwean author, Stanley Nyamfukudza, takes on this theme in a short story called 'Posters on the Wall' in his collection, *If God Was a Woman* (Harare: College Press, 1991).

The story of the evolution of the sexual orientation clause towards its inclusion in the South African constitution is best told in two books. The most detailed, and with insider perspectives on the struggle going back to gay rights activism in the apartheid era, is *Sex and Politics in South Africa* by Neville Hoad, Karen Martin and Graeme Reid (Cape Town: Double Storey, 2005). We can also recommend Carl Franklin Stychin's *A Nation by Rights: National Cultures, Sexual Identity Politics, and the Discourse of Rights* (Philadelphia: Temple University Press, 1998). This is a scholarly book that it places the South African experience in comparative perspective to other gay rights struggles around the world, including places where they have been extremely successful such as Quebec and the Netherlands. Neville Hoad's *African Intimacies: Race, Homosexuality and Globalization* (Minneapolis: University of Minnesota Press, 2007) includes a close analysis of a homosexual character in one of Wole Soyinka's novels, a re-examination of the case of the Christian martyrs in Buganda, a discussion how homosexuality nearly tore the world Anglican community apart in 1998, and an analysis of the long-term impact of imperialism in shaping responses to the HIV/AIDS crisis. Marc Epprecht's *African Heterosexuality: The History of an Idea from the Age of Exploration to the Age of AIDS* (Athens OH: Ohio University Press, 2008) will cover some of the same ground, with particular focus on how same-sex issues were written out of colonial-era anthropology, psychiatry and the early scientific studies of HIV in Africa.

The former Portuguese and French colonies of Africa have not been well researched on this topic. The very first academic book to investigate male–male sexuality in French-speaking Central Africa is Charles Gueboguo's *La Question homosexuelle en Afrique: Le cas du Cameroun* (Paris: Harmattan, 2006). Another first from Cameroon is an edited collection of articles and book reviews by philosopher Fabien Eboussi Boulaga entitled *Dossier: L'Homosexualité est bonne à penser* ('Homosexuality is good to think about' – special issue of *Terroirs, revue africaine des Sciences Sociales et de Philosophie*, Nos 1–2, Yaoundé, 2007). What makes this especially important is that it highlights the work of African-based African scholars, a breakthrough for the continent.

Gay-themed literature

Homosexual characters and themes crop up in interesting ways in African literature. The earliest reference in English-language novels seems to be in *Blanket Boy's Moon*, co-authored by Peter Lanham and A. S.

Mopeli-Paulus, a Mosotho chief (London: Collins, 1953). It tells the story of a naïve young man from Lesotho who migrates to Johannesburg where he is shocked to witness male–male sex in prison. Later, under the influence of marijuana, he becomes sexually infatuated with a young male hustler. What makes the novel all the more remarkable is its uneven homophobia. It hints, for example, that male–male sex was known and was not controversial in traditional, rural settings.

Yambo Ouologuem's *Le Devoir de violence,* published in English as *Bound to Violence* (London: Heinemann, 1971), is also important for its early and uncertain homophobia. Similar to a technique used by many African novelists, Ouologuem begins with scenes of cruel sexual abuse of African boys by corrupt 'Arab' elites. But this is then contrasted with a tender, loving homosexual relationship between the main African character and a European man in Paris. In addition to the frank depictions of male–male sex, the book made a very controversial implication at the time: that is, Arab abuse and imperialism in Africa have been worse than European abuse and imperialism.

The literary technique of showing homosexuality as coming from outside to corrupt or trouble Africans is also used by several important African novelists, including Nigerian Wole Soyinka in *The Interpreters* (London: Heinemann, 1970), by South African Motswana Bessie Head in *A Question of Power* (London: Heinemann, 1974), by Ghanaian Ama Ata Aidoo in *Our Sister Killjoy* (London: Longman, 1977), by Cameroonian Calixthe Beyala in *Your Name Shall Be Tanga* (Portsmouth NH: Heinemann, 1996), and by Zimbabwean Dambudzo Marechera in *Mindblast!* (Harare: College Press, 1984). In most cases, the homosexual character or encounter is of minor importance and used by the author only to make some small moral point or plot advancement. Yulisa Amadu Maddy's *No Past, No Present, No Future* (London: Heinemann, 1973) is unusual in that one of its three main characters is openly gay. The young Joe in the story is turned off heterosexuality by a weird combination of sexual betrayal by a woman and seduction/corruption by a white priest. He is then subjected to some strongly homophobic attacks throughout the book. But, remarkably, Joe eventually emerges as the most mature and moral among the three friends of the story, saved from alienation and self-hatred by the love of his English boyfriend.

Homosexuals are portrayed with different levels of sympathy or revulsion in these novels; from 'diseased', in Head's case, to insane, in Beyala's. What they have in common, though, is that the main source of sexual uncertainty is Europe or America. For a rare exception to this pattern, see the short novel by the Mosotho author Mpapa Mokhoane, *Teba* (Manzini: Macmillan Boleswa, 1995). Here the main African character angrily defends his loving sexual relationship with another man at the mines. He questions the sanity of the African Christian minister who preaches against homosexuality.

Beyala herself radically revises the common picture of African women's sexuality as being more or less passive and subservient to men's needs with her latest novel. *Femme nue, femme noire: roman* (Paris: Albin Michel, 2003) is a dark comedy that recalls both the Marquis de Sade and African traditions of controlled sexual and gender inversion to make a political point. Not yet translated into English, this novel probably contains more – and more varied – descriptions of sexual acts than any other example of African literature, including oral sex by various combinations of men and women, several scenes of group sex, and even a (heterosexual) sex act with a chicken! There is also a remarkable scene where a man's virility with his wife is restored after being anally penetrated by another man. All of this activity is witnessed or experienced by the young female narrator. She does not judge morally but constantly reflects on the meaning of desire. Her own aggressive, 'masculine' sexuality serves for Beyala to comment on oppressive gender roles and hypocrisies in African and Islamic traditions. The International Monetary Fund takes its share of knocks as well. Beyala seems to be saying that the achievement of pleasure, by whatever means, is a radical and necessary political act in the contemporary context.

The Zimbabwean author, Charles Mungoshi, also wrote a provocative short story about male–male sex between African men called 'Of Lovers and Wives' in his book *Walking Still* (Harare: Baobab, 1997).

What makes this especially fascinating is that the main character is married to a woman while having an affair with a male friend (while this happens all the time in the real world, it almost never appears in fiction). The story gives strong insight into why African women may sometimes be more homophobic than men because of fears about their husbands' bisexual infidelity. Another short story from Zimbabwe is 'Mea Culpa' by Rory Kilalea in the collection of stories called *Writing Still* (Harare: Weaver Press, 2003). This portrays a sexually and politically confused white man at the University of Rhodesia during the liberation struggle. He is seduced by a fellow student (black), with bitter consequences that lead us to reflect on both internalised homophobia and racism. In fact, the story could be interpreted as a neat illustration of those very qualities in the author himself, who seems to want to feel guilty about or to take pleasure in his morally bad nature.

Homosexual themes are more common in white South African literature. Stephen Gray's *Time of Our Darkness* (London: Frederick Muller, 1988) in one of the more important early treatments. At its heart is an affair between a gay white teacher and one of his black pupils. This novel is often grim, with discomforting descriptions of what amounts to child abuse and prostitution. But it also uses comedy to challenge the stereotype of a rigid homo/hetero opposition. Gray makes the point that human sexuality is fluid, which can be confusing and upsetting but also funny and liberating. His *Born of Man*, (London: Gay Men's Press, 1989), also used comedy to mock hypocrisy and prejudice in white South African attitudes toward sexuality – a gay man becomes pregnant. More seriously, Damon Galgut sets his first novel in a boys' reformatory school where two graphic scenes of male gang rape take place. *A Sinless Season* (Johannesburg: J. Ball, 1982) suggests that violent homophobia grows organically out of the racism and patriarchy of white South African society. That theme is also developed in relation to racial conflict in *The Beautiful Screaming of Pigs* (London: Scribners, 1991) in which a spontaneous male–male sexual embrace takes place after the trauma of battle against Namibian freedom-fighters.

Since 1994 there has been an explosion of gay-themed literature from South Africa, some of it borderline pornographic. Mark Behr, for example, is unlikely to win converts to the cause of gay rights with his lengthy novel *Embrace* (Boston: Little, Brown, 2000). It tells a coming-of-age story of a boy with strong bisexual feelings. In addition to its explicit gay, bisexual and hints-of-lesbian eroticism, the novel contains graphic scenes of sexual intercourse and fantasies with animals. One character is a morally corrupt teacher. Sello Duiker's *The Quiet Violence of Dream* (Cape Town: Kwela, 2001) is also troubling in its depictions of male rape, prostitution and racism in post-apartheid Cape Town. Yet, what makes both Behr and Duiker important is that they show homosexual characters with the full range of human emotions, from ugly to admirable. In that way, they surmount the kind of stereotyping found in many earlier novels from Africa.

There is also the work of Tatamkhulu Ismail Afrika, which includes fascinating insights into tensions around homophobia/homoeroticism within 'struggle masculinity'. Afrika grew up in the Transvaal where he was classified as a white person. But, in 1964, he converted to Islam and founded the militant group al-Jihaad. Themes of self-doubt about his race and sexuality come out in short stories such as 'The Quarry' (in *Tightrope,* Cape Town: Mayibuye Books, 1996). His novel, *Bitter Eden* (London: Arcadia Books, 2002), involves a love triangle between men in a World War II prisoner-of-war camp that may be autobiographical. A common tension in his work is between men who violently deny feelings of homosexual attraction yet at the same time voyeuristically and explicitly describe male physiques and genitals.

Nigeria has also produced its first gay-themed novel with Jude Dibia's *Walking with Shadows* (Lagos: BlackSands Books, 2005). It is the story of a man, Adrian, who hides his homosexual desire within a normal-appearing marriage and the emotional turmoil that this causes both himself and his wife when the secret is outed. Interestingly, Adrian's predicament is not portrayed as unique: several other characters in the novel are men who have sex with men but who publicly claim to be heterosexual and whose wives either do not know or are not really bothered by it.

Lesbian themes are rare in African literature. Nonetheless, they do exist. Rebecca Njau in *Ripples in the Pool* (London: Heinemann 1975) portrays an erotic relationship between a married woman and her young servant that eventually leads to madness and tragedy. By contrast, Mpho 'M'atsepo Nthunya fondly remembers intimate female friendships in 'When a Woman Loves a Woman' from her memoir, *Singing away the Hunger: Stories of a Life in Lesotho* (Pietermaritzburg: University of Natal Press, 1995). David Sweetman tells a very different story in his examination of the life of the influential, English-born, South African immigrant, Mary Renault. His *Mary Renault: A Biography* (London: Chatto and Windus, 1993) sheds light on a time when the vocabulary of gay rights and lesbian identity did not yet exist, up to the early struggles against apartheid efforts to criminalise homosexuality. There is also a fascinating chapter by Unoma N. Azuah on 'The emerging lesbian voice in Nigeria' in *Body, Sexuality and Gender*, edited by Flora Veit-Wild and Dirk Naguschewski (Amsterdam: Rodopi, 2005). This is a very recent development, and a potentially dangerous one given the extreme homophobia expressed by several Nigerian leaders. But it contains important insights that strengthen our understanding of how 'normal' African women may rationalise having sex with women. Similar boundaries are pushed in a rich collection by African women authors edited by Ama Ata Aidoo called *African Love Stories* (Banbury: Ayebia Clarke Publishing, 2007). Among these stories is Monica Arac de Nyeko's prize-winning 'Jambula Tree', in which two young Ugandan women have a loving sexual relationship. The story has them exposed and denounced by an older woman but in the process much hypocrisy in the community is also exposed.

Finally, a resource for high school 'life experience' or 'sex education' teachers is a slim volume of personal stories given by young South African gays and lesbians called *Balancing Act: South African Gay and Lesbian Youth Speak Out* (Johannesburg: New Africa Education, 2005). Edited by Karen Martin and Joanne Bloch, and produced by the Gay and Lesbian Archives of South Africa, the balance refers to the difficulties faced by being gay in a homophobic environment as well as the positives of developing self-esteem, leadership potential, and concrete strategies for making healthy life choices about gender and sexuality.

Heterosexuality and Gender

A great deal has been written about human sexuality. Unfortunately, much of it is simply incorrect or twists the scientific knowledge in order to promote preferred behaviours and moral agendas. The Kinsey report in the 1940s is still shocking to many who read it precisely because it approaches human sexuality without an obvious moral agenda. Meanwhile, science is continually expanding our awareness of the physiology of sex and sexuality – for example, identifying genes that could influence sexual orientation. Political and cultural assumptions about what is normal, healthy and proper are also constantly changing, particularly as research on sexuality by scholars and activists in the South begins to challenge the domination of research by the developed countries of the North.

For all these reasons, and because of the difficulties in obtaining scholarly books in much of Africa, the Internet is probably the most effective tool for finding solid information on sexuality in Africa. The *Sexual Health Network* (www.SexualHealth.com) and *Sexuality and You* (www. sexualityandu.ca) are good places to start for information about human sexuality in general. They include detailed discussions of the physical aspects of sexuality, contraception, and sexually-transmitted diseases, emotional aspects of love and relationships, educational resources and teaching methods, and much more. *Sexuality and You* is especially convenient in that it has different sections clearly addressed to different audiences (teens, parents, professional health workers, and so on).

The Society for Human Sexuality out of Seattle, USA, also maintains a strong website which includes references for how-to books, erotic literature, and ideas on safer sex (www.sexuality.org). The Love Life Campaign from South Africa (www.lovelife.org.za) is directed primarily at teenagers and their parents. Through an emphasis on peer education, it promotes knowledge about how to build and negotiate healthy sexual and emotional relationships in an environment where the risks and pressures are high.

Gender-based and sexual violence are not just criminal offences in most countries. They also carry huge health and social costs. The World Health Organization (www.who.int) has estimated that the physical injuries caused by gender-based violence directly adds as much as 15% of the developing world's burden of ill-health. Indirectly, violence against women and children adds even more by contributing to the spread of HIV/AIDS and other sexually-transmitted diseases. The United Nations Development Fund for Women, or UNIFEM, maintains global statistics on women's status, and lobbies for improvements in women's rights (www.unifem.org).

There are now many excellent histories of women and gender in Africa, as well as debates around African feminisms. To direct you to just one study for each of the three countries that this book is mostly focused on, see Elizabeth Schmidt, *Peasants, Traders and Wives: Shona Women in the History of Zimbabwe, 1870–1939* (Portsmouth NH: Heinemann, 1992), Marc Epprecht, *'This Matter of Women is Getting Very Bad': Gender, Development and Politics in Colonial Lesotho, 1870–1965* (Pietermaritzburg: University of Natal Press, 2000), and Pamela Scully, *Liberating the Family?: Gender, Labor, and Sexuality in the Rural Western Cape, South Africa, 1823–1853* (Ann Arbor: University of Michigan Press, 1993). One among many thought-provoking efforts to develop a specifically African understanding of feminism is Nigerian scholar Oyèrónké Oyéwùmí's, *The Invention of Women: Making an African Sense of Western Gender Discourses* (Minneapolis: University of Minnesota Press, 1997). Directly from Nigeria with a contemporary and practical or policy-oriented focus is the magazine *Sexuality in Africa*. The publisher is the Africa Regional Sexuality Resource Centre in Lagos, founded in 2003 to promote public dialogue, learning, leadership, and 'positive change' around sexuality at a pan-African level. In addition to the quarterly magazine, the Centre puts out occasional academic papers with a generally pro-feminist analysis. Issues discussed ranged from media representations of sexuality, Islam, impotence, disabled people, old people, and many others (see the centre's website: http://www.arsrc.org/).

Men and masculinity in Africa are the subjects of a growing literature, including Robert Morrell (ed.), *Changing Men in Southern Africa* (Pietermaritzburg: University of Natal Press, and London: Zed Press, 2001), L. Lindsay and S. Miescher (eds). Men and Masculinities in Modern Africa (Portsmouth NH: Heinemann, 2003), and Lisa Richter and Robert Morrell (eds). Baba: Men and Fatherhood in South Africa (Cape Town: Human Sciences Research Council Press, 2006).and L. Lindsay and S. Miescher (eds), *Men and Masculinities in Modern Africa* (Portsmouth NH: Heinemann, 2003). Graeme Reid's and Liz Walker's *Men Behaving Differently: South African Men since 1994* (Cape Town: Double Storey/Juta Academic, 2005) may be of particular interest as it contains interviews with Basotho gay men, gay rural South African hairdressers, and men who have sex with men in prison. This last chapter (by Sasha Gear) is helpful to understanding homophobia and misogyny (woman-hating) among men who re-enter society after prison. Lahoucine Ouzgane and Robert Morrell (eds) *African Masculinities: Men in Africa from the Late Nineteenth Century to the Present* (London: Palgrave Macmillan, 2005) is also of interest in that it contains chapters from all around the continent, including several that touch on male sexuality, men's violence against women, and men's pro-feminist activism. Three chapters on Egypt reveal strong parallels between the Islamic north of Africa and Africa south of the Sahara.

The history of sexuality in Africa has also been gaining critical attention in recent years. Andrew and Harriet Lyons chart the history of professional anthropological writing about 'primitive' sexuality in *Irregular Connections: A History of Anthropology and Sexuality* (Lincoln and London: University of Nebraska Press, 2004), including how European and American anthropologists sometimes twisted evidence to score points in debates back home. Diana Jeater offers a close case study of how white settlers manipulated and exploited African sexuality for their own political and economic ends (*Marriage,*

Perversion and Power: The Construction of Moral Discourse in Southern Rhodesia, 1890–1920. Oxford: Clarendon, 1993). Signe Arnfred provides a solid theoretical introduction to a number of articles on different aspects of African heterosexuality, including female genital cutting, prostitution and HIV interventions (*Re-thinking African Sexualities.* Uppsala: Nordiska Afrikainstitutet, 2004). In *Female Circumcisions and the Politics of Knowledge* (Westport, CT, and London: Praeger, 2005) Obioma Nnaemeka and (mostly) African contributors make a strong argument against both female genital cutting and the arrogance of Western 'interventionists and insurgents' who have trampled on African women's dignity in the name of emancipating them from custom.

Films and Videos

Turning to the visual media, there are now several fascinating video documentaries and feature films that focus on lesbian themes. For example, Beverley Palesa Ditsie and Nicky Newman's *Simon and I* (Cape Town/Johannesburg: See Thru Media/Steps for the Future, 2004) looks at the sometimes-tense relationship between Simon Nkoli and Ditsie. Ditsie was one of the first out black lesbians in South Africa and a powerful feminist voice on the international scene. She fell out with Nkoli over his seeming lack of interest in feminist politics, although they came together in friendship once again just before his death from HIV/AIDS. Mpumi Njinje and Paolo Alberton provide a close look at a very different type of lesbian life in *Everything Must Come to Light* (Johannesburg: Out of Africa Films, 2002). Njinje, an anthropologist, follows three African lesbian couples through their lives together in Soweto where they are well regarded as traditional *sangoma*s or healers.

Idol Pictures of Cape Town has also produced a number of powerful videos on both LGBT history and HIV activism (www.idol.co.za). *A Normal Daughter: The Life and Times of Kewpie of District Six* (Jack Lewis, director, Cape Town: Idol Productions, 1998) focuses on the pre-gay rights moffie community in one of Johannesburg's black and coloured townships. In 1999, Zackie Achmat, the well known HIV/AIDS activist, teamed up with Jack Lewis to produce a thorough two-hour-long historical documentary for the South African Broadcasting Corporation. Entitled *Apostles of Civilised Vice*, after an influential academic article written by Achmat several years earlier, it dramatises a number of key moments in the history of same-sex sexuality in South Africa. This includes the story of the doomed prison affair between Rijkaart Jacobse and the 'Hottentot', Claas Blank, back in the 1700s, Junod's campaign against mine marriage, an interview with the gangster Nongoloza Mathebula from 1912, and parliamentary debates on perversion in the 1960s.

Achmat himself is the focus of another documentary, *It's My Life*, directed by Brian Tilley (Cape Town: Steps for the Future, 2001). The camera follows Achmat around in his capacity as a leader in the Treatment Action Campaign to win access for Africans to cheap anti-retroviral drugs. It includes dramatic, David-versus-Goliath scenes of the court case where the TAC challenged the multinational drug companies, as well as Achmat's subsequent campaigns to protest his own government's approach to HIV/AIDS.

Another important video is *Dark and Lovely, Soft and Free*, written and directed by Paulo Alberton and Graeme Reid (Johannesburg: GALA, 2000). This takes us off the beaten path of South African gay life by means of a road trip into the black townships and 'rural areas'. There they discover black gay men who live more or less openly homosexual lives, whether as a *sangoma*, as a mine wife, or as a hairdresser.

By contrast, John Scagliotti takes a fairly negative overall view of the human rights situation for LGBT in six developing countries, including Namibia and Egypt, in his video and DVD called *Dangerous Living: Coming Out in the Developing World* (New York: After Stonewall Productions, 2003). Interviews with LGBT political refugees living in Canada and the United States add to a gloomy picture of homophobic violence and seemingly growing intolerance.

Greta Schiller directed *The Man Who Drove with Mandela* (London:

Jezebel Productions, 1998), a tribute to the life and political struggles of Cecil Williams. The British-born South African theatre producer and openly gay Communist activist has been credited by some for sensitizing the ANC leadership to gay rights back in the early days of the anti-apartheid movement. From a bit later in that era comes Jack Lewis and Thulanie Phungula's *Sando to Samantha, aka The Art of Dikvel* (Cape Town: Idol Productions, 1998). This takes an amusing look at gay life in one of the places you might least expect to find it – the South African military.

Two other films from West Africa cut new ground in the treatment of homosexuality in African cinema. First came Mohammed Camara's feature, *Dakan* (Conakry: ArtMattan, 1997). This provided a sympathetic look at two young gay men who fall in love in Conakry, Guinea. *Dakan* is notable not only for its sensitive treatment of the theme but also for the first male–male erotic kiss ever to be shown in African cinema. But this is not a celebration of coming out in the Western sense. On the contrary, in realistic African style, there is a strong celebration of family in traditional terms, including marriage and children, something to which Western audiences often react with confusion. *Woubi Cheri* by Philip Brooks and Lawrent Bocahut (Paris and Abidjan: ARTE-France, 1998), meanwhile, is a documentary that comes closer to representing the modern gay scene. It examines the ups and downs of life in a transgender community in the very chic city of Abidjan.

Finally, the first-ever feature film from Africa to depict a lesbian relationship is *Karmen Gei,* a musical directed by Joseph Gaï Ramaka (Dakar: Les Ateliers de l'Arche, 2001). Set in Senegal, the movie is an adaptation of Bizet's famous opera (*Carmen*). Ramaka's Karmen, however, is not just a physically stunning and extremely sensual character who tempts men. She actually opens the movie by seducing the warden of the women's prison, Angelique. Karmen subsequently has affairs with men, but her real love interest (and the most erotic scene in the movie) is unquestionably with the sad, strikingly beautiful Angelique. As with the films above, *Karmen Gei* is available through the website of California Newsreel (www.newsreel.org). *Emotional Crack* and other 'Nollywood' films that touch on gay themes are available through the Internet Movie Database (www.imdb.com).

Theatre

In the world of theatre, there have been several African plays that depict or discuss homosexual themes. Among the most sympathetic are two that were written and directed by Robert Colman. *After Nines!* has not yet been published, although the full script is available on the *Behind the Mask* website. The transcripts of the oral interviews upon which it drew for its characters and themes are also available at the Gay and Lesbian Archives. Written as a form of community outreach, and performed by LGBT members of the Hope and Unity Metropolitan Community Church in Johannesburg, it tells the story of a young African girl in the townships who wants to come out as a lesbian but faces the homophobic hostility of her parents. The living characters are then advised by ancestral spirits to overcome their homophobia and to love each other in a non-judgemental way as, they say, used to be the way in African traditions. *Your Loving Simon* is also based on actual historical evidence, in this case the letters of Simon Nkoli from prison to his lover on the outside. It shows Nkoli's ultimately successful struggles to overcome the homophobia of his fellow political prisoners.

Less sympathetic, but still important, are *The Hill* by Zakes Mda, in Andrew Horn (ed.), *The Plays of Zakes Mda* (Johannesburg: Ravan, 1990) and *Too Late* by Gilbert Kente in Robert Mshengu Kavanagh (ed.), *South African People's Plays* (Johannesburg: Heinemann, 1992). *Too Late* was first performed in Johannesburg in 1963, when it was banned for a scene that showed a more or less forced homosexual relationship between African men in prison. Poverty, corruption, and the sex lives of Basotho migrant workers are the main themes of *The Hill*. First performed in Cape Town in 1980, it shows the men living in caves above Maseru where they wait to sign up for new contracts to take them back to the mines in South Africa. There is considerable, sometimes quite crude, discussion of mine marriage with a curious mix of homophobic disgust and matter-of-fact acceptance.

Performing Queer, Shaping Sexuality: 10 Years of Democracy in South Africa, edited by Melissa Steyn and Mikki van Zyl (Cape Town: Kwela Books, 2005) is not about theatre in a literal sense, but about the ways that people have understood, discussed and performed their sexuality in a society undergoing rapid social and political change. It includes chapters based on interviews with black MSM and lesbians which tend to support the views put forth in *After Nines!*

LGBT literature from elsewhere in the world

Of course, we cannot fully appreciate African experiences and perspectives unless we understand what has been going on elsewhere in the world. So much has been written and produced that it would require another whole book to do justice to the topic. However, let us just mention a handful of classic studies that relate directly to the material discussed in this book. Annick Prieur brings an anthropologist's eye to a small queer community in a poor, underdeveloped country in her book, *Mema's House, Mexico City: On Transvestites, Queens, and Machos* (Chicago: University of Chicago Press, 2000). From India, we have Serena Nanda's *Neither Man Nor Woman: The Hijras of India* (Belmont CA: Wadsworth, 1990), and from Brazil, Richard Parker's, *Beneath the Equator: Cultures of Desire, Male Homosexuality, and Emerging Gay Communities in Brazil* (New York: Routledge, 1999). Jarrod Hayes discusses gay themes in North African Arab writing during the period of colonialism in his book, *Queer Nations: Marginal Sexualities in the Maghreb* (Chicago: University of Chicago Press, 2000). What makes this study particularly interesting is that homosexuality emerges as a means for Arab writers to establish an anti-colonial or even revolutionary identity to counter the oppressive moralism, machismo, and racism of the French settlers.

Robert Aldrich's *Colonialism and Homosexuality* (London: Routledge, 2004) sometimes reads like a gossip column. It nonetheless makes a convincing case that both repressed and active homosexuals played an important role in building the European colonial empires. This included conquerors, authors and businessmen (Cecil Rhodes is included as a closet case). Aldrich also draws attention to a number of strong defenders of African human and political rights against the abuses of colonial rule in Africa who were practising homosexuals, including Roger Casement and Jean Sénac.

Wesley Crichlow breaks new ground with his study of black MSM in Canada, *Buller Men and Batty Bwoys* (Toronto: University of Toronto Press, 2004). Based largely on interviews, the book shows some striking parallels to Africans' struggles against homophobic 'bionationalism' in the African-Canadian and Caribbean communities.

For understanding the history of homophobia, meanwhile, you cannot go wrong by starting with Byrne Fone, *Homophobia: A History* or Warren Blumenfeld's edited collection, *Homophobia: How We All Pay the Price* (Boston: Beacon Press, 1992). The Blumenfeld book remains one of the clearest explanations of how prejudice and fear of homosexuality helps to channel the majority population into narrow, often dehumanizing or repressive gender roles and identities. *Pink Blood: Homophobic Violence in Canada* by Douglas Janoff (Toronto: University of Toronto Press, 2005) meanwhile offers a powerful analysis of how extreme homophobic violence can remain a cultural influence long after laws and official rhetoric have accepted sexual diversity and minority rights. It is a sobering lesson for those who might feel complacent about the power of the South African constitution to rectify deep homophobic sentiments in the wider society.

Rudi Bleys may be heavy reading for some, but his book, *The Geography of Perversion* (New York: New York University Press, 1995) gives an important, wide-ranging examination of the intellectual origins of homophobia in the Western imagination. This includes looking for references and descriptions of male–male sexuality in books and travel accounts by Europeans in all the major imperial languages over nearly two hundred years. His bibliography alone (with over 1000 references) is invaluable for tracking down early mention of non-European homosexualities in the published literature. Jennifer Terry's *An American Obsession: Science, Medicine and Homosexuality in Modern Society* (Chicago: University of Chicago Press, 1999), and Dagmar Herzog, *Sex after Fascism: Memory and Morality in Twentieth-Century Germany* (Princeton and Oxford: Princeton University Press, 2005) are other important academic studies. As with *Pink Blood*, they provide a strong caution against the presumption found in much of the South that the West is somehow 'naturally' a gay-friendly culture.

Two 'must-have' reference books for LGBT organisations are George F. Haggerty (ed.) *Gay Histories and Cultures* (New York: Garland, 2000) and *Routledge International Encyclopedia of Queer Culture* edited by David Gerstner (New York and London: Routledge, 2006). The first takes a long historical view, with a tendency to focus on the Western experience: there are only four entries on Africa south of the Sahara, for example. The second focuses on the post-1945 period and contains a broader appreciation of non-Western cultures.

HIV/AIDS

With respect to HIV/AIDS, there is an almost overwhelming amount of resources available. *The Body* (www.thebody.com) is a good place to start. Updated daily, it contains state-of-the-art information on 'best practices' for a range of different heavily affected communities, including MSM. Although it tends to be American or west-focused, there are also regular articles on developments in Africa. *Behind the Mask's* HIV/AIDS Discussion Forum is a rich source for personal insights from LGBT activists and people living with HIV/AIDS in Africa, as is SAfAIDS (send for information about resources to info@safaids.org). Another excellent source of information on the struggle to gain access to medicines in Africa is from the Treatment Action Campaign's website: www.tac.org.za. On the controversial question of where HIV came from in the first place, Edward Hooper's *The River: A Journey to the Source of HIV and AIDS* (Boston: Little, Brown, 1999) has been hotly disputed by many scientists. It nonetheless provides a thought-provoking investigation into the abuses and carelessness of the colonial health system in Africa that may have contributed to creating a new virus.

As Cary Alan Johnson has closely documented in *Off the Map: How HIV/AIDS Programming is Failing Same-Sex Practicing People in Africa* (NY: International Gay and Lesbian Human Rights Commission, 2007), the bulk of material on HIV/AIDS in Africa is blind to same-sexuality. However, many non-government organisations around Africa have begun to publish excellent materials in a wide range of formats for their own counsellors and local audiences. One of the best is fairly widely available through Kwela Books (Cape Town) and Weaver Press (Harare) – *ABC of All the Questions We Never Dare to Ask* (2003). This is a book structured around questions raised by real teenagers in Zimbabwe and South Africa. It is directed both at youth themselves and at teachers and parents who need help to overcome their shyness around talking about sex. Idol Productions of Cape Town (www.idol. co.za) also has a series of videos called *Beat It: Your Guide to Better Living with HIV/AIDS.*

To give another example of this type of action-oriented material, GALZ published in 2004 'An Organisational Manual for Gay and Lesbian Organisations in Africa' in PowerPoint format available on CD-ROM. The Training and Research Support Centre in Harare has also published a series of cards and a facilitator's guide by 'Auntie Stella' for use in promoting free-flowing discussions in schools and youth groups (available on CD-ROM and through the website, www. auntiestella.org). Some of the cards deal directly with gay rights. Others normalise the issue of sexual choice simply by including homosexuality in general discussions around topics such as masturbation, abortion, sex before marriage, contraception, and forced sex. They do not provide single, clear-cut answers to complex and sensitive questions; rather, they encourage youth to work together in fun ways so as to break down prejudices, taboos, and unhealthy decisions faced by growing up in today's environment. The training manual for counsellors offers brilliant insights on how to manage youth groups using such different methods as role playing and drama, debates, art, letter- and short story-writing, quizzes, and open discussions.

Faith-based organisations are controversial. In some cases they have been shown to promote dangerous myths about sexuality. There is no denying, however, that they are very active in Africa today and that they have scored some successes in promoting certain kinds of safer sex. One of these is the Mennonite Central Committee. It has produced a simple, non-judgemental resource called *Join Hands, Stop AIDS Toolkit* that can be downloaded from its website (www.mcc.org/aids/resources).

In terms of books, a ground-breaking collection of studies in both English and French is *Vivre et Penser le Sida en Afrique: Experiencing and Understanding AIDS in Africa*, edited by Charles Becker, Jean-Pierre Dozon, Christine Obbo, and Moriba Toure (Dakar: CODESRIA, 1999). Same-sexuality is only mentioned in passing in a few chapters, although one makes a very suggestive comment that homosexuality is 'widespread' in Sudan. *HIV/AIDS in Africa: Beyond Epidemiology* (London: Routledge, 2004) is another valuable collection with 25 chapters by well known scholars from different disciplines offering case studies from right across the continent and addressing a wide range of issues. Edited by Ezekiel Kalipeni and other well established social scientists in the field, the bibliography contains over 50 pages of other publications and helpful resources. Another important collection of studies that is focused specifically on South Africa is *AIDS in Context* edited by Peter Delius and Liz Walker (special issue of the journal *African Studies*, vol. 61, no. 1, 2002). *Global AIDS: Myths and Facts* (Boston: South End Press, 2003) walks readers through the main controversies and debates, including those around access to treatment, harm reduction, vaccine development and the role of structural adjustment and international trade. While global in scope, it is introduced by Zackie Achmat of South Africa and has a sharp, focused chapter entirely devoted to Africa. The first historical overview of the disease in French is an edited collection by Philippe Denis and Charles Becker. *L'Épidémie du sida en Afrique subsaharienne* (Paris: Karthala, 2006) includes chapters from countries like Burundi and Congo, which tend to get overlooked in general overviews.

All of these books carefully analyse the social, cultural, economic and other historical factors that have contributed to the pandemic and that continue to frustrate efforts to stop the spread of the disease. These include racist and sexist prejudices that were built into supposedly scientific studies in colonial and apartheid eras. Unfortunately, however, like most of the work on HIV/AIDS in Africa, these books tend to be quite heterosexist. *HIV/AIDS in Africa* contains just one short chapter by Oliver Phillips on 'The Invisible Presence of Homosexuality'. Elsewhere in the book there is virtually no discussion of homophobia, anal sex (either heterosexual or homosexual), and gay sex. One chapter even goes out of its way harshly to mock scholars who have speculated about the existence of homosexuality and bisexuality in Africa. Scholars who have demonstrated that existence with an abundance of evidence are simply ignored.

AIDS in Context does contain a fascinating chapter by the anthropologist Isak Niehaus on male–male sexuality in labour compounds and prisons. But otherwise it, too, makes surprisingly little reference to LGBT-specific issues. In that way it quietly, if unintentionally, contributes to erasing public knowledge about the role of homophobia and gay sex in spreading HIV, and of the role of LGBT groups in the fight against AIDS.

May these gaps, like the book that you are holding at this very moment, inspire others to pick up those lines of research and start to give them the attention they so desperately require.

notes on contributors

Lindsay Clowes is a graduate of Historical Studies at the University of Cape Town and teaches on the Women's & Gender Studies programme at the University of the Western Cape, South Africa. Her recent research explores media representations of race, gender and sexuality in South Africa's *Drum* magazine.

Dumisani Dube is a member of GALZ and a former Publications Officer with the organisation.

Chris Dunton has taught at universities in Nigeria, Libya and Lesotho and is currently Professor of English and Dean of Humanities at the National University of Lesotho. He has published widely on African literature and especially on Nigerian theatre. His collection of short stories, *Boxing*, is available through the African Books Collective.

Marc Epprecht is an Associate Professor in the Department of Global Development Studies at Queen's University, Kingston, Canada. He has published on the history of gender and sexuality in southern Africa, including *'This Matter of Women Is Getting Very Bad': Gender, Development and Politics in Colonial Lesotho, 1870–1965*. His book *Hungochani* was the winner of the 2006 Joel Gregory Prize for best book on Africa published by a Canadian or an African scholar based in Canada in 2004/05.

Keith Goddard is the Director of the Gays and Lesbians of Zimbabwe (GALZ). Although originally trained as a musician and composer and still active in the field of promoting Zimbabwean culture, he moved into the field of LGBT activism in the early 1990s and was a member of the small GALZ task force which helped transform the association from an underground social club to a force in the struggle for lesbian and gay rights throughout Africa.

Poliyana Mangwiro (Tsitsi Tiripano) rose to prominence within the gay and lesbian movement in when she stood up at the Zimbabwe International Book Fair in 1996 and defended the rights of lesbian and bisexual women. She died of AIDS-related illnesses after a two year struggle in 2001.

T. Dunbar Moodie is a professor of sociology at Hobart and William Smith Colleges, Geneva, New York. He is the author, with Vivienne Ndatshe, of *Going for Gold: Men's Lives on the Mines*, as well as numerous other studies of the impacts of industrialisation on working class Africans in South Africa.

Ruth Morgan holds a doctorate in linguistic anthropology from the American University, Washington D.C. Since 2002 she has been the director of the Gay and Lesbian Archives, Johannesburg. She co-edited *Tommy Boys. Lesbian Men and Ancestral Wives: Female Same-sex Practices in Africa*. She has been collecting life stories of same-sex identified women and men for GALA since 1997 with a particular focus on same sex *sangoma*s (traditional healers) and deaf gays and lesbians in South Africa.

Nkunzi Zandile Nkabinde had just started to study journalism when she received her calling to become a *sangoma* (traditional healer). Since that time she is also named for her ancestor Nkunzi (the Bull) who gives her her healing powers. She is proud of being a lesbian and a *sangoma*. All her life she has dreamt of becoming a writer, which she achieved with a chapter in *Tommy Boys* entitled 'This has happened since ancient times ... it's something you are born with': Ancestral wives amongst same-sex *sangoma*s in South Africa.'

Taiwo Oloruntoba-Oju has taught Stylistics, Language and African Literature at the University of Ilorin in Nigeria for about two decades. He has also taught Creative Writing and is himself a published poet and playwright. His current research is in language, gender relations and sexuality in Nigerian literature and film, and he was recently engaged in a research project titled 'Male, Female and the Other Sex in Nigerian Video Films' conducted at the Nordic African Institute, Uppsala, Sweden.

Drew Shaw is a Zimbabwean by birth and upbringing, now living in London. A graduate of the University of Toronto, the University of Cape Town and Queen Mary, University of London, his Ph.D. thesis, *Transgression and Beyond: Dambudzo Marechera and Zimbabwean Literature* (2004), contains the first comprehensive study of lesbian, gay, bisexual and transgendered themes and their significance in Zimbabwean writing. He continues to write essays, reviews and short stories.

index

Abidjan 237
abortion 27, 148, 190, 242
abstinence (*see also* celibacy) 26,
   38, 142, 149–50, 198
Achmat, Zackie 15–16, 73, 197,
   224, 236, 243
adultery 28, 52, 80, 97–8, 140, 163,
   172–3
African Christian Democratic
   Party 190
African National Congress (ANC)
   (Rhodesia) 140
African National Congress (ANC)
   (South Africa) (*see also* Mbeki,
   Thabo; Mandela, Nelson; Man-
   dela, Winnie) 183, 188–92, 237
African nationalism (*see also*
   African National Congress,
   ZANU(PF), individual African
   leaders) 132–55
Afrika, Tatamkhulu Ismail 230
Afrikaners 52, 82, 92, 116–17, 121,
   125
After Nines! 238–9
AIDS (*see* HIV/AIDS)
AIDS Action Group (South Africa)
   197
AIDS Law Project (South Africa)
   195–7
AIDS-phobia 198
AIDS Township Project (South
   Africa) 197
Akinola, Peter 212

All-Africa Rights Initiative 194–95
Alliance Rights Nigeria 6
American Psychiatric Association 185
anal sex (*see also* sodomy) 25, 35,
   42, 53, 56, 58, 79–80, 84, 101,
   138, 192, 216, 228, 244
ANC (*see* African National Congress)
Angela 35–6
Anglican church 4, 116–17, 140,
   198, 226
Angola 14, 24, 35, 36, 50–1
aphrodisiacs 29
Arabs (*see also* Islam) 10, 13, 37,
   135, 144, 227, 239
Aschwanden, Herbert 26, 35–6
aversion therapy 124, 186, 190
Azande 40, 135

Banana, Canaan 4, 140, 153
BaSili, *see* Bushmen
Basotho (*see also* Basutoland,
   Lesotho, Sesotho) 54, 56, 81, 83,
   92, 96, 116, 161–76
Basutoland (*see also* Basotho,
   Lesotho, Sesotho) 52, 64, 67,
   161, 163, 166
Behind the Mask 194, 220, 224,
   238, 241
Behr, Mark 230
Beirousky, Carl 119
berdache 217

bestiality 28, 214
Beyala, Calixthe 113, 227–8
Big Five gang 78, 80 83
Big Six gang 78
Bikinosi 99
biphobia 215
birth control 143, 216
Bisamu 100
bisexuality 1–2, 8, 11, 18, 107, 109, 118, 135, 171, 187, 206–9, 211, 215, 229, 230, 244
Black Peril 103
Black Sash 184
blackmail 4, 101, 123, 127, 149, 154, 184, 192, 193, 200, 213
Blank, Claas 53, 74, 236
Blanket Boy's Moon 169, 226–7
Boaz, Mike 193
Boers *See* Afrikaners
Boesak, Revd Allan 198
bohali (*see also lobola*) 163, 171, 172, 173
Botswana (*see also* Tswana) 6, 25, 194
boxing 101, 139
Brand, J. H. 116
Britain 4, 10, 13–14, 52–5, 58, 60, 75, 92, 94, 116–18, 126–7, 153, 161
Burrell, Brenda 196
Burton, Sir Richard 12–13
Bushmen (*see also* Khoi) 16, 24–5, 32, 42, 102

Calvinism 52, 116
Camara, Mohammed 237
Cameroon (*see also* Beyala, Calixthe) 226
Canada 226, 236, 240
canaries 81–2
Candomblé 35
Cape Town (*see also* Robben Island) 51–4, 108, 116, 119, 149, 182, 187, 192, 197, 230, 238
catamites 59, 75, 117

Catholic church (*see also* inquisitions) 10, 118
celibacy 30, 34, 56, 175
Chewa 96
chibado 35
chibanda 35
chibeura 138
Chicken Run (nightclub) 186
chidhoma 29
Chihota 34
Chikunda 96
chikwambo 29
China 33, 59, 143
Chinese 14, 59, 75, 117
chiramu 28
chitsina 30
Chitungwiza 194
Chopi 62, 135
Christianity (*see also* Calvinism, Anglican church, Catholic church, Dutch Reformed Church, inquisitions, *likopano*)
gay-friendly, 8, 117, 185–6, 191, 198, 222–3, 243; anti-homosexual 9, 52, 115, 117–19, 135–6, 149–50, 153, 166, 169, 176, 183, 198, 214; missions 15, 40, 134, 163, 174; and African nationalism 139–43, 183
Chung, Fay 143
circumcision, male 27, 37, 38, 54, 139; female 235
Clark, Bev 111–12, 196
clothing (*see also* cross-dressing) 35–6, 137, 147
Cold War, 9, 10, 123, 124, 126, 167, 213–14
Colman, Robert 238
Coon Carnival 119, 182
coons 142
cross-dressing (*see also* transvestism) 2, 31, 35–6, 51, 119, 126, 186

Dabengwa, Dumiso 152
Dakan 237

Dakar 64, 119, 149
dances, homoerotic 61, 69, 99, 125, 142, 167, 177
Davis, John Gordon 127
Dawn Mine 99
Dhlamini (a prisoner) 77
Dhlamini, Gugu 198
Dhuri 101
dildo 111–12, 125
Ditsie, Bev 187, 235
diviners (see also n'naga, sangoma, spirit mediums, traditional healers) 13, 28, 35, 39
divisi rakaipa 37, 39, 40
Dlamini, Moses 72–3, 78, 83, 145, 184, 225
drag, see cross-dressing
Dube, Jefta 4
Duiker, Sello 230
Dutch, see Netherlands
Dutch Reformed Church 122

Early, Robert 127
Eddy, Fanny Ann 194–5
Egypt 221, 234, 236
Emotional Crack 206–9, 237–8
End Conscription Campaign 189
Equality Project (South Africa) 5, 195
Equus 185
eshengi (Ovambo) 3
Ethiopia 5
Evershina 196

Falk, Kurt 24–5
Fanon, Frantz 14, 144
fascism 121, 241
fertility 25–6, 33, 60, 114
Forest Town raid 124–5, 184
France 64, 95, 118, 226, 239
Free State (South Africa) (see Orange Free State)
Freed, Louis 121–2
Freudian psychology 118, 121, 123, 143, 144

Galgut, Damon 229
GALZ, see Gays and Lesbians of Zimbabwe
gangisa (see also thigh sex, hlobonga) 27, 57
gangs (see also names of individual gangs) 14, 60, 72–3, 76–86, 96, 101, 119, 123, 145, 162, 236
Garlake, Peter 24, 42
GASA (see Gays and Lesbians of South Africa)
gay pride marches 188–9
Gay, Judith 174
Gayle, 123–4, 224–5
Gay-related Immune Deficiency (GRID) 211
Gays and Lesbians of Matabeleland 194
Gays and Lesbians of South Africa (GASA) 185–6, 187–8, 197
Gays and Lesbians of Witwatersrand (GLOW) 188–9, 193
Gays and Lesbians of Zimbabwe (GALZ) 6, 18, 23, 72, 106, 151–3, 155, 186, 193–6, 198, 199, 217, 223–4, 242
Gaza-Ngoni (see also Shangaan) 39, 40
Gelfand, Michael 13
Gezi, Border 115
Gibbon, Sir Edward 12
Globe and Phoenix mine 98
GLOM, see Gays and Lesbians of Matabeleland
GLOW, see Gays and Lesbians of Witwatersrand
Goddard, Keith 223–4
Gray, Stephen 229
GRID, see Gay-related Immune Deficiency
Guinea, 237
Gungunyana, King 61

Harries, Patrick 15, 222
Hayes, Jarrod 239

Head, Bessie 227
hermaphrodites, *see* intersex
heterosexism 210, 215–19, 223, 244
HIV/AIDS (*see also* sexually transmitted diseases) 1, 6, 15–16, 18,
  73, 149–51, 175, 197–200, 210–
  19, 224, 226, 233, 235–6, 241–4
hlobonga (*see also* thigh sex) 27,
  55, 57, 58, 62, 98, 134, 139, 162
Hlohoangwane, Pule 170–1
hlonepha 162, 168, 174, 176
Hogoza 55, 117
Hollywood 123, 126
homophobia (*see also* Christianity, anti-homosexual) 3–4, 9–10,
  18–23, 210–19; in settler society
  114-128; in the African nationalist movement 132–55
Homosexual Law Reform Fund
  (South Africa), *see* Reform
  Movement
homosexuality: definition 1–3;
  causes 7–8; in European and
  North American history 8–9,
  51–3, 87–8, 117–18, 121, 183,
  216–17, 222–3; in African historiography 12–17; in the developing
  world outside Africa 239–41
Hope and Unity Metropolitan Community Church 191, 238
Hottentot (*see also* Khoi) 53, 54,
  96, 236
hungochani (*see also* inkotshane) 3,
  4
Hunzvi, Chenjerai 199
hygiene 120, 138

Idol Productions 235, 242
Imbangala 50
Immigration Act (Southern Rhode-
  sia) 122, 126
Immorality Act (South Africa) 184–
  5, 190
Immorality Amendment Bill (South
  Africa) 125, 129

impotence 29–30, 31–2, 37, 234
incest 28, 34–5, 37
indecent assault 31, 98, 103, 104,
  119, 140, 147, 153, 165, 190
initiation 27, 36, 54, 63, 87, 139,
  167
Inkatha Freedom Party 190
Inkotshane (*see also* ngochani) 12,
  56–8, 60–3, 72, 75, 85, 93, 98,
  135, 136, 165–6, 168
inquisitions (Catholic) (*see also*
  Catholic church) 9, 35, 115
Internet 220, 232, 238
inter-racial sex 120–1, 122, 141
intersex 2, 30
Islam (*see also* Arabs, Muslims) 37,
  214, 217, 221, 223, 228, 230, 234

Jacobse, Rijkaart 53, 236
Jagas 50–1
January, Adam 54
Jews 52, 116, 125
John of Lesotho, *see* Shubela
Jumbo mine 99
Junod, Henri 166, 222, 236

Kaapstadt, *see* Cape Town
Kalipeni, Joseph 243
kaMbengwana, Ndukwana 56
Karanga 26, 33, 35–6
karanga 35, 36
Karmen Gei 237
Kendall, K. Limakatso 176
Kenya 4, 108, 222
Khoi (*see also* Bushmen) 24, 52–3,
  54
Kimberley 56
Kinsey Report 232
Kitchener, Lord 94
Kololo 38
kupinga nyika 34
kusenga (*see also* labia majora) 27

labia majora, stretching 27, 54,
  163, 173–4

Ladysmith 56
Lagemaat, Jolande 192
Leary, J. Glenn (see also Leary–Taberer inquiry) 59
Leary–Taberer inquiry, 59–63, 65–71, 72, 93, 98, 100 133, 135, 162, 165–6
LeGaBiBo 6, 194
lesbianism 1–7, 11–12, 14–15, 18, 24, 27, 32–3, 43–8, 72, 78, 83, 85, 94, 106–13, 126–7, 136, 147–9, 172–6, 182, 183, 185–96, 206–9
Lesotho (see also Basutoland, Basotho, Sesotho) 5, 6, 108, 161, 162, 165, 168–72, 175, 176, 224, 227, 231, 233
Liddicoat, Renée 183
lifaqane, see mfecane
Ligueey (Senegal) 6
likopano 172
literature, gay-themed 87–91, 112–13, 217, 221, 226–32
Lobengula 22, 39
lobola (see also bohali) 33, 36, 38, 43–8, 60, 67, 70, 99, 100, 139, 140, 163, 177
Lovedu 36
Lozi 38, 96
Lozikeyi 39
Lyautey, Hubert 94–5

'Maggie' 31
Maama, Albert 166–7
Mabala, James 101
McCarthy, Joseph 213
Maboma 32
Machida, Tina 193
Maddy, Yulisa Amadu 227–8
Madikizela-Mandela, Winnie see Mandela, Winnie
Malawi (see also Nyanja, Ngoni) 62, 93, 96–8, 101, 143, 169, 212
mamuna (see also mbonga) 34
Mandela, Nelson 5, 153, 183, 189, 236

Mandela, Winnie 145, 189, 193, 200
mangoromera 101
Mangwiro, Poliyana 18–20, 193
manyano 172
Manyika 34, 96
maotoane (see also thigh sex, hlobonga) 3, 164
mapoto (see also marriage) 99
MaRashea 81, 162
Marriage (see also mapoto; mine and prison marriage; woman–woman marriage): heterosexual 19, 26–30, 37–9, 80, 114, 117, 133, 139–40, 163, 172–4; gay 9, 191–2, 198, 230, 237
Marxism-Leninism 124, 143, 146
Maseane 164
mashave 29–30
Mashonaland 52, 92, 95, 96
Mashumba 32, 102
masturbation 25, 27, 52, 80, 121, 242
Matabeleland 92, 146, 148, 165, 194
matanyera 3, 97, 137, 217
matanvola 97
Mathebula, Nongoloza 14, 72, 76, 78, 81, 236
Mazinge, Nomxadana ('Maggie') 31
Mazrui, Ali 144
Mbeki, Thabo 189, 200
mbonga 34, 39
Mbuya, C. 155
MDC, see Movement for Democratic Change
medicine, see muti
mfecane 38–40
migrant labour 14–15, 25, 55, 56, 58, 63, 81, 93, 96–8, 135, 142, 162, 164–9, 172, 174–5, 212, 222, 238
mine marriages (see also inkotshane) 15, 58, 60–1, 64, 72–3, 85, 93, 119, 143, 167–70, 184, 221, 222, 236, 239
mines (see also mine marriages)

14–15, 56–64, 75, 81, 92–3, 97–99, 104, 162, 165–6
Miscellaneous Offences Act (Southern Rhodesia) 126
misogyny (*see also* sexism) 5, 150, 188, 217, 234
Mkhumbane 119
Moba 164–5
Moffatt, Robert 39
moffies 119, 123, 144, 182, 224, 235–6
Moffietaal 123, 225
Moira 107
Mokete 166–7, 168
Monday Club (Zimbabwe) 187
Mondhlani, Herbert 199
Moodie, T. Dunbar 15, 143, 171, 221–2
Mopeli-Paulus, A. S. 168–9, 227
Movement for Democratic Change (Zimbabwe) 196
Mozambique (*see also* Tsonga, Ngoni, Shangaan, Portugal) 15, 38, 57, 58, 61–3, 84, 93, 135, 169, 222
Mpofu, Alum 154
Mpondo (*see also* Xhosa) 63, 81, 221–2
Mugabe, Robert 3–4, 84, 114, 140–1, 145–6, 152, 196, 199–200, 202
Mullard, Julie 107, 183
mummy–baby relationship 174–6
Mungoshi, Charles 228–9
mupfuhwira 29–30, 150
muroyi 28
Murray, Stephen O. 221
Museveni, Yoweri 200, 212
Muslims (*see also* Arabs, Islam) 135
Mutasa, Diymus 141
Muteza, Obed 142
muti (*see also* aphrodisiacs, *mupfuhwira*) 34, 37, 40, 41, 101
Mwanga of the Buganda 135
Mzengeli, Charles 142–3
Mzilikazi 39

n'anga (155 *see also sangoma*, spirit mediums, traditional healers) 28, 30, 35, 37, 40,
Namibia (*see also* Bushmen, Khoi, Ovambo) 4–6, 24–5, 35, 110, 187, 194, 222, 224, 229, 236
Nare, Paulus Matjaka 145–6
Natal 38, 52, 55–7, 117, 120–1, 164–5, 185
National Coalition for Gay and Lesbian Equality (South Africa) 191–2, 195, 197
National Party (South Africa) 83, 122, 183, 189, 190
Native Adultery Punishment Ordinance (Southern Rhodesia) 97–8
Natsios, Andrew 151
Ncube, Archbishop Pius 153
Ndebele 3, 39–41, 54, 93, 96–98, 101, 132, 146
Ndongo 36, 50–1
Ndungane, Revd Njongonkulu 198
Netherlands 10, 51–3, 74, 116, 226
ngaka 77–8, 164
NGO Network Alliance 196, 221
ngochani (*see also inkotshane*) 4, 12, 40, 137, 217
Ngoni (*see also* Malawi; Mozambique) 38–40, 96
Ngoni Chaidzo 152, 193
Ngonyana, James 62, 65–8
ngozi 28–30, 32, 146
Nhiwatiwa, Naomi 140
Nigeria 4, 6, 40, 112, 194, 206–9, 221, 227, 230, 231, 233
Ninevites, *see* 28s
Njau, Rebecca 231
Njebe 32, 102
Njinga, *see* Nzinga, Anna
njuzu 35–6
Nkoli, Simon 188–9, 197, 224, 235, 238
Nkomo, Joshua 140, 145, 147
nkotshane, *see ngochani*
Noble, James 104–5

Nollywood 206–9, 238–9
Nongoloza, see Mathebula, Nongoloza
Northern Rhodesia, see Zambia
nsati (see also umfaan, wyfie) 58
Nthunya, Mpho 'M'atsepo 108, 173, 231
Nujoma, Sam 200, 212
Nupe 40
Nyambura, Freedom 143
Nyampule, Phillip 63, 68–71
Nyanja (see also Malawi) 3, 62, 96–7
Nyasaland see Malawi
Nyerere, Julius 156
Nzinga, Anna 36, 50–1

Old Hartley mine 165
Operation Clean-up (Zimbabwe) 148
oral sex 80, 215, 228
Orange Free State 57, 84, 116–17, 137
Organization of Lesbian and Gay Activists (OLGA) 188
orgasm 26, 58, 80, 83, 173
Ovambo 3

paedophilia 3
pederasty 3, 136
Pelser, P. C. 125
Perspective 186
police 4, 9, 57, 84, 104–5, 124–7, 130–1, 190, 192–3, 195, 217
polygamy 26–7, 38, 116, 139–40, 172–3, 174, 187
pornography 124, 215, 230
Porter Reformatory 81
Portugal 10, 13–14, 33, 35, 38, 50–1, 58, 67–9, 115–16, 118 121, 138
prisons 53, 72–86, 93, 98, 104, 119, 121, 145, 192, 225, 227, 234, 236, 237, 238 244
prostitution: female with males 53, 56, 60, 82, 93, 99, 101, 169–70,

179; lesbian 149; male–male, 56, 121–2, 148–9, 167, 170; equated to homosexuality 152
psychological theories (see also Freudian psychology) 94, 118, 121, 143–4, 183–5

Qalizwe 56
Quebec 226
queens (see also Coon Carinval, moffies, transgender) 2, 123, 138, 187, 193
queer politics 2–3

Rainbow (Chitungwiza) 194
Rainbow Project (Namibia) 6, 194–5
Rand Gay Organization 188
rape: male 56, 59, 64, 72–3, 77–9, 82–5, 103, 124, 134, 144–5, 165, 229–30; of lesbians 4, 114; of men by women 150; of political prisoners and opponents 83–5, 145; of virgins 150; of women by men 102, 110, 124, 141–2, 162, 174
Reform Movement (South Africa) 184–5
religion, African traditional 25–30, 33–7, 39–41, 43–8
Renault, Mary 107, 183, 231
Rhodes, Cecil 94, 240
Rhodesia see Zimbabwe
Robben Island 53, 72–5, 78, 83, 145, 225
Roman Catholic church, see Catholic church
Roman-Dutch law, 52, 55, 92, 93, 94, 192
roora (see also lobola) 33
Russians (gang), see MaRashea

Sade, Marquis de 87–91, 118, 228
sangoma (see also n'anga, spirit mediums, traditional healers) 35, 43–8, 109–10, 235, 236

Santeria 35
Scotland gang, *see* 27s
Sea Point 192
Sena 96
Senegal 6, 118–19, 237
SePedi 97
Sesotho (*see also* Basutoland, Basotho, Lesotho) 3, 97, 108, 136, 162, 164, 166, 172–3
setsualle 83, 173, 176
sex tourism 149, 190
sex, inter-racial, *see* inter-racial sex
sex-change operations 2
sexism (*see also* heterosexism) 5, 10, 74, 128, 150–1, 219 244
sexual rights 2–3, 182–200, 207, 219
sexually transmitted diseases (*see also* HIV/AIDS, syphilis) 60, 63, 96, 138, 175, 210, 214, 216, 232, 233
Shaka 38–9, 144
Shangaan 3, 27, 39, 57, 62, 66–7, 69, 96, 162, 165–6, 222
Shona 13, 16, 18, 25–9, 37, 39–41, 54, 62, 96–8, 101, 102, 115, 132, 136–7, 146, 165, 233
Shubela 165
Sierra Leone, 194
Simonas 99
Sister Namibia 6, 194
Sithole, Ndabaningi 140–2, 145
skesana 3
slavery 35, 37, 50–3, 116
sodomy (*see also* anal sex) 3, 9, 10, 12, 31, 35, 40, 52, 54-9, 62, 75, 76, 81, 96, 99, 100, 103–5, 115–19, 136, 140, 147, 153, 192
Sokisi 58, 61, 134
Sotoma 56
South Africa (*see also* Cape Town, individual ethnic groups) 13–15, 55–9, 71–85, 107–10, 117, 119–28, 131–4, 137, 143, 145, 147, 152–3 177–81; constitution, 5–6,

225–6, 240
Spain (*see also* inquisitions) 10, 148
spirit mediums (*see also* n'anga, sangoma, diviners, traditional healers) 35, 164
Sudan 40, 94, 221, 243
Sunday Mail (Harare) 147, 152
Swahili 3, 37, 135, 221
Swaziland 4, 38, 67, 222, 225
syphilis (*see also* sexually transmitted diseases) 49, 60, 162

Taberer, Henry (*see also* Leary–Taberer inquiry) 59
TAC, *see* Treatment Action Campaign
Tanzania 38, 156–60, 194, 222
Tekere, Edward 140
terminology 2–4, 10–11, 136, 218
Thandekiso, Revd Tsietsi 191
theatre, gay-themed 238–9
thigh sex (*see also* hlobonga) 27, 54, 57, 97, 101, 164, 166
Tiripano, Tsitsi, *see* Mangwiro, Poliyana
Tokai 81
tokoloshi 29
Toms, Ivan 189, 224
Tonga 96
traditional healers (*see also* n'anga, sangoma, spirit mediums) 13, 30, 43–8, 109–10, 155, 164
transgender 2, 215, 220, 237
Transkei 63
transvestism (*see also* cross-dressing) 2, 138
Treatment Action Campaign (TAC) 16, 197, 236, 241
Tsonga (*see also* Shangaan) 3, 57–8, 222
Tsouroullis, Evan 148
Tswana 97
Tutsi 40, 135
Tutu, Bishop Desmond 5, 153, 169, 223

Twells, Edward 116–17
28s (Ninevites) 14, 76–7, 80–1, 101, 119
27s (Scotland gang) 81, 119

ubunkotshani 3
UDF, *see* United Democratic Front
Uganda 4, 110–11, 135, 144, 195, 222–3, 226, 231
ukumetsha (see also thigh sex, *hlobonga)* 27, 57, 180
umfaan (see also wyfie) 58, 61, 76, 77, 80, 82
Umteto ka Sokisi 58
United Democratic Front (UDF) (South Africa) 188–9
United States of America 113, 115, 123, 149–51, 184–5, 197, 211, 213–14, 216–17, 236
University of Zimbabwe (formerly University of Rhodesia) 140, 149, 229
uranism 118
USSR 143

Vambe, Lawrence 141
van Onselen, Charles 14–15
VaNyemba 34
VaRemba 37
VaShandi 143
Venda 36
virginity 29, 34, 36, 134, 150, 172
Williams, Cecil 124, 183–4, 236–7
Williams, Gertie 82–3, 107–8
witchcraft (*see also n'anga, ngozi)* 10, 28, 30, 37
Women's Cultural Club (Zimbabwe) 187
World War I 63, 121
World War II 9–10, 121–3, 126, 182, 185, 230
Woubi Cherie 237
wyfies (see also umfaan) 76–81

xenophobia 10, 195, 212

Xhosa (*see also* Mpondo) 27, 54, 59, 92, 96, 136, 165

Zambia 4, 38, 143, 224
Zandemela, Bob 135
ZANU(PF) (*see also* Mugabe, Robert) 140, 143, 146, 151–3
Zidji 166
Zimbabwe African National Union (Patriotic Front), *see* ZANU(PF)
Zimbabwe International Book Fair 152–3, 194–5, 223
Zimbabwe (*see also* Gays and Lesbians of Zimbabwe (GALZ)): pre colonial 24–5, 42, 87, 134; colonial period 40–1, 66, 92–105, 119, 122, 125; compared to South Africa, 105; ethnography and historiography, 13–16; gay identity in 2–4, 18–23, 110–12, 193–200; in South Africa, 84–5, 169; settler culture, 122, 126–8; prisons in, 72, 79–80, 84–5
Zingha, *see* Nzinga, Anna
Zulu 3, 14, 27, 38–40, 43–8, 54–7, 76, 96, 144, 165, 190
Zvibengu 101